Commission of the European Communities

Sixteenth Report
on Competition Policy

(Published in conjunction with the
'Twentieth General Report on the
Activities of the European Communities 1986')

Brussels • Luxembourg • 1987

This publication is also available in the following languages:

ES	ISBN	92-825-6953-5
DA	ISBN	92-825-6954-3
DE	ISBN	92-825-6955-1
GR	ISBN	92-825-6956-X
FR	ISBN	92-825-6958-6
IT	ISBN	92-825-6959-4
NL	ISBN	92-825-6960-8
PT	ISBN	92-825-6961-6

Cataloguing data can be found at the end of this publication

Luxembourg: Office for Official Publications of the European Communities, 1987

ISBN 92-825-6957-8

Catalogue number: CB-48-86-060-EN-C

Contents

Introduction

The purpose of the European Community is to foster economic and social progress in its member countries by breaking down the barriers dividing them and creating a genuine common market. The removal of the remaining barriers by 1992 has been made the top priority of the Community. After the Commission's proposals to this end had been accepted by the European Council in March 1985, the seal was set on this commitment by the Single European Act signed in February 1986. Considering the historical, cultural and economic diversity of the Member States, creating a common market was always an ambitious undertaking. A further formidable challenge was added by enlargement: in 35 years the Community has grown from a group of six countries with a relatively homogeneous economic structure to one of 12 countries of more than 300 million inhabitants, covering the majority of Western Europe and showing marked regional disparities.

1986 saw a major step in this growth: with the accession of Spain and Portugal the European Community has attained a geographical extent and an economic potential comparable to the great world powers. All our efforts must now be applied to the task of strengthening the cohesion of this unit.

A barrier-free internal market is an essential basis for increased prosperity in the Community as a whole. Only when the various kinds of barriers which currently limit their operations are removed will firms be able to take full advantage of the Community's size and to deploy their human, material and financial resources more efficiently. The resulting improvement in industrial efficiency and competitiveness and in overall economic performance should also make it possible to develop new ways of tackling the problem of unemployment.

But there is more to unifying the common market than dismantling the physical, technical and tax barriers between our countries. Many other supporting measures are needed to transform the space thus created into a single dynamic and flexible market. In fact this is a goal to which all Community policies in their various ways must contribute.

Competition policy has a key role to play in ensuring that the opening of the market yields all the benefits expected of it. It must ensure that these barriers are not replaced by divisions of markets resulting from restrictive business practices or protectionist measures taken by the Member States. The control of State aid is of particular importance in this context. Member States may use aid to give their industry an advantage over industry elsewhere in the Community. Public funds may also be used to prop up uncompetitive businesses and industries. This generally only renders ultimately more difficult the task of finding a genuine solution and in the meantime tends to cause difficulties for more competitive firms that are providing real jobs. Hence it is essential to ensure that government funds are not used to confer a competitive advantage on some firms at the expense of others.

Creating a genuine common market also implies reinforcing efforts to bring about economic and social cohesion and contributing to reducing disparities between the regions. In the Single European Act special attention is paid to achieving this objective both through the operation of the Community's own structural funds and in the conduct of national economic policies. The Commission's policy of State aids has an important role to play in this respect by ensuring that regional aid is only granted in the areas of greatest need in order to limit distortions of competition and by ensuring a correlation between the degree of structural handicap and the intensity of aid granted.

Competition policy fosters market integration in a positive way as well. Subject to the maintenance of an adequate level of competition, it allows scope for cooperation between firms likely to further technical and economic progress, especially in research and development and the transfer of technology. Hence the Commission can take favourable decisions on inter-company cooperation or government intervention that is in the wider Community interest and not just the interest of the firms or countries concerned. This is especially evident in the case of measures which stimulate R & D and innovation, as well as boosting dynamic growth, or which help realize the growth protential of underdeveloped areas.

These two sides of the Commission's competition policy, control of the action of governments and of firms, thus pursue the same aim of ensuring open, efficient markets in which firms determine their prices and output independently according to market conditions. It is this type of environment in which firms can best develop and can take on world competition.

A major task of competition policy in 1986 was to consolidate the new geographical dimension of the Community by integrating the new Member States. Negotiations on the reform of the State monopolies in Greece continued and talks were started with the Spanish and Portuguese Governments which

Ireland and Italy because they increased the efficiency of the banking system. It took care that the agreements did not contain provisions fixing actual charges to the consumer for the services.

Also in the area of cooperation between firms, the Commission pressed ahead with the preparation of a notice on joint ventures which will in particular specify which types of arrangements are not caught at all by Article 85 and which are exemptable. It also continued work on a block exemption for know-how licensing agreements, which will supplement the patent licensing regulation adopted in 1985. At the same time, it pursued its policy of authorizing arrangements that enable firms to take advantage of the wider Community market. It thus exempted an agreement between a number of computer manufacturers which established a standard operating system. Such standards help to make European hardware and software manufacturers more internationally competitive. Operations exploiting the complementary resources of firms in different Member States, especially those involving the transfer of high technology, were also given the seal of approval, as were agreements for rationalization in industries suffering from overcapacity such as petrochemicals and steel.

In the field of distribution, another area of prime importance for market integration, 1986 saw the Commission's first two decisions on franchising agreements. This type of arrangement, which is assuming increasing importance in the Community where there were over 83 000 franchisees even in 1983, in the Commission's view helps to integrate the common market by making it easier for comparatively small firms to develop cross-frontier distribution networks. Here too the Commission intends, on the basis of the experience built up from dealing with individual cases, to set out a favourable general approach in the form of a block exemption.

Finally the Commission tried to ensure that the Member States did not interfere with the free play of competition in ways detrimental to the Community interest. It took action, for example, to open up public telecommunications markets by moving against restrictive practices. In this sector where technology is evolving rapidly it is particularly important that Member States should not seek to maintain technical or administrative barriers to trade to protect their domestic industry.

The greatest power the Commission has to prevent government action that distorts competition without sufficient justification, however, is its control of State aid. A look at the statistics for 1986 shows that the number of notifications, which peaked in 1982, has since steadily declined. The decrease in notifications is especially marked in industries in chronic difficulty (in particular steel, textiles and man-made fibres) for which the Commission has worked out comprehensive criteria for aid in order to promote restructuring of these industries. On the other hand, the number of notifications has increased in other sectors. It should be stated, however, that the machinery for obtaining the notification of cumulation of aid awards has so far not been effective. Lastly, in 1986 the Commission confirmed its policy of requiring governments to recover aid provided illegally.

In April 1986, the Commission adopted a framework which sets out its generally favourable approach to aid for R & D. The framework defines the limits of what is acceptable in the Community interest.

The various facets of competition policy thus form an interlocking whole. The policy seeks to keep the market economy working as satisfactorily as possible through the twin instruments of anti-trust and control of government aid, which need to be supplemented by action to remove distortions caused by differences in national legislation. Competition policy itself is an integral part of the Community's other endeavours, one of whose top priorities was stated by the European Council of March 1985 as 'to achieve a single large market by 1992, thereby creating a more favourable environment for stimulating enterprise, competition and trade'.

Part One

General competition policy

Chapter I

EC competition policy and the contribution from socio-economic and political circles

European Parliament

1. The European Parliament has been actively involved in the field of competition policy during the past year. On 14 November it adopted a resolution on the Fifteenth Report on Competition Policy.[1] The general conclusions of the resolution echo the Commission's sentiment that a vigorous application of the Community competition rules is fundamental in creating economic incentives to promote the necessary restructuring of European industry thereby increasing its competitiveness.

The problems identified by the Parliament as requiring immediate attention are, for the most part, areas in which the Commission is working actively and in which concrete solutions are expected within a realistic period of time. However, it must be pointed out that certain matters, such as distortions in the fiscal policy of the Member States and the failure to make progress in the adoption of the ninth company law directive, do not come within the ambit of the competition rules. Whilst such matters do have a tangible effect upon the proper functioning of competition policy, the Commission cannot comment upon them in this Report, the purpose of which is to set out how the competition rules have been implemented during 1986.

Specific matters raised in the resolution will be treated in the separate chapters allocated to them in this Report. However, two general points will be dealt with here:

---

[1]   OJ C 322, 15.12.1986, reproduced in the Annex to this Report.

(i)   *The establishment of a two-tier system of judicial review*
(Points 5 (viii), 57, 58)

The Commission has frequently spoken out in favour of a two-tier system of judicial review.[1] This demand has found a response in the Single European Act which provides[2] that '...at the request of the Court of Justice, and after consulting the Commission and the European Parliament, the Council may, acting unanimously, attach to the Court of Justice, a court with the jurisdiction to hear and determine at first instance, subject to a right of appeal to the Court of Justice on points of law only, ... certains classes of action brought by natural or legal persons.' That court would not have jurisdiction in actions brought by Member States or the Community institutions or to determine questions referred for a preliminary ruling under Article 177 of the EEC Treaty.

While the Commission welcomes the prospect of the creation of another tribunal which would relieve the Court of Justice of some of the heavy burden of cases it currently bears, it must be stressed that it is for the Court of Justice to take the initiative to create such a tribunal.[3]

(ii)   *Dialogue with the Parliament* (Point 12)

The Commission is ready to intensify the existing dialogue with the Parliament. However, the specific responsibilities of both institutions ought to be respected.

Relations between the two institutions are already close.

During the course of 1986 the Parliament submitted 193 written questions to the Commission relating to competition matters (1985: 197 written questions) and 37 questions were put to the Commission for oral reply.

On 13 March 1986 a resolution was adopted the object of which was to close the procedure for consultation in the European Parliament on the communication from the Commission of the European Communities to the Council for new Community rules for State aids to the coal industry.[4]

A resolution on the crisis in the shipbuilding industry was adopted on 12 June 1986.[5]

On 16 December 1986 the Parliament adopted a resolution on the Commission's proposal for a sixth directive on aids to the shipbuilding industry.[6]

---

[1]   Fifteenth Competition Report, point 45.
[2]   Articles 4, 11 and 26.
[3]   See reply by the President of the Commission to Written Question No 1114/86. OJ C 54, 2.3.1987.
[4]   OJ C 88, 13.3.1986.
[5]   OJ C 176, 14.7.1986.
[6]   OJ C 7, 12.1.1987.

The Commission always considers carefully the resolutions of the Parliament in deciding whether and to what extent it is appropriate to modify its proposals to the Council and in the formulation of its policy.

Economic and Social Committee

2.   The Economic and Social Committee (ESC) has also played an active role in the development of Community competition policy in the past year.

3.   On 23 October 1986, the ESC, sitting in plenary session, adopted an opinion on the Fifteenth Report on Competition Policy. [1]

From the discussions leading up to the adoption of the final opinion it emerged that the Commission and the ESC agree that the competition rules must be applied in such a way as to ensure the promotion of dynamic, innovative competition designed to promote the global competitiveness of European industry, whilst at the same time maintaining a system of undistorted competition. The specific points raised in the opinion are dealt with in the relevant sections of this Report.

4.   In the field of air transport, after consultation by the Council, the ESC delivered, on 27 November, an opinion on the proposed amendments to Council Regulation No 2821/71 of 20 December 1971 on the application of Article 85(3) of the Treaty to categories of agreements, decisions and concerted practices. [2]

5.   In the shipbuilding sector the ESC adopted an own-initiative opinion dealing with Community policy in the shipbuilding sector [3] and one opinion after consultation by the Council on the Commission's proposal for a sixth directive on shipbuilding aids. [4]

Advisory Committee on Restrictive Practices and Dominant Positions

6.   In the course of 1986 the Advisory Committee met five times. The meetings, on average of two days' duration, were concerned with the Commission's draft decisions in individual cases applying Article 85. A total of 22 opinions were issued.

---

[1]   OJ C 333, 29.12.1986; the opinion is reproduced in the Annex to this Report.
[2]   OJ C 333, 29.12.1986.
[3]   OJ C 281, 7.11.1986.
[4]   OJ C 7, 12.1.1987.

On 22 May, the Commission met the heads of the national competition authorities, in an extraordinary meeting of the Advisory Committee to discuss general matters of competition policy.

Recent developments both at Community level and within different Member States were presented. Discussion concentrated on current problems such as merger control, joint ventures, know-how licensing agreements, franchising and the application of the competition rules to the air and sea transport sectors. This exchange of views once again demonstrated the increasing convergence of the competition policies of the Community and its Member States.

In addition, Member State officials attended nine oral hearings which took place this year in individual cases.

Conference of National Government Experts

7.   The Conference of Government Experts met three times to discuss general policy issues such as the assessment of joint ventures under the competition rules, the modification of the notice on agreements of minor importance, and the treatment of know-how licensing under the competition rules.

Other contacts

8.   The Commission contacted governments, industrial organizations and other interested circles during the course of the year to discuss the various policy priorities announced in previous competition reports and in the Commission's working programme, as well as other issues of general interest.

Colloquium on competition policy
and research and development cooperation

9.   In view of the increasing cooperative efforts in research and development within the Community and in order to ensure fuller understanding between the Commission and industry on the role of competition policy with respect to this cooperation, the Commission invited leading European industrialists, most of whom were actively involved in research and development projects under-

taken within the framework of such programmes as Esprit, Brite, RACE and Eureka, to a colloquium. [1]

This colloquium, the first of its kind, provided a useful forum for increasing the mutual understanding of European industry and the Commission on the impact of competition policy on R&D cooperation between firms. Attention was drawn to the Commission's efforts in the field of competition policy to facilitate cross-frontier research and development designed to increase the competitiveness of European industry.

The Commission, however, stressed the importance of the limits to R&D cooperation in order to ensure that the free market system required by the Treaties is not undermined by a dense network of collaborative arrangements between firms ranging from joint R&D, through to joint production and even joint sales.

Some of the projects so far submitted to the Commission involve a certain danger of 'prevention, restriction or distortion of competition within the common market' within the meaning of Article 85(1). A more detailed analysis reveals the following categories:

1. Some of the projects clearly involve only cooperation on R&D and are confined to the pre-competitive phase. These either do not fall within Article 85(1) and are unobjectionable from the competition point of view or fall within the scope of the R&D block exemption Regulation. [2]

2. Others involve cooperation between competitors in areas close to the market-place and therefore potentially fall within Article 85(1). Here, two sub-categories can be distinguished:

   (a) Projects where the cooperation extends to joint exploitation of the results of the R&D in the form of either joint production or joint licensing to third parties: here, Eureka projects undertaken by firms whose combined market share for the relevant products is less than 20% are covered by the block exemption for R&D cooperation agreements, those involving firms with combined market share of over 20% require individual exemption.

   (b) Projects where the cooperation extends also to joint sales: such agreements can only be exempted after close individual scrutiny.

---

[1] Held on 17 June 1986 in Brussels.
[2] Regulation (EEC) No 418/85 of 19 December 1984. OJ L 53, 22.2.1985.

10. The Commission will also have to examine cooperation projects in the context of Eureka. When State aids are involved with respect to Eureka projects they have to fulfil the general conditions laid down in the 'Community framework on State aids for reseach and development'. [1] Moreover, it must be pointed out that, according to Article 130 F paragraph 3 of the Single European Act, particular account should be taken of the connection between research and technological developments and competition policy.

BEUC

11. In November the Commission met representatives of the European Bureau of Consumer Associations (Bureau européen des Unions de Consommateurs — BEUC) to discuss, in particular:

(i)   the continuing problem of parallel imports in the automobile sector;

(ii) the advantages and disadvantages for the consumer of distribution franchises;

(iii) the importance for the consumer of Community-wide acceptance of after-sales guarantees.

On a more general note, the BEUC representatives emphasized the intense interest of consumers in the Commission's policy to liberalize the air transport sector.

The Commission, for its part, pointed out that consumers could seek effective application of the Community competition rules in their national courts in most sectors of economic activity.

It should be noted that the Commission in its communication to the Council entitled 'Integration of consumer policy into other common policies' [2] sets out clearly how consumers' interests could be furthered in competition policy. The Council in its resolution of 15 December [3] welcomed the Commission's proposals and emphasized the necessity of taking consumers' interests into account in drafting proposals.

---

[1]   See point 247 of this Report.
[2]   COM(86) 540 final.
[3]   OJ C 3, 7.1.1987.

Unice

12.   In September 1986, the Commission met Unice (Union des Industries de la Communauté européenne) for an exchange of views on the Commission's administrative practices in the field of competition. The following points, in particular, were raised: the setting-up of a two-tier level of jurisdiction in the Court of Justice, acceleration of Commission procedures, the Commission's powers and methods of investigation and decision making.

Chapter II

EC competition policy and international contacts

OECD

13. The OECD Committee of Experts on Restrictive Business Practices celebrated its 25th anniversary. In a speech to mark the occasion, the Secretary-General of the OECD stressed the importance of the Committee's work in a world where restrictive business practices were becoming more and more complex and internationalized and said that competition was still an essential condition for ensuring that the rules of international trade functioned effectively. He also reiterated his belief in competition as the best means of combating structural rigidities as it gave enterprises maximum scope to engage in competitive behaviour. The Commission representative stressed, in this context, that in the current economic climate competition plays an essential role in developing healthy industrial structures, stimulating the transfer of technology and promoting international trade.

14. On 21 May the OECD Council adopted a revised Recommendation on cooperation between member countries on restrictive business practices affecting international trade.

The Recommendation and the attached guiding principles which member countries are advised to follow confirm the basic principles of prior notification and mutual consultations underlying the original 1979 Recommendation. [1] These seek to ensure that a country taking action to enforce its restrictive practices law which may affect important interests of another country informs that country and takes its views into account to an extent consistent with the safeguard of its own national interests. The new Recommendation also formally records the commitment of member countries to exercise moderation and restraint in the extra-territorial application of their competition laws, by

---

[1]   Third Competition Report, point 40, and Ninth Competition Report, point 33.

recognizing the 'need for member countries to give effect to the principles of international law and comity and to use moderation and self-restraint in the interest of cooperation in the field of restrictive business practices'. The Commission, for its part, has always interpreted the original Recommendation in this sense. [1]

15.   On 23 October the OECD Council adopted a Recommendation on cooperation between member countries in areas of potential conflict between competition and trade policies. The Recommendation incorporates a checklist of questions which national authorities should ask in evaluating the economic costs and benefits of proposed trade policy measures. Also, to avoid or minimize conflicts between laws, regulations and policies in the fields of trade and competition, it provides for consultations with other member countries concerned on proposed official trade policy measures affecting competition such as export limitation arrangements and on private restrictive practices affecting international trade which may well be legal under national law, such as export limitation arrangements and export or import cartels. The Recommendation answers the call made by the Council in 1982 for development of an improved international framework for dealing with problems arising at the frontier of competition and trade policies.

Committee on International Investment and Multinational Enterprises (CIME)

16.   Work in this Committee and its Working Group on International Investment Policies takes on a new interest with the opening of the new GATT Round, on the agenda of which are subjects closely related to work in the CIME, for example trade-related investment measures and services.

The periodic reviews of the application of national treatment to foreign controlled enterprises continued. In July the OECD Council adopted recommendations concerning discriminatory measures motivated by public order and essential security interests, which further strengthen and clarify the national treatment instrument.

The new surveys of measures related to national treatment in connection with investment by established foreign-controlled enterprises and of international investment incentives and disincentives will be completed in the near future.

---

[1]   Eleventh Competition Report, point 37.

Unctad

Restrictive business practices

17.   The fifth meeting of the Intergovernmental Group of Experts on Restrictive Business Practices, established to monitor the operation of the Restrictive Business Practices Code (the set of multilaterally agreed equitable principles and rules for the control of restrictive business practices, adopted by the United Nations General Assembly on 5 December 1980) took place in Geneva from 15-24 October. Following the absence of an agreement at the United Nations Conference held in November 1985 to review the Code, it was agreed to recommend that the General Assembly should convene under the auspices of Unctad a new Review Conference in 1990.

The Community reiterated its position that its participation in the Group as an observer only was not in keeping with the responsibilities it has under the Treaty of Rome for the control of restrictive business practices. It indicated its intention to seek the inclusion of this matter on the agenda of a forthcoming meeting of the United Nations Trade and Development Board.

The Group reviewed the application and implementation of the Code, the progress of studies on restrictive business practices related to the provisions of the Code, the arrangements for technical assistance and the preparation of a handbook on restrictive business practices legislation and of a model law for control of restrictive business practices. The Group was unable to reach conclusions as to the continuation of its work. It was however understood that the Secretariat-General of Unctad would make proposals in that respect.

Cooperation between the Commission and the anti-trust authorities of non-member countries

18.   The annual bilateral talks with representatives of the Japanese Fair Trade Commission were held in Brussels on 1 October. The topics discussed included the FTC's anti-trust policy in relation to the improved access of foreign goods to the Japanese market and the progress made in deregulating air transport in Japan and in the EEC.

Later an FTC delegation visited the Commission to learn about its policy on parallel imports, a subject the FTC was also studying.

19.   In mid-October bilateral talks were held in Washington with the US anti-trust authorities. One of the topics discussed was the experience of the EC and the US in dealing with predatory pricing. The conclusion was that predatory pricing was rarely found alone but usually formed part of a global strategy by a firm to drive a competitor from or to prevent it entering a market. The two sides also discussed the importance of international competition for the evaluation of the effect of mergers. Here too, the US and EC policies converged in regarding the domestic EC or US market as the relevant geographical market, although the impact of international competition on the market also had to be considered.

20.   Delegations of the New Zealand and Australian competition authorities visited the Commission to discuss problems relating to the treatment of firms in dominant positions and to merger control. Both delegations were interested in obtaining information about the Commission's policy in this field in order to prepare amendments to their national legislation.

GATT

21.   In September a new round of multilateral trade negotiations, christened the 'Uruguay Round', was launched at Punta del Este, Uruguay.

The new round, which it is aimed to complete within four years, covers trade in services as well as trade in goods. The ministerial declaration adopted at the Punta del Este meeting stressed, among other things, the determination of the GATT contracting parties to halt and reverse protectionism, to remove distortions to trade, and to develop a more open, viable and durable multilateral trading system.

Several of the subjects announced for negotiation are to a greater or lesser extent directly relevant to Community competition policy. Thus, the Commission has begun preparatory work on the improvement of GATT disciplines on subsidies and countervailing duties that affect international trade; other relevant topics are the effect of investment policies on trade, intellectual property rights and counterfeiting and indirect taxation. Despite the great importance of these issues, the Commission's thinking is still at too formative a stage to predict what the eventual implications of the work will be for Community competition policy. Only after a period of reflection will the effect of the new trade round on competition policy, and vice versa, become clear.

Chapter III

EC competition policy and small and medium-sized enterprises

22.   Small and medium-sized entreprises (SMEs) have a vital role to play in the development of the European economy. In March the Heads of State or Government meeting in the European Council, therefore, resolved that the creation and survival of such businesses should be encouraged and that all obstacles which could prejudice their existence should be minimized as far as possible. [1]

Accordingly, the Commission has set up an inter-departmental group on small businesses and cooperatives to study three basic issues: Community or national schemes to promote the creation or expansion of small businesses; the simplification of legislation and the removal of barriers to the setting-up of small businesses; and the impact of Community financial instruments on small businesses.

The work of this group in general is dealt with in other Community publications, notably the General Report on the Activities of the European Communities. [2]

23.   A study has been commissioned to identify the obligations imposed on SMEs by Community and national legislation taking account of the costs and benefits for businesses. Five legislative areas are being examined: taxation, environment, consumer protection, competition and social legislation.

In each of these areas the study will examine Community legislation and national implementation measures. The obligations arising out of these legislat-

---

[1]   Bull. EC 3-1985, point 1.2.3.
[2]   Nineteenth General Report, points 315-317; Twentieth General Report, points 349-355.

ive measures for SMEs will be examined and the overall impact of such legislation on SMEs will be assessed. The study is expected to be available in February 1987.

The most important contribution in the competition area to the welfare of SMEs made this year is the new notice on minor agreements which do not fall under Article 85(1), which is discussed in detail elsewhere in this Report. [1]

---

[1]   Point 24 of this Report.

Part Two

Competition policy towards enterprises

Chapter I

Main developments in Community policy

§ 1 — New Notice on agreements of minor importance which do not fall under Article 85

24.   On 3 September the Commission adopted a new Notice [1] on agreements of minor importance which has replaced the previous Notice of 19 December 1977. [2]

The purpose of the Notice is to indicate to undertakings which agreements the Commission considers, by virtue of their impact on competition within the common market and on trade between Member States, not to fall within the scope of Article 85(1).

The Commission believes that, in general, an agreement will not have an appreciable impact on market conditions when the market share of the firms involved does not exceed 5% and where their combined annual turnover does not exceed 200 million ECU.

The new Notice differs from its predecessor in three respects:

(i)   The market share of participating firms is no longer calculated by reference to a 'substantial part of the common market', i.e., in practice a national market, but rather to the 'area within the Community in which the agreement has effect'. With the increasing integration of the Community into a single market, this area will more frequently be the whole of the Community.

(ii)   The turnover limit is increased from 50 million ECU to 200 million ECU. More firms will, therefore, benefit from the Notice.

---

[1]   OJ C 231, 12.9.1986.
[2]   OJ C 313, 29.12.1977.

(iii) The scope of the Notice has been extended to services. This reflects the increasing importance to the economy of the service industries, in which small and medium-sized firms (SMEs) play a particularly significant role.

Detailed explanations are given as to how to calculate market share and combined turnover, thereby making it easier for firms involved to understand and apply the Notice.

The Notice will relieve many SMEs of the burden of notifying their agreements and will facilitate cooperation between them. Moreover, it will give them legal security in the conduct of their commercial operations.

§ 2 — Operation of the block exemption regulations

25. The purpose of the block exemption regulations is to grant automatic exemption from the competition rules to certain classes of agreements thereby making individual notification of such agreements unnecessary.

During 1986 the Commission continued its policy of examining to what extent agreements and practices already notified or cases brought to its attention by complainants fall within the scope of the existing six block exemptions. In 25 of these cases the Commission was able to close the file because the agreements or practices were covered by one of the block exemption Regulations either in their original form or after modifications suggested by the Commission.

Exclusive distribution and exclusive purchasing agreements

26. In one case the Commission had to examine whether the pricing policy of Shell[1] towards its petrol station tenants led to restriction of competition going beyond the scope permitted by Regulation No 1984/83[2] and, if so, whether it constituted an abuse of such a nature as to warrant the withdrawal of the block exemption. After investigation the Commission found that Shell's policy as modified at the request of the Commission was in fact compatible with the competition rules, making intervention unnecessary.

27. Furthermore, the Court's ruling in the Pronuptia[3] case has clarified the scope of Regulation No 67/67 by indicating that franchising agreements constitute a special type of agreement different from exclusive distribution contracts.

Specialization, research and development

28. As to Regulation No 417/85[4] on specialization and No 418/85[4] on research and development the Commission examined a certain number of notifications of such contracts in particular those in which the parties had invoked the opposition procedure.

---

[1] Point 55 of this Report.
[2] OJ L 173, 30.6.1983. Corrigendum OJ L 281, 13.10.1983.
[3] Case 161/84, not yet reported. See point 107 of this Report.
[4] OJ L 53, 22.2.1985.

Little use has been made so far of the opposition procedure. Only two notifications have been received under Article 7 of Regulation No 418/85 and only one under Article 4 of Regulation No 417/85.

Patent licensing

29.   Experience with the patent licensing Regulation has shown one of the main questions to be the practical operation of the opposition procedure.

Since the entry into force of the patent licensing Regulation   on 1 January 1985 32 notifications requesting the opposition procedure have been received. These have been dealt with as follows. Four cases were closed because the agreements were 'intra-group' and thus did not fall under Article 85; in four cases the opposition procedure was inapplicable because the agreements did not concern valid patents but know-how and trade marks; in one case the Regulation was deemed inapplicable because it concerned a cross-licensing agreement which is excluded from the scope of the Regulation pursuant to Article 5; in six cases the opposition procedure was not available because the agreements contained black clauses. In 12 cases, all relating to exclusive patent licensing and sublicensing agreements between the same parties for various Member States, the Commission decided not to oppose as the agreements were deemed to be in line with the Regulation. Finally, in five cases the Commission decided to oppose exemption because of restrictions on the use of the accompanying know-how and of an exclusive grant-back of improvement inventions. The Commission is examining these cases on an individual basis: in one of them the procedure has been suspended at the request of the parties who wish to renegotiate the terms of the agreement.

Distribution in the motor vehicle sector

30.   The Commission has so far not had reason to withdraw the exemption under Regulation No 123/85[2] in any case.

Complaints from consumers or intermediaries about difficulties in purchasing new vehicles in the exporting country or with importation, registration, free servicing or warranty claims in the importing country were passed on to the manufacturers, importers or dealers concerned with a request for an immediate

---

[1]   Regulation No 2349/84 of 23 July 1984, OJ L 219, 16.8.1984; Corrigendum OJ L 113, 21.4.1985.
[2]   OJ L 15, 18.1.1985; OJ C 17, 18.1.1985.

reaction to the complaint. In the majority of cases the cause for complaint could be removed in this way. The remaining cases were investigated by the Commission.

In dealing with complaints the Commission checks that certain ground rules are observed:

1. The manufacturer or importer in the exporting country must quote his prices, conditions and specifications for right-hand-drive (RHD) vehicles to the prospective customer on request. Delivery times should normally not exceed the longer of the two delivery times for the vehicles in the exporting or importing country.

2. The manufacturer or importer in the importing country may not withhold his assistance in registering the vehicle, take an unreasonably long time over providing that assistance or impose unreasonable conditions (e.g., high charges) for it. No interference with warranty rights is tolerated.

3. Where intermediaries are involved, the Commission has always refused to accept as a valid ground for refusing to sell to an intermediary who has a written order to purchase a new vehicle the fact that he is collecting orders professionally or is charging for his services.

§ 3 — Franchising

31. The Commission continued its work on franchising. [1] As was announced in previous work programmes, the Commission is preparing a block exemption on the basis of the general lines already developed and in the light of the indications given by the Court of Justice in the Pronuptia case. In preparing this regulation it took two decisions concerning the franchising systems of Yves Rocher [2] and Pronuptia. [2]

Three categories of franchising agreements can be distinguished:

(i)   industrial franchises, where the franchisee manufactures products according to the franchisor's instructions and sells them under the franchisor's trade mark;

(ii) service franchises, where the franchisee offers a service under the business name or trade mark of the franchisor in accordance with the latter's instructions;

(iii) distribution franchises, where the franchisee sells certain products in a shop bearing the franchisor's business name, in accordance with the commercial methods developed by the franchisor. Two situations must be distinguished: where the products are manufactured by, or according to the specifications of the franchisor and sold under its trade mark, and where the products are selected according to criteria defined by the franchisor and sold under their original trade mark.

The future regulation will probably cover distribution and service franchises only.

---

[1]   Fifteenth Competition Report, point 25.
[2]   See point 53 of this Report.

§ 4 — Joint ventures

32.   The Commission's approach to joint ventures (JVs) and other forms of industrial cooperation is designed to ensure that the right balance is struck between the need for coordination of industrial effort in order to increase the competitiveness of European industry and to create a single market, and the necessity of ensuring that competition in the common market is not distorted and allowed to fulfil its function of bringing about a more efficient allocation of resources.

The Commission continued its work on JVs.[1] The broad lines of a future notice on the assessment of JVs under the EEC competition rules were discussed with government experts on 17-18 February. Almost all the Member States endorsed the idea of a notice, but wanted it to be made as comprehensive and precise as possible.

In addition, discussions with industry provided useful information and encouraged the Commission to pursue its general line in this field. Industry, however, requested a more detailed and clearer presentation.

The suggestion of both the Member States and industry will be taken into account in drawing up the future notice.

33.   The notice will confirm the Commission's previous policy towards JVs,[2] as exemplified in the block exemption regulations and individual decisions and adapt it to the changed economic environment.

The Notice could, if necessary, deal in particular with the following points or questions:

(i)   JVs which might not fall within the scope of Article 85(1), because they do not have any appreciable effects on competition within the common market or on trade between Member States;

(ii) JVs which are taken out of the scope of Article 85(1) by a block exemption regulation (specialization agreements, R&D agreements);

(iii) JVs which can only be exempted from Article 85(1) on a case-by-case basis;

(iv) Specific obligations undertaken in connection with JVs;

---

[1]   Fifteenth Competition Report, point 26.
[2]   Thirteenth Competition Report, points 53-55.

(v)   JVs which might be caught by Article 85(1) because they restrict competition between the parties or foreclose market access opportunities for third parties;

(vi) the possibilities of applying Article 86 to JVs.

34.   The Commission is currently preparing a new draft of the notice. This text will take into account the experience gained from a number of individual decisions during the past years.

§ 5 — Know-how licensing agreements

35.   The Commission continued its work, which started in 1985,[1] on the provision of a legal framework to facilitate technology transfer in an open competitive market of which the Regulation on patent licensing was the first step.

Intensive discussions took place between Member States, representatives of industry and the Commission. After these discussions, the Commission started to prepare a draft block exemption regulation. They could include amongst other elements, the following points:

(i)   the regulation should relate only to know-how which is not in the public domain and consists of substantial technological information relating to the whole or part of a manufacturing process or a product;

(ii)   obligations on the licensee to preserve the confidentiality of the licensed know-how and not to grant sub-licences without the licensor's consent could be regarded as not falling within Article 85;

(iii)   as to clauses concerning territorial protection, field-of-use restrictions, and customer and quantity restrictions, a solution similar to that provided for in the patent licensing Regulation could be envisaged;

(iv)   with respect to royalties, an obligation to continue turnover-related payments could be allowed in certain cases at least for a limited period after the know-how has become publicly known.

In 1986 the Commission decided several individual cases relating to know-how licensing, thereby further developing its policy in this field.[2] These decisions will be taken into account in the preparatory work for the block exemption regulation.

---

[1]   Fifteenth Competition Report, point 24.
[2]   See points 71 and 72 of this Report.

§ 6 — Air and sea transport

Air transport

36. With a view to adding fresh impetus to discussions in the Council on Civil Aviation Memorandum No 2 [1], the Commission made several new proposals during the year. In July it drew up a new framework, based on the objectives set by the Commission in Memorandum No 2,[2] for liberalization of government controls over tariffs and capacity.

Also in July the Commission amended the draft Article 87 Regulation on air transport [3] by extending the list of technical agreements in Article 2 to include *inter alia* arrangements relating to the leasing of aircraft, aircraft parts, equipment and fixed installations as well as arrangements relating to the establishment, operation and maintenance of technical communication networks and the exchange, pooling and training of personnel. [4]

It also added to the list of agreements covered by the draft Council Regulation arrangements concerning slot allocation at airports and airport scheduling. Finally, an amendment was proposed to Council Regulation No 2821/71 on the application of Article 85(3) to categories of agreements, decisions and concerted practices by adding the following further categories of agreement to the list:

(a) the common purchase, operaton of or access to computer systems relating to timetabling, reservations and ticketing by air transport undertakings,

(b) technical and operational ground handling at airports such as push-back, refuelling, cleaning and security,

(c) the handling of passengers, mail and baggage at airports,

(d) services for the provision of in-flight catering.

The Transport Council met on several occasions during the year to discuss the Commission's proposals for liberalization of capacity controls and tariff setting procedures as well as the proposals relating to competition. In June the

---

[1] OJ C 182, 9.7.1984.
[2] COM(86) 338 final/2. These amendments were made in accordance with the Commission's proposal for a Council Regulation laying down the procedures for the exercise of implementing powers conferred on the Commission, COM(86) 35 Final, 29.10.1986.
[3] OJ C 317, 3.12.1982, p. 3, COM(86) 328.
[4] COM(86) 328 final.

Transport Council confirmed 'the need for a coherent Community air transport system based on a balanced set of instruments promoting increased competition in intra-Community air services as regards tariffs, capacity and market entry, in conformity with the competition rules of the Treaty'. The Ministers further agreed that such a system should apply for an initial period of three years during which the Council would 'review developments and take decisions on further steps in order to achieve the objective of the completion of the internal market by the year 1992'. Although progress was made during the year the Council was unable to reach a unanimous agreement on all elements of the package of liberalization measures.

On 18 July the Commission formally charged, pursuant to Article 89(1), 10 Community airlines (Aer Lingus, Air France, Alitalia, British Airways, British Caledonian, KLM, Lufthansa, Olympic Airways, Sabena and SAS) with having infringed the competition rules. The alleged infringements embrace capacity and revenue sharing arrangements as well as joint ventures, tariff concertations and agreements.

Sea transport

37. On 22 December the Council adopted four regulations in the maritime transport sector.[1] Regulation No 4056/86 lays down detailed rules for the application of Articles 85 and 86 to maritime transport. A block exemption is granted in respect of liner conferences. Conditions and obligations are attached to the exemption to protect the interests of transport users. The block exemption will be withdrawn if outside competition is eliminated owing to an act of a third State, but only after negotiations with such a State. The Regulation enters into force on 1 July 1987.

The other three regulations concern the principle of freedom to provide services in maritime transport within the common market and between the Member States and third countries: unfair pricing practices in maritime transport and the coordination of measures to safeguard free access to cargoes in ocean trades.

---

[1] Council Regualation (EEC) No 4055/86 of 22 December 1986 applying the principle of freedom to provide services to maritime transport between Member States and between Member States and third countries OJ L 378, 31.12.1986.
Council Regulation (EEC) No 4056/86 of 22 December 1986 laying down detailed rules for the application of Articles 85 and 86 of the Treaty to maritime transport OJ L 378, 31.12.1986.
Council Regulation (EEC) No 4057/86 of 22 December 1986 on unfair pricing practices in maritime transport OJ L 378, 31.12.1986.
Council Regulation (EEC) No 4058/86 of 22 December 1986 concerning coordinated action to safeguard free access to cargoes in ocean trades OJ L 378, 31.12.1986.

The Council invited the Commission to consider whether it is necessary to submit proposals regarding competition in passenger transport, tramp shipping, consortia in liner shipping and agreements between transport users. The Commission has undertaken to report to the Council within a year on whether it is necessary to provide for block exemptions for passenger transport services and consortia in liner shipping. Meanwhile, any request for an individual exemption of an agreement relating to passenger transport services will be carefully examined to see whether the agreement contributes to the facilitation of services.

With respect to consortia, the Commission held a hearing in which the shipping industry and representatives of the Member States were heard. The objective was to clarify the replies to the questionnaire distributed by the Commission and to obtain additional information.

Shipowners, represented by CAACE and CENSA met again with the Commission in December. It was agreed that further meetings should take place with the object of defining the concept of 'consortium'.

§ 7 — Merger control

38.   In the course of 1986, the Council's Economic Questions Working Party and the Committee of Permanent Representatives did not succeed in making any progress on the four outstanding issues contained in the draft proposal, namely: (i) scope of application; (ii) derogation; (iii) prior notification; (iv) procedures. [1] With respect to the last issue, the Commission modified its initial proposal. [2] It now proposes to organize cooperation between the Commission and the Member States in the decision-making process through the establishment of a traditional advisory committee similar to that provided for in cartel cases.

39.   In fact there will only be a decisive step towards pre-merger control on a Community level when all these issues are finally resolved. Unfortunately, there has been no meeting in the Council to discuss these matters. This situation is difficult to understand in the light of persistent increases in concentration [3] and the commitment of the Community to achieve an integrated internal market by 1992. In such a market a sound structural policy needs a means of controlling mergers having a Community-wide dimension. Both of these considerations lead the Commission to consider carefully Parliament's advice to withdraw the proposal and to make a fresh start in filling this lacuna in the Commission's competition policy. [4]

---

[1]   Fifteenth Competition Report, point 37.
[2]   OJ C 324, 17.12.1986,   p. 5. These amendments were made in accordance with the Commission's proposal for a Council Regulation laying down the procedures for the exercise of implementing powers conferred on the Commission, COM(86) 35 Final, 29.10.1986.
[3]   See point 317.
[4]   Point 29. Resolution on the Fifteenth Report of the Commission of the European Communities on Competition Policy reproduced in the Annex to this Report.

§ 8 — Anti-dumping

40.   For as long as there are transitional measures of protection for certain products in relations between the Community of Ten and Portugal and Spain, there is no complete free movement of goods. Consequently Article 380 of the Act of Accession provides that, if before the expiry of the transitional period the Commission, on application by a Member State or by any other interested party, and in accordance with rules of procedures to be adopted upon accession by the Council acting by a qualified majority on a proposal from the Commission, finds that dumping is being practised between the Community of Ten and the new Member States or between the new Member States, it addresses recommendations to the responsible persons for the purpose of putting an end to them. If the practices continue, the Commission authorizes the injured Member States to take protective measures, the conditions and details of which it determines.

In implementation of this provision, the Council adopted on 14 March Regulation (EEC) No 812/86 and Decision No 813/86/ECSC [1] on protection against imports which are the subject of dumping between the former Community of Ten and the new Member States themselves or between the new Member States during the period throughout which the transitional measures laid down by the said Act apply.

These texts are based, as the rules on protection against dumped or subsidized imports from third countries, [2] on the notions expressed in Article VI of the General Agreement on Tariffs and Trade (GATT). Dumping is characterized by the fact that the export price of a product is less than its normal value. Anti-dumping duties may be imposed where dumped imports cause a material injury to an established industry in the Community of Ten, in Spain or Portugal, if the interests of the Community require Community action. The regulation and decision lay down detailed rules for the calculation of normal value, export price, the calculation of a dumping margin and the establishment of an injury.

The procedures differ from those applied in case of dumping from third countries to take account of the fact that all countries involved are Member States of the Community. To obviate consultation of all Member States in cases mainly concerning the bilateral relations between two Member States,

---

[1]   OJ L 78, 24.3.1986.
[2]   Regulation (EEC) No 2176/84 of 23 July 1984 and Decision No 2177/84/ECSC of 27 February 1984, OJ L 201, 30.7.1984.

only interested Member States are consulted in the course of proceedings. Interested Member States are those which have an economic interest in the proceedings and have declared such interest to the Commission. Where there is evidence of dumping and injury and where the interests of the Community require Community action, the Commission first addresses recommendations that the dumping be terminated to the parties responsible. If they do not give an undertaking to this end or fail to comply with such undertaking, the Commission may authorize the injured Member States to introduce anti-dumping duties or conditions determined by the Commission.

Eight cases have been examined under the new Regulation in 1986, two were new complaints. The other cases concern anti-dumping measures taken or proceedings opened before Accession which are also dealt with under Regulation No 812/86 in conformity with Article 380(3) of the Act of Accession by the Community or by the new Member States.

In four of those cases, the Commission has taken a decision or published a notice. The two proceedings opened by the Commisssion before Accession have been terminated: in one case, concerning imports of hardboard from Portugal, on the ground that the Act of Accession does not provide for any transitional measures for the product concerned [1] and in the other case, concerning imports of Portland cement from Spain, because the complainants have withdrawn their complaint. [2]

Proceedings opened by Spain before Accession, concerning imports of refrigerating units for transport from France are being continued by the Commission and a notice inviting interested parties to comment has been published. [3]

Proceedings have been re-opened after a request for review by Spain of Council Regulation (EEC) No 2109/85 of 25 July 1985, which had imposed definitive anti-dumping duties imposed on imports of certain kinds of polystyrene sheet originating in Spain. [4] A notice inviting interested parties to comment has also been published in this case. [5]

---

[1]   OJ L 81, 26.3.1986.
[2]   OJ L 282, 3.10.1986.
[3]   OJ C 241, 25.9.1986.
[4]   OJ L 198, 30.7.1985.
[5]   OJ C 238, 20.9.1986.

§ 9 — Application of Community competition law by national courts

41. The Commission has continued to press ahead with its policy of stressing the role of national courts in the enforcement of the EEC competition rules as set out in the EEC Treaty. National courts can play a useful role in the application of Community competition policy where such policy is already clearly defined by block exemption regulations, general notices or established case law. The Commission should be able to concentrate on the further development of Community policy and the treatment of complex cases with Community-wide dimensions should be reserved for the Commission.

A detailed questionnaire was sent to the authorities of the Member States in December 1985. [1] The picture that emerges from the replies to the questionnaire is as follows:

(i)   In the Federal Republic of Germany, civil law courts are obliged to inform the Bundeskartellamt of proceedings in which questions of national competition law are raised. In practice information is also given to the Bundeskartellamt in respect of cases involving Articles 85 and 86.

In all other Member States, there is no systematic gathering of information relating to proceedings involving Articles 85 and 86 of the EEC Treaty which are pending before national courts or tribunals. National authorities become aware of these proceedings through informal contacts with undertakings or parties involved in litigation or their legal advisers;

(ii) In most Member States, the national cartel authorities cannot take the initiative to intervene in proceedings before national courts or tribunals. However, they may be able to do so at the invitation either of the parties to the litigation or of the judge;

(iii) It was felt that the problem of obtaining evidence located in other jurisdictions might possibly be overcome by existing procedures;

(iv) The national cartel authorities were of the opinion that members of the judiciary in their Member States were aware of Community competition law so as to be able to deal with points which might be raised in the course of proceedings before them. Nevertheless, any activities designed to enhance their knowledge are always appreciated, such as training courses for judges, seminars and publications.

---

[1]   Fifteenth Competition Report, point 42.

An analysis of the replies to the questionnaire confirmed the Commission's view that, in principle, there are no fundamental obstacles to the application of Community competition law by national courts and that some kind of cooperation between the Commission and national jurisdictions can be organized. Until now it is clear that the Community competition rules have generally been pleaded as a basis for obtaining an injunction or other interim relief or as a defence to an action for a breach of contract. There does not appear, to the Commission's knowledge, to be any case in which damages have been awarded by a national court for a breach of either Article 85 or Article 86 of the EEC Treaty.

42.   As was mentioned in the Fifteenth Competition report [1] the Commission has begun to prepare a guide on the enforcement of the EEC competition rules by national courts.

The purpose of this guide is to set out which cases coming within the scope of Articles 85 and 86 of the EEC Treaty can best be dealt with by national judges. The guidebook will be addressed to all those likely to be involved in competition litigation: undertakings, lawyers and members of the judiciary as well as individual citizens or consumers.

In order to maximize the practical use of the guide the Commission has requested the Consultative Committee of the Bars and Law Societies of the European Community (CCBE) to assist in its preparation.

---

[1]   Point 43.

§ 10 — Procedural issues — Locus standi

BP/TGWU — Llandarcy Refinery

43. In June 1985 the Transport and General Workers Union (TGWU), one of the largest trade unions in the United Kingdom, lodged a complaint to the Commission pursuant to Article 3(2) of Regulation 17/62. Two allegations were made: the first was that BP had entered into a concerted practice with Texaco to close down the BP refinery at Llandarcy; the second allegation was to the effect that the oil-processing arrangements between BP and Texaco were a breach of the Community competition rules.

The Commission took the view that the TGWU as a representative of the workers made redundant by the closure of the refinery had a legitimate interest within the meaning of Article 3(2) of Regulation 17 entitling it to make a complaint.

The existence of such interest was obvious with respect to the first allegation. However, the Commission came to the conclusion that the closure of the refinery had been decided by BP unilaterally. Consequently there was no infringement of Article 85 of the EEC Treaty and hence that part of the complaint was unfounded.

With respect to the processing contracts the legitimate interest of the TGWU only existed to the extent to which these arrangements had a bearing on the closure of the refinery. Since there was no link between the two elements that part of the complaint was inadmissible.

Chapter II

Main decisions and measures taken
by the Commission

Part I

Articles 85 and 86 of the EEC Treaty

44.   In 1986 the Commission adopted 21 formal decisions and two further
decisions rejecting complaints under Article 85 or 86 of the EEC Treaty. It also
took 2 decisions under Article 65 of the ECSC Treaty and 14 decisions applying
Article 66 of the ECSC Treaty. Seventy-four cases were dealt with by way of
administrative letter.

Furthermore, 283 cases were settled without formal decision because the agreements or other activities of the parties involved were either altered to conform
with the competition rules or were terminated or had expired.

On 31 December there were 3 522 cases pending, of which 3 032 were applications or notifications (384 made in 1986), [1] 330 were complaints from firms
(75 made in 1986) and 160 consisted of proceedings started by the Commission
on its own initiative (33 started in 1986). The breakdown of notifications and
applications currently pending is as follows:

50% concern industrial property rights, 32% distribution agreements and 18%
so-called 'horizontal' agreements.

---

[1]   A total of 149 notifications were received from Spanish undertakings and four notifications were made
by Portuguese undertakings. 17 notifications concerned agreements made with Spanish undertakings and
11 notifications concerned agreements with Portuguese undertakings.

Until recently the Commission has been able to reduce the backlog of notifications in particular by means of the block exemption regulations. However, this year, in spite of its best endeavours, the backlog has actually increased. This is regrettable, but inevitable, given the numbers of staff as compared with the volume of work.

§ 1 — Prohibited horizontal agreements

45.   The Commission adopted four decisions relating to horizontal agreements in which it confirmed that the partitioning of geographical markets, quotas and price fixing run counter to a fundamental principle of Community law and policy and accordingly merit heavy fines. Furthermore, it was reaffirmed that this policy extends to agreements made between undertakings established within one Member State if the object or effect of such an arrangement is to protect a national market against competition from other parts of the Community.

Polypropylene [1]

46.   The Commission imposed fines totalling 57.85 million ECU on 15 major petrochemical producers for infringements of Article 85 of the EEC Treaty. Thirteen of them were firms whose head office and production facilities are located inside the EEC; the other two have their polypropylene marketing headquarters outside the Community although they have subsidiaries and sales networks within it. The Commission found that these undertakings had operated a market-sharing and price-fixing cartel in the polypropylene market from the end of 1977 until at least November 1983.

Polypropylene is a thermo-plastic product and is an important input to the plastics processing industry. It has an extensive range of uses which include the manufacture of packaging film and tape, rope, clothing, automotive parts, household goods and other consumer articles. It can also be a substitute for products such as wood, metal, paper, textiles or jute and other plastics such as polystyrene and polyvinyl chloride (PVC).

Most of the 15 producers held regular 'bosses' (directors or senior managers) and 'experts' (marketing managers) meetings twice monthly in order to set target prices and to decide on how to concert efforts to raise prices and to implement and monitor, where appropriate, a system of annual quotas. There were also local meetings in which producers discussed the detailed implementation of the agreed measures in national markets.

The four largest producers — Montepolimeri (part of Montedison), Hoechst, ICI and Shell — which account for some 50% of the polypropylene market in

---

[1]   Decision of 23 April 1986, OJ L 230, 18.8.1986. An application for annulment of this decision by 14 of the 15 addressees has been lodged before the Court of Justice.

the Community constituted a kind of self-appointed directorate of the cartel. From 1982 they held meetings — known as the 'Big Four pre-meetings' — the day before the 'bosses' meetings. The other firms implemented the decisions adopted at such meetings.

The pervasive nature of these restrictive practices was such as to affect seriously trade between Member States and to pose a threat to competition within the common market. Thousands of industrial users of polypropylene were adversely affected by the manipulation of the selling price of what is, for many industries, an important input.

The evidence, both direct and circumstantial, upon which the decision was based was obtained by investigations at the premises of most of the undertakings pursuant to Article 14(2) and 14(3) of Regulation 17 coupled with requests for information under Article 11 of Regulation 17. The investigations revealed details of the cartel meetings, and of the way in which target prices had been fixed and markets shared out. Following the meetings, the measures adopted were implemented by the producers themselves or by their subsidiaries and their selling agents. The totality of this evidence indicated a clear violation of Article 85.

Considering the serious and deliberate nature of the infringement, which caused grave damage to processors of polypropylene in the common market, the Commission imposed fines at a level calculated to deter such serious violations of the competition rules. (Montepolimeri: 11 million ECU; ICI: 10 million ECU; Hoechst: 9 million ECU; Shell: 9 million ECU; Hercules: 2.75 million ECU; Huels: 2.75 million ECU; DSM: 2.75 million ECU; BASF: 2.5 million ECU; Solvay: 2.5 million ECU; Ato Chem: 1.75 million ECU; Linz: 1 million ECU; Statoil (successor of Saga Petrokjemi): 1 million ECU; Anic: 0.75 million ECU; Petrofina: 0.6 million ECU and Rhône-Poulenc: 0.5 million ECU).

It should be noted that in imposing these fines the Commission took into account the fact that the undertakings involved had incurred substantial losses on their polypropylene operations over a considerable period, that price targets did not in general achieve their objectives in full and that in the last resort there were no measures of constraint to ensure compliance with quotas and other measures.

Meldoc

47.   The Commission imposed substantial fines [1] totalling 6 565 000 ECU for infringement of Article 85(1) on five Dutch dairies in respect of a cartel known as 'Meldoc' which involved market-sharing through quotas combined with a

---

[1]   Decision of 27 November 1986, OJ L 348, 10.12.1986.

compensation system, cooperation on sales and prices on a nationwide scale and the protection of the home market against imports.

The cartel agreement set up a joint policy for prices and conditions of sale for liquid milk and other dairy products, both fresh and long-life. Quotas based on the parties' 1977 sales levels were allotted to each member; levies were imposed for exceeding the allotted quotas, and compensation was paid where there was a failure to reach quota level. The proportion of the Dutch market controlled by the Meldoc cartel rose from approximately 68% in 1978 to over 90% in 1983. The home market was protected against imports from other Member States which threatened the market share of the participants or their profits on pasteurized milk. Aldi, a large German supermarket chain with branches in the Netherlands, was forced to discontinue imports of low-priced UHT milk from Germany after Meldoc had dropped the price of its UHT milk. With respect to fresh milk Meldoc launched a dumping operation on the Belgian market which consisted in offering milk at unprofitable prices to Belgian retailers, in order to persuade Belgian dairies to stop their exports to the Netherlands. The losses resulting from these actions were shared amongst the members of the cartel. The result of the cartel was to exclude virtually all competition on a nationwide scale.

Trade between Member States was affected in that the agreement covered almost the whole of the territory of the Netherlands, making penetration of the Dutch market by producers from other Member States more difficult than would have been the case otherwise. The size of the cartel, coupled with the intensive cooperation in terms of sales and prices, had an inherently adverse effect on the possibilities for foreign suppliers to enter the Dutch market. These suppliers were confronted with a market controlled jointly by members of a cartel which ultimately covered 90% of the relevant product market and who acted together to defend their sales volume against outsiders.

The infringements of the competition rules by those involved in the Meldoc cartel were serious and merited substantial fines. However, the Commission took into account certain mitigating factors such as the serious situation prevailing in the dairy sector, the fact that four of the five undertakings were cooperatives of small farmers, the concentration of market power in the hands of the big retailers and the vulnerability of the Dutch producers to imports because of the relatively high minimum price for fresh milk of Dutch origin. Individual fines were imposed as follows: Melkunie: 3 150 000 ECU; Coberco: 1 360 000 ECU; DOMO Bedum: 600 000 ECU; Campina: 1 020 000 ECU; Menken Landbouw: 425 000 ECU.

Belasco

48. A fine of 1 million ECU was imposed by the Commission[1] on seven Belgian producers of roofing felt, who entered into and operated a cartel from 1978 to early 1984 contrary to the provisions of Article 85(1). The parties to the agreement were members of the Société Cooperative des Asphalteurs Belges (Belasco) and two other undertakings. All the parties are producers of roofing felt, bitumen coated sheeting used extensively in the building industry for waterproofing, in particular flat roofs. Some had other business activities including roofing work and road works.

The agreement was designed to organize the Belgian market for roofing felt and to protect it from external competition. It provided for the adoption of a common price list and minimum prices for all roofing felt supplied in Belgium, the allocation of quotas between members for deliveries to the Belgian market, and joint action to deal with any disturbance to the collective interest of members arising out of new entrants to the market, increased foreign competition or the development of substitute products. There were restrictions on the sale or leasing of production facilities and on the production of roofing felt on behalf of non-members for delivery to the Belgian market. The members also agreed to coordinate product ranges and to carry out joint sales promotion.

The agreement was administered by a 'general meeting' at which each member was represented. An accountant monitored compliance with quotas and prices. Penalties were imposed for deliveries in excess of agreed quotas.

Furthermore, the members of the cartel decided to take joint counter-measures against Belgian producers and importers of roofing felt who were selling at prices below those fixed by the cartel. The whole scheme tended to isolate the Belgian market and maintain rigid market structures.

In view of the very serious nature of the restrictions on competition practised over a period of five years, the Commission imposed fines, which in relation to the turnover of firms were high. However, in determining the level of the fines imposed account was taken of two mitigating factors: the small size of the firms involved who may not have fully appreciated the Community competition rules and their applicability to them and the economic difficulties faced by the firms as a result of a recession in the building industry.

The individual fines were as follows: Antwerpse Teer- en Asphaltbedrijf: 420 000 ECU; Lummerzheim & Co.: 200 000 ECU; Compagnie Générale des

---

[1]   Decision of 10 July 1986, OJ L 232, 19.8.1986.

Asphaltes: 150 000 ECU; Kempisch Asphaltbedrijf: 75 000 ECU; De Boer & Co.: 75 000 ECU; Vlaams Asfaltbedrijf Huyghe & Co.: 50 000 ECU; Limburgse Asfaltfabrieken: 30 000 ECU; Société Coopérative des Asphalteurs Belges ('Belasco'): 15 000 ECU.

Fatty acids

49.   This decision confirms the attitude of the Commission to the exchange of information between competitors. [1] The Commission does not object, in principle, to market information systems. However, where these systems enable the participants to coordinate their market strategies, it may come within the scope of Article 85(1). This case is the first in which the Commission has imposed fines in respect of an exchange of information agreement. [2]

Three major European producers of oleine and stearine (fatty acids) within the Community were fined for having operated an exchange of information agreement contrary to Article 85(1). The parties to the agreement — Unilever, Henkel and Oleofina — held around 60% of the market for the products in question. Fatty acids are used in the manufacture of soap and detergents, cosmetics, toiletries, paints and resins as well as industrial lubricants and processed foods. They are also used in the manufacture of plastics and rubber and the treatment of paper and textiles. In 1979, faced with structural overcapacity and stagnant growth rate, the three undertakings agreed to exchange confidential information about their sales of fatty acids in Europe. Under the agreement the parties first established their respective average market shares over a preceding three-year period and subsequently exchanged information about their sales of fatty acids in each quarter. They were thus able to monitor each others' activities and adjust their own behaviour accordingly. The agreement was terminated in 1982 upon the recommendation of the Commission after an investigation had been carried out.

The Commission considered that such an agreement, operated by three major producers in a market in recession which on the one hand provided for exchange of confidential information, about traditional market positions and on the other hand set up means of monitoring their future performance had an inherent restrictive effect upon competition. The exchange of information made for artificially increased transparency between the parties to the agreement about each other's activities, thereby enabling them to react more rapidly and

---

[1]   See Seventh Competition Report, points 5-8.
[2]   Decision of 2 December 1986, OJ L 3, 6.1.1987.

efficiently to one another's actions. It dissuaded the parties from adopting aggressively competitive lines of behaviour towards one another and aimed at stabilizing their relative positions on the market.

Trade between Member States was affected in that the producers in question supplied the major part of the need for European industry for fatty acid. All three producers marketed their products in several or all Member States; one had production facilities in several Member States.

A fine of 50 000 ECU was imposed on each of the three undertakings involved.

§ 2 — Distribution agreements

50.   The Commission continued its policy of favouring the establishment of efficient distribution systems even where they contain some restrictions on the commercial freedom of manufacturers and traders. It insists, however, that these systems should operate in such a way as to ensure that parallel imports remain possible, that no catagory of purchasers is excluded from supply in a discriminatory manner and that any interference with the parties' individual price policy is excluded.

On the basis of these principles, the Commission intervened against export bans on cars and a resale ban on coffee and investigated an allegation of resale price maintenance. It also adopted its first decisions on franchising agreements. More generally, the Commission reaffirmed its conviction that a Community-wide product guarantee is essential for free and undistorted competition within the common market and for consumer protection.

Parallel imports

Peugeot-Talbot

51.   The Commission decided [1] that the standard agreement on which the distribution network of Peugeot-Talbot was based, as applied in the Benelux between 1 May 1982 and 30 June 1985, infringed Article 85(1) and did not qualify for an exemption under Article 85(3). [2] Furthermore, the Commission imposed a fine of 4 000 ECU on Peugeot-Talbot because it had supplied incorrect information in the course of the investigation. In its decision the Commission found that this system was operated in such a way as to prevent United Kingdom and Irish residents from obtaining right-hand-drive (RHD) cars from Peugeot-Talbot distributors in the Benelux where they were available at much lower prices. The main features of Peugeot-Talbot strategy were the following:

(i)   in order to control the supply of cars (including RHD cars) to persons not resident in the country of purchase, Peugeot-Talbot created a new company, the Société de Distribution et d'Exportation Automobile (Sodexa);

---

[1]   Decision of 25 September 1986, OJ L 295, 18.10.1986.
[2]   OJ L 15, 18.1.1985.

(ii) orders for such vehicles had to be sent to Sodexa which sold them direct to the purchaser; the dealer was treated as an agent and received a small commission as opposed to the usual profit margin;

(iii) Sodexa consistently tried to dissuade potential buyers of RHD vehicles resident in the United Kingdom from ordering such vehicles on the Continent. Persons who contacted Sodexa were systematically referred to the British Dealer Network.

52.   Following an increase in demand for RHD vehicles, additional measures were taken to discourage orders for such vehicles from customers resident in the United Kingdom. Dealers in the Netherlands were no longer supplied with RHD cars. The list prices for such vehicles in Belgium and Luxembourg were increased to approximately the price level in the United Kingdom with the result that a sharp price difference between RHD and left-hand-drive (LHD) cars was created, which amounted to 31% for Peugeot vehicles and 47% for Talbot cars. Moreover, the profit margin for dealers was limited to 10%. As a result of these obstructions a large number of orders for RHD cars were cancelled and in fact parallel imports from the Benelux of Peugeot-Talbot models into the United Kingdom were sharply reduced.

The decision is in line with the Commission's policy previously set out in the Ford case, [1] which was upheld by the Court of Justice. [2]

It makes clear that a refusal to supply RHD vehicles and measures of equivalent effect such as the introduction of price differentials between LHD and RHD vehicles in the operation of a distribution network for cars is contrary to Article 85(1) and will lead to a refusal of an exemption under Article 85(3) for the distribution system in question.

Fines were not imposed in respect of the above-mentioned restrictive practices for two reasons: the distribution agreement in question gave Peugeot and Sodexa the exclusive right to sell RHD vehicles, so that the notification extended to the refusal to supply and therefore precluded the imposition of a fine (Article 15(5) Regulation No 17). Secondly, it was not entirely clear until the judgment of the Court of Justice in the Ford case, [3] handed down on 17 September 1985, what were the obligations of Continental dealers with respect to the sales of RHD cars to customers resident in the United Kingdom.

---

[1]   Decision of 16 November 1983, OJ L 327, 24.11.1983. Thirteenth Competition Report, point 96.
[2]   Joined Cases 25 and 26/84 *Ford-Werke AG and Ford of Europe Inc. v Commission*, not yet reported. Fifteenth Competition Report, point 125.
[3]   Ibid.

Franchising

Pronuptia/Yves Rocher

53. In two decisions [1] the Commission granted an exemption under Article 85(3) in respect of standard form distribution contracts made between Pronuptia and Yves Rocher with the franchised retailers of their products, wedding dresses and cosmetics respectively, in several Member States.

In each case the contracts obliged the franchisor to grant the franchisees the exclusive right, within a defined geographical area, to use its industrial property rights (shop signs, trade marks, symbols and registered designs and models) for the retailing of its products. The franchisor undertook to transfer to its franchisees its commercial know-how and to supply them with technical and commercial assistance. The franchisees, in both cases, were legally independent traders carrying on business at their own risk. They were responsible for the cost of fitting out their premises in accordance with the specification stipulated by the franchisor. Their obligations consisted in operating their outlets in accordance with the trading methods laid down by the franchisor and in selling only under the franchisor's sign. The franchisees further undertook to pay certain sums of money over to the franchisor and not carry on a competing business during the lifetime of the agreements and for a period of one year after their termination, within a specified territory.

The franchisees were free to set their own resale prices although guidelines were laid down by the franchisors. Franchisees were able to buy from or to sell to one another.

Several obligations imposed on the franchisees did not restrict competition since they were a necessary prerequisite for the proper functioning of the networks: they were designed either to safeguard their uniformity and reputation or to prevent the use by competitors of the know-how and commercial knowledge transferred by the franchisor to the franchisee under the terms of the contracts.

Although the franchising contracts provided for a certain degree of market sharing and restricted competition by granting exclusive territorial protection to each franchisee, their overall effect was to improve and strengthen competition rather than to restrict it. The agreements permitted the franchisor to set up and expand distribution networks with similar business methods and to

---

[1] Decisions of 17 December 1986, OJ L 8 and 13, 10 and 15.1.1987.

make available merchandise of a uniform quality and range to the public, without having to invest in numerous individual sales outlets. The franchisees had access to proven business methods and an established name and reputation.

Resale ban

Brazilian coffee

54. Acting on a complaint logded in December 1985 by the European Federation of Associations of Coffee Roasters, the Commission requested the Instituto Brazilero do Café (IBC) in July 1986 to delete certain clauses in its contracts with coffee roasters forbidding the resale of green coffee, which it held to amount to restrictions contrary to the Community competition rules since they discriminated between coffee processors according to where they were established and resulted in unreasonably higher prices for the consumer.

This is not the first time that the Commission has had to intervene to enforce the competition rules in the coffee sector. The present case reinforces the position adopted by the Commission on earlier occasions. [1]

Resale price maintenance

VEB/Shell

55. The Commission formally rejected a complaint by the Vereniging Exploitanten Benzinestation (VEB), an association of tenants of petrol stations which are owned by the Dutch sales subsidiary of Shell, that Shell's contract with its petrol station tenants in the Netherlands infringed the competition rules in that the discount system operated by Shell amounted to indirect resale price maintenance and price discrimination.

The Commission established that the discount system in question was operated to support the margin of retailers who were forced to reduce their pump prices to counter local competition. A retailer could ask for an extra discount off the wholesale price in order to meet the reduction in his margin caused by a lowering of prices. Shell appraised local competitive conditions when deciding

---

[1] Fifth Competition Report, point 33. Decision of 10 December 1982, OJ L 360, 21.12.1982; Twelfth Competition Report, point 76.

on whether or not to grant such a discount. The Commission did not consider that this practice involved indirect resale price maintenance.

Although the Commission rejected this particular complaint, it has drawn Shell's attention to the fact that the scheme must not lead to discrimination between retailers of the same brand competing with one another.

Consumer guarantees

56.   The Commission has repeatedly stated that guarantees offered as part of after-sales service by manufacturers of consumer durables must be valid throughout the Community regardless of the Member State in which the product is purchased. [1]

Refusal to honour a guarantee in respect of a product which has not been imported or exported through the manufacturer's established network may constitute a substantial barrier to trade within the Community.

In authorizing distribution agreements, the Commission has at all times insisted upon the availability of Community-wide product guarantees. In a series of decisions concerning clocks and watches, [2] motor vehicles, [3] consumer electronics, [4] electrical appliances [5] and personal computers, [6] the Commission has ensured that where the manufacturer gave a guarantee on branded goods, the service covered by that guarantee would be available from any approved dealer, not merely the dealer from which it was purchased. This position has been confirmed by the Court of Justice in the *Hasselblad* [7] and *Swatch* [8] cases.

This policy is mirrored in the block exemption regulation on distribution in the motor vehicle sector in which it is provided that the exemption granted by the regulation applies only where dealers honour guarantees and perform free services and vehicle recall work in respect of vehicles supplied in the common market by another dealer in the distribution network.

The Commission has been informed by the European Bureau of Consumer Unions (BEUC) that certain distribution networks, in spite of numerous

---

[1]   Seventh Competition Report, points 17-20.
[2]   Decision of 28 October 1970, *Omega*: OJ L 242, 5.11.1970; First Competition Report, point 56.
[3]   Decision of 13 December 1974, *Bayerische Motoren Werke AG*: OJ L 29, 3.2.1975; Fourth Competition Report, point 86.
[4]   Decision of 15 December 1975, *SABA*: OJ L 28, 3.2.1976; Fifth Competition Report, point 54.
[5]   Decision of 23 October 1978, *Zanussi*: OJ L 322, 16.11.1978; Eighth Competition Report, point 116.
[6]   Decision of 18 April 1984, *IBM Personal Computer*: OJ L 118, 4.5.1984, p. 24; Fourteenth Competition Report, point 63.
[7]   Judgment of 21 February 1984, Case 86/82 *Hasselblad* [1984] ECR, 883.
[8]   Judgment of 10 December 1985, Case 31/85 *Swatch*.: OJ C 347, 31.12.1985.

unequivocal statements of policy by the Commission, still refuse to honour guarantees for produce purchased in another Member State.

The Commission is investigating the cases brought to its attention by BEUC. In the light of these complaints, the Commission, in early November, felt it to be its duty to warn [1] manufacturers that unless consumers could obtain Community-wide guarantees on products purchased in any Member State, the distribution agreements covering such product might be declared to be incompatible with the competition rules.

---

[1]   Bull. EC 11-1986, point 2.1.77.

§ 3 — Services sector

57.   In 1986 the activity of the Commission in the services sector was mainly concentrated on banking. The Commission furthermore continued its policy on commodity markets and adopted five decisions.

Banking

58.   The Commission has consistently maintained that the competition rules are applicable in the banking sector in the same way as in other sectors of the economy, a policy upheld by the Court of Justice in the *Züchner* case. [1] The Commission's decision of 10 December 1984 to exempt agreements on the international use and clearing of uniform Eurocheques under Article 85(3) was its first formal decision in the banking sector. [2] Three decisions adopted in the course of 1986 break new ground in that they determine the compatibility of an entire range of agreements concluded within national banking associations of Member States with the competition rules. None of the decisions is concerned with interest rates: the Commission has decided for the present to reserve its position on this matter pending an enquiry into the relationship between interest rates and the monetary policy of the individual Member States.

Irish banks

59.   The Commission decided [3] that a number of agreements between members of the Irish Banks Standing Committee (IBSC) do not appreciably restrict competition in the common market within the meaning of Article 85(1) and therefore granted them a negative clearance. The banks are the Allied Irish Banks plc, Bank of Ireland, Northern Bank Ltd and Ulster Bank Ltd. They are generally known as the associated Banks and are the main clearing and retail banks in Ireland. The agreements relate to common opening hours, clearing rules and a direct debiting system. Previous agreements relating to commissions for services to customers had already been voluntarily abandoned by the Associated Banks following a Community-wide investigation by the Commission into such agreements in the banking sector.

---

1   Case 172/83 *Züchner v Bayerische Vereinsbank AG* [1981] ECR 2021.
2   Decision of 10 December 1984, OJ L 35, 7.2.1985. Fourteenth Competition Report, points 77-79.
3   Decision of 30 September 1986, OJ L 295, 18.10.1986.

Belgische vereniging der banken/
Association belge des banques

60. Following Commission intervention, a wide range of restrictive practices in the Belgian banking sector were abandoned. At the same time, the Commission exempted [1] under Article 85(3) three agreements which were notified to it by the Belgian association of banks (Belgische vereniging der banken/ Association belge des banques BVB/ABB) — because they were beneficial to the fluidity of transactions in the banking sector.

The BVB/ABB, which at the end of the first half of 1986 comprised 84 of the 86 banks in Belgium, had notified a series of restrictive practices, concluded on the Associations' initiative. These agreements were the subject of a statement of objections issued by the Commission in spring 1985. The objections concerned restrictive practices in respect of commissions charged by the banks for their services. Following discussions held between the BVB/ABB and the Commission, the BVB/ABB decided to abandon the agreements to which the Commission objected with effect from 1 April 1986, except for three, which were retained in part.

These three agreements apply to interbank relations and no longer concern the relations between banks and their customers. They govern transactions which involve at least two banks in Belgium, one acting as intermediary for the other. The relevant transactions are of two kinds: they relate either to securities or to international monetary movements and trade. In the first case, one bank undertakes various securities dealings on behalf of its customers instead of another bank which had been made directly responsible by the issuer as registrar bank for those securities. In the second case, one bank forwards to another bank, also in Belgium, an order which it has received as correspondent from a bank abroad.

The three agreements restrict competition within the meaning of Article 85(1) for the following reasons: two of them (the agreement on securities dealings and the one on international payments in foreign currencies or originating abroad) contain provisions concerning, respectively, the actual amount of the rebates, and of the commissions charged for acting as intermediary in these operations. As regards the third agreement (which concerns the collection of cheques and commercial bills originating abroad), its restrictive provisions consist in laying down the principle of charging a commission and the procedure for doing so.

---

[1]   Decisions of 11 December 1986, OJ L 7, 9.1.1987.

Nevertheless, these three agreements were exempted, in particular because they contribute to an appreciable improvement of the services provided to customers and because the commissions are only maxima and not necessarily charged to customers.

The Commission attached an obligation to the decision: the BVB/ABB is required to inform the Commission immediately of any addition or amendment to the three agreements in question and of any new agreement concluded between its members within the Association. The exemption applies for 10 years from 30 May 1986, the date of notification of the final version of the three agreements.

Associazione bancaria italiana

61. The Associazione Bancaria Italiana (ABI) is a non-profit-making association of all banks and other financial institutions established in Italy. In 1984 it notified 15 agreements and recommendations, to the Commission. Five of these were subsequently abandoned following the Commission intervention. Of the remaining 10, seven have been declared not to restrict competition to an appreciable extent and thus not to violate Article 85(1); the remaining three, although restrictive of competition, were granted an exemption under Article 85(3). [1]

With respect to those agreements granted negative clearance, one was concerned with technical matters only, whilst four dealt with the standardization and rationalization of banking operations on a national level, a matter which concerned operations in Italy only and hence did not appreciably affect trade between Member States. Two more agreements on minimum charges for safe deposits, although restrictive of competition, could not, in the Commission's view, be deemed to have an appreciable effect on trade.

Three agreements relating to the collection and acceptance of Italian bills and documents, the collection of cheques and assimilated instruments, and an interbank agreement on a new uniform type of lire travellers' cheque were considered by the Commission to be contrary to Article 85(1) in that they eliminated the freedom of members of the ABI to determine individually charges for banking services, thereby restricting competition between banking institutions and consumer choice. Trade between Member States was affected since the agreements extended to foreign operations. Consequently although

---

[1]   Decision of 12 December 1986, OJ L 43, 13.12.1987; Bull. EC 12-1986, point 2.1.97.

the agreements were clearly within the scope of Article 85(1), the Commission found that the conditions for the granting of an exemption under Article 85(3) were fulfilled. The agreements achieved the necessary standardization and rationalization of banking and credit services. As a result, a more efficient service at a reasonable cost could be provided. The fixing of a uniform rate for services was essential for the collaboration between banks and centralized clearing. Moreover, the agreements in question do not concern relations between banks and their customers, the extent to which the value date and commissions are passed on to customers being left to the discretion of the banks. They, therefore, constitute only one element of the final cost of the service provided to customers.

The exemption was granted for a period of 10 years from the date of notification and was made subject to the obligation of the ABI to inform the Commission immediately of any changes in the commissions and value dates indicated in the notified agreements and of any new agreement concluded between the members of the association.

Commodity markets

The London Grain Futures Market

The London Potato Futures Association Limited

The London Meat Futures Exchange Limited

The Gafta Soya Bean Meal Futures Association Limited

The International Petroleum Exchange of London Limited

The five decisions [1] relating to the Rules and Regulations of the above-mentioned terminal markets follow the previous decisions taken by the Commission with respect to the commodity markets last year. [2]

Under the original Rules and Regulations as notified to the Commission, a fixed minimum commission for transactions carried out on the 'floor' of the market was applicable. Furthermore, the rules on membership did not contain

---

[1]   Decisions of 10 December 1986, OJ L 19, 21.1.1987 and 4 December 1986, OJ L 3, 6.1.1987.
[2]   Decisions of 31 December 1985, OJ L 369, 31.12.1985 and Fifteenth Competition Report, point 70.

clear and objective criteria to be fulfilled by applicants for membership, making the markets so-called 'closed shops'.

As a result of the Commission's intervention the following amendments have been made to the Rules and Regulations:

(i)   the references to the system of fixed minimum commission rates have been deleted; the rates of commission are now freely negotiable;

(ii)   the membership rules have been altered; membership is now regulated on the basis of objective criteria. In the interest of the protection of the rights of actual or potential members, an appeal procedure has been introduced.

Under these circumstances the Commission felt able to grant negative clearance in all five cases.

Broadcasting

European Broadcasting Union

62.   A number of members of the European Broadcasting Union had planned to group together to fix joint rates and conditions for the use of television news items taken from the network by third parties. Upon being advised by the Commission that this would restrict competition within the common market, [1] in that intended purchasers would no longer be able to negotiate separately with individual broadcasters, the broadcasters abandoned their plans. They have reverted to their previous practice of negotiating separately with purchasers.

---

[1]   Bull. EC 7/8-1986, point 2.1.61.

§ 4 — Permitted forms of cooperation (including joint ventures)

63.   In 1986 the Commission dealt with seven cases in which it took a favourable view of horizontal forms of cooperation. The key issues of these cases were the rationalization of fairs and exhibitions for office equipment, cooperation to develop an open industry standard for computer software systems, industrial restructuring in the petrochemical industry, the joint exploitation of complementary techniques in the fields of optical fibres and air filters and cooperation in the field of safety in oxide fuel reprocessing services. In all these cases the Commission reiterated its established policy of accepting agreements even between competitors which are designed to develop and transfer new technology or to restructure industry.

Fairs and exhibitions

Vifka

64.   The Commission, in accordance with its general policy of approval of measures which tend to render more efficient the organization of fairs and exhibitions, provided that restrictions on the freedom to exhibit are not excessive, granted an exemption to the rules governing participation in a major office equipment exhibition called the 'Efficiency beurs' held every other year in Amsterdam. [1] The exhibition is organized by Vifka, the Vereniging van importeurs en fabrikanten van kantoormachines (Association of office equipment importers and manufacturers), the major organization of its kind in the Netherlands. Under the rules approved by the Commission, exhibitors at the 'Efficiency beurs' may not participate in any other office equipment fair or exhibition not organized or approved by Vifka in the same calendar year.

The initial version of the rules provided that Vifka members, whether or not they exhibited at Efficiency beurs, would be banned from participating in any other office equipment fair. Non-members wishing to exhibit at the 'Efficiency beurs' had to undertake not to participate in any other office equipment fair in the following two years. These restrictions were found to be excessive and could not be exempted.

---

[1]   Decision of 30 September 1986, OJ L 291, 15.10.1986.

Industrial standards

X/Open Group

65.   An exemption [1] under Article 85(3) was granted to the members of the X/Open Group who are currently: Bull, France; DEC International (Europe), Switzerland; L.M. Ericsson, Sweden; ICL, United Kingdom; Nixdorf, Federal Republic of Germany; Olivetti, Italy; Philips, the Netherlands; Siemens, Federal Republic of Germany and Unisys, USA. The aim of the Group is to establish a standard interface for use in Europe between applications software and a particular version of the Unix operating system.

The X/Open Group was established by an agreement ('Group Agreement') in 1984 with the aim of increasing the volume of application programs available on the members' computer systems. In the eyes of users it is the application programs that determine the use of their machines and, therefore, the range and quality of such software is a determining factor for them when deciding which make of machine to acquire. Many application programs are written by independent software companies which naturally concentrate their efforts upon the biggest markets. Although the members of the X/Open Group are companies of a considerable size, each of them offers the software industry only a limited potential market. However, by agreeing upon a common application interface to a particular version of the Unix operating system, the members offer the software industry a much bigger market. Software houses should therefore be interested in designing application programs which implement the Group's interface definitions. This, in turn, may also make other hardware manufacturers interested in implementing them.

In its Decision the Commission finds that the members of the Group have a considerable competitive advantage *vis-à-vis* their competitors who are not members *inter alia* because their earlier knowledge of the Group's interface definitions enables them to implement these interfaces before they are made publicly available. This advantage is different in nature from the advantage resulting from participation in a research and development project because of the situation of dependence in which non-members are placed. Membership of the Group is primarily open only to major manufacturers with a considerable turnover and is conditional upon approval by a majority of the members. In an industry where lead time can be a factor of great importance the circumstances of the case mean that an appreciable distortion of competition may

---

[1]   Decision of 15 December 1986, OJ L 35, 6.2.1987.

result from the Group's decisions on interfaces in combination with its decisions on admission of new members.

The negative effects of this distortion are, however, easily outweighed by the advantages resulting from the activities of the Group. It is the professed aim of the Group to make its interface definitions available as widely and quickly as possible. The interfaces which the group defines will therefore constitute an open industry standard.

The advantages for users resulting from the creation of open industry standards are set out in considerable detail in the Commission's Decision. Until now users have tended to be locked into a particular system. The interfaces which the X/Open Group defines mean, however, that users are likely to get a wider choice of application programs and that programs which implement these definitions can be moved from the machine of one member to that of another ('portability'). Users will thus have the possibility of changing between hardware and software from different sources and of protecting their investments in application programmes in the future if their requirements as to machine capacity should change with business growth.

The activities of the X/Open Group mean, moreover, that small and medium-sized companies in this important sector may compete for the supply of goods and services which implement the Group's definitions.

For the above-mentioned reasons the Commission granted an exemption for six years. However, it obliged the addressees to furnish it with an annual report on cases where applications for membership are refused, and to inform it immediately of any changes in membership.

Industrial restructuring

ENI/Montedison

66.   An exemption [1] was granted under Article 85(3) in respect of a series of agreements between Ente Nazionale Idrocarburi (ENI) and Montedison SA, the objective of which was a major restructuring of the Italian petrochemical industry. They provided for the reciprocal transfer of parts of the petrochemical businesses of ENI and Montedison, notably cracking products, thermoplastics and certain rubbers. Supply and plant management contracts were concluded

---

[1]   Decision of 4 December 1986, OJ L 5, 7.1.1987.

to cope with the new situations created by the dual ownership of plants or complexes of plants following restructuration. Although competition that previously existed between ENI and Montedison has been substantially reduced as a result of the agreements, the Commission decided that they warranted an exemption under Article 85(3) since they were essential to the restructuring of an industry suffering from serious structural overcapacity throughout the entire common market. The agreements enabled the two undertakings to rationalize more quickly and radically than would otherwise have been the case in their absence. They ensure that, although the degree of competition on the relevant markets is diminished, it is still maintained at a workable level. Furthermore, the benefits of the rationalization would be passed on to the consumer.

The exemption was granted for a period of 15 years. A report on the implementation of the agreements must be submitted every three years to the Commission.

Joint exploitation of complementary technology

Optical fibres

67.   The Commission has granted an exemption under Article 85(3) [1] in respect of two sets of agreements involving the US corporation, Corning Glass Works. Under the agreements Corning has set up joint ventures in the United Kingdom with BICC plc and in Germany with Siemens AG for the production and sale of optical fibres.

Corning Corporation is one of the major producers and distributors of optical fibres in the world and its joint ventures in the European Community account for almost 50% of productive capacity in the Community. BICC plc and Siemens AG are leading cable makers in the United Kingdom and Germany respectively.

Optical fibres are high-technology carriers of information. The main use of optical fibres is in the field of telephone communications, where they are tending to replace the more traditional copper wire or coaxial cables.

The Commission found that the individual joint venture agreements notified to it did not as such restrict competition between Corning and its partners. They did not contain obligations which went beyond what would be admitted in licensing agreements between non-competitors.

---

[1]   Decision of 14 July 1986, OJ L 236, 22.8.1986.

However, the Commission found that there was a distortion of competition in the relationship between the joint ventures, and the existence of other similar joint ventures in which Corning participated actively. The joint ventures had substantially the same activity, namely the production and marketing of optical fibres. They were therefore direct competitors. The agreements taken together with other agreements which do not form part of the decision created a network of inter-related joint ventures in an oligopolistic market in which Corning as owner and supplier of the relevant technology held an influential position.

This network of joint ventures distorted competition between the individual joint ventures and was, therefore, likely to lead to market sharing between them. This brought the agreement within the scope of Article 85(1). However, following amendments to the agreements the Commission found that they fulfilled the conditions for exemption under Article 85(3). They enabled several European companies to manufacture a high-technology product with significant advantages over traditional cables in the Community, thereby promoting technical progress and benefiting consumers. The agreements were essential to achieve these objectives. Corning's participation in the joint venture made possible the rapid transfer of fast moving technology. There was no possibility of eliminating competition. Although competition between the joint ventures was distorted, they were not able to eliminate competition entirely since there were several other producers of optical fibres in the common market, and producers in the common market were subject to global competition. Optical fibres, in spite of their advantages over other forms of cable, did not supplant the latter and in effect remained in competition with them.

The exemption was granted for a period of 15 years in order to enable the parties to enforce the agreements and to obtain a satisfactory return on their capital.

Mitchell Cotts/Sofiltra

68.   The Commission exempted [1] under Article 85(3) a joint venture agreement made between Mitchell Cotts (Engineering) Ltd, a United Kingdom undertaking and a French firm Sofiltra Poelman SA and also held that some of its provisions fell outside Article 85(1).

The objective of the agreement was to create a company, Mitchell Cotts Air Filtration Ltd, in the United Kingdom, for the manufacture and marketing of

---

[1]   Decision of 17 December 1986, OJ L 41, 11.2.1987.

high efficiency air filters using microfine glass fibre for the nuclear, biological, chemical and computer markets. Sofiltra manufactures high efficiency particulate air filters from small pleated paper media which are composed of submicronic glass fibres. Mitchell Cotts (Engineering) has been involved since 1976 in the manufacture and marketing of air filtration devices incorporating pleated glass fibre paper purchased from Sofiltra. Unlike the manufacture of pleated glass fibre paper, no advanced technology is involved in the assembly of the final product, which merely entails the provision of a metal or plastic casing. The pleated glass fibre paper represents the major cost component and the key technical element in the finished product. Mitchell Cotts Engineering did not possess either the relevant technology or the research and development facilities necessary to manufacture these high-efficiency air filters independently.

Under the joint venture agreement Sofiltra agreed to grant an exclusive know-how licence relating to technology and expertise necessary for the manufacture of air filtration devices to the newly created company. The licence included the grant of the exclusive right of sale to the joint venture in respect of a sales territory comprising the United Kingdom, Ireland and seven non-EEC countries. Sofiltra could not manufacture the product in the United Kingdom or appoint other licensees there. Similarly, Sofiltra and other possible future licensees were prohibited from actively selling air filters in the joint venture's territories.

The Commission found that the parent firms were, as regards manufacturing, neither actual nor potential competitors. They were, however, competing at sales level. In addition, the arrangements setting up the joint venture did contain certain restraints upon the commercial freedom of the parties. The grant of an exclusive licence in the United Kingdom to the joint venture company meant that Sofiltra would not manufacture air filtration devices in that territory or appoint other licensees there. Similarly, Sofiltra and other possible future licensees were prohibited from actively selling air filters in certain countries. These restrictions which were not limited in time could not be considered indispensable for the creation and proper operation of the joint venture.

The Commission held that the mutual ban on active sales, although it allowed for passive sales by the licensor and licensees in each other's territory must be considered to fall under Article 85(1), since such a restriction resulted in the sharing of markets between Sofiltra and the joint venture which had become competitors. Trade between Member States was affected in view of the strong position of Sofiltra within the common market.

The Commission found, however, that the agreement, in so far as it led to restrictions on competition, merited an exemption under Article 85(3) because it substantially improved production and distribution and promoted technical progress. The territorial restrictions provided for in the agreement were found to be necessary for the joint venture to establish itself and to develop in a competitive market. As a matter of fact these restrictions on the one hand led the new company to concentrate its efforts on its exclusive territory and on the other hand protected it against direct competition from Sofiltra or from other licensees.

Consumers benefited from the operation of the agreements in that the products in question were manufactured by an integrated production process and technological improvements were made available widely and rapidly.

Obligations regarding confidentiality in respect of the know-how and disclosure of improvements to one another as well as the obligation not to grant sublicences were considered not to be appreciable restrictions of competition within the meaning of Article 85(1). The obligation on the joint venture company not to manufacture or deal in competing products was also considered in the context of integrated industrial cooperation within a joint venture not to be an appreciable restriction within the meaning of Article 85(1).

Nuclear safety

United Reprocessors GmbH (URG)

69.   The Commission reviewed a cooperation agreement between the three European undertakings involved in nuclear oxide fuels reprocessing services. British Nuclear Fuels plc (BNLF), Compagnie générale des matières nucléaires (Cogena), Deutsche Gesellschaft für Wiederaufarbeitung von Kernbrennstoffen (DWK) agreed to establish a joint subsidiary called United Reprocessors GmbH which was similar in nature to a professional association. The main purpose of the cooperation is the exchange of information on specific technical matters such as R&D programmes, the furtherance of common interests in the field of public relations and legal, economic and political matters.

The cooperation does not, however, extend to investments in production, marketing and licensing. Under these circumstances the Commission declared by means of a 'comfort letter' that there were no grounds for action under Articles 85 or 86.

This cooperation agreement replaces a previous agreement of 1971 concluded between BNFL, the French commissariat à l'énergie atomique (CEA) and

Kernbiennstaff-Wiederaufarbeitungsgesellschaft mbH (KEWA) which was exempted under Article 85(3). It should be stressed that this form of cooperation is quite different from that which existed previously. [1] The principal purpose of the previous arrangement concerned the coordination of investment, the joint marketing of oxide fuel reprocessing services and associated transport.

---

[1]   Decision of 23 December 1975, OJ L 51, 26.2.1976.

§ 5 — Industrial and commercial property rights

70.   The Commission decided two cases concerning the transfer of technology by way of mixed licence agreements, in which know-how licensing was the principal feature. These decisions contributed to the preparation of the envisaged block exemption regulation on know-how agreements. [1]

Boussois/Interpane

71.   A licensing agreement between the German firm Interpane and the French firm Boussois was granted an exemption under Article 85(3). [2] The agreement licenses Boussois to use the know-how Interpane has developed for a process applying fine thermal insulation coatings to flat glass for double glazing units. The know-how is secret and of substantial importance, being indispensable for the use of Interpane's technology. Only one of the types of coatings developed by Interpane is patented and only in seven Member States.

Three clauses in the contract were capable of restricting competition within the meaning of Article 85(1). These are:

(a) the exclusive right to manufacture and sell coated glass granted to Boussois for France,

(b) the prohibition to manufacture by Boussois outside France, and in particular in other Member States, although it is allowed to sell in any other country until such time as Interpane appoints another exclusive licensee there, and

(c) the prohibition on direct exports, active or passive, by Boussois and Interpane's future licencees into each others' territories outside France.

In view of the special circumstances of the case and in particular the economic background, the Commission, however, found that the three restrictions fulfilled the conditions for exemption under Article (85)(3). The exemption was granted from the date of notification until the end of the five-year period from the date of the contract. The parties regard this period as the average life cycle of technology in the industry and they have agreed to take it as the duration

---

[1]   See point 35 of this Report.
[2]   Decision of 15 December 1986, OJ L 50, 19.2.1987.

of the various contractual obligations, in particular those of secrecy and exclusivity.

This agreement was not covered by the block exemption on patent licensing agreements for two reasons: the know-how was a dominant element in the licence package, and parallel patents did not exist in five Member States.

ICL/Fujitsu

72. The Commission viewed favourably several notified agreements made between ICL and Fujitsu in the field of computer components. The agreements consist of a framework for collaboration between both firms and a number of specific agreements relating to the licensing of know-how and industrial property rights for design and production, the supply of design services and the delivery of components. Most of the industrial property rights involved under the specific agreements are licenced on a non-exclusive basis. In more technical terms the collaboration involves the use of Fujitsu's LSI chip and computer-aided design technology, in conjunction with ICL's VME software and other ICL technology, in ICL's computers.

Initially, there was also an agreement whereby ICL bought large mainframe computers on original equipment manufacturer (OEM) terms from Fujitsu (this means that ICL bought Fujitsu computers to sell under an ICL name as if they were ICL products). But ICL only had the right to resell in a named territory, which excluded Germany and Greece. For its part, Fujitsu undertook to supply these computers in the United Kingdom exclusively to ICL (exception being made for one other EEC competitor of ICL which had prior UK rights) with the result that any other computer manufacturer that wished to complete its own range of computers by buying Fujitsu's computer systems on OEM terms was prevented from entering this specific market. The parties claimed this to be an exclusive distribution agreement worthy of exemption.

In discussion the Commission made clear that an OEM purchase agreement does not constitute a distribution agreement and therefore is not covered by the block exemption on exclusive distribution agreements. It furthermore indicated that the above-mentioned restrictions could have a serious effect on competition and so probably would not even have qualified for an individual exemption. The parties subsequently cancelled this agreement.

Considering that the agreements in their modified form contributed to an important transfer in the field of high technology and that the remaining restrictions were indispensable to the achievement of that aim the Commission decided that they merited an exemption under Article 85(3). A 'comfort letter' to this effect, following publication of the relevant facts in the Official Journal, [1] has been sent to the parties.

---

[1]   OJ C 210, 21.8.1986.

§ 6 — Abuse of a dominant position

73. The Commission intervened in two cases of alleged abuse of dominant position, the first in order to protect a small firm from being eliminated from the market by unfair methods, and the second to ensure the supply of vital raw materials. In both cases the Commission accepted undertakings by the firms concerned which restored the status quo. It has also followed up the undertaking given by IBM in 1984.

British Sugar/Napier Brown

74. In 1985 Napier Brown and Company Limited complained that British Sugar plc had engaged in various activities which amounted to an abuse of its dominant position. It had tried to drive Napier Brown out of the retail sugar market in Great Britain by an aggressive pricing policy and refusing to supply industrial sugar to Napier Brown. Napier Brown packages and supplies sugar for the retail trade.

Furthermore, British Sugar refused to sell industrial or retail sugar to any client unless it was delivered at a uniform price irrespective of the location of the client. British Sugar is the largest sugar producer in the United Kingdom and the sole United Kingdom producer of sugar from beet. At the end of 1985, Napier Brown requested the Commission to take interim measures. In July 1986 the Commission issued a statement of objections concluding that on the basis of evidence before it, there was a prima-facie abuse of dominant position by British Sugar and that it had made several agreements which infringed Article 85(1). Accordingly it stated that it intended, subject to any observations that British Sugar might care to put forward, to adopt interim measures against British Sugar. Following discussions between British Sugar and the Commission, British Sugar offered undertakings to the Commission which the latter believed would restore normal conditions of competition in the retail sugar market in Great Britain. The proceedings for interim measures were then suspended.

The acceptance of these undertakings will not of course, prejudice the final outcome of the case.

IBM

75. The IBM undertaking is now in its third year of operation. It was made on 1 August 1984, and resulted in the suspension of the Commission's proceeding against IBM initiated on 6 December 1980, under the EEC rules of

competition. IBM undertook that it would provide certain interface information at the request of competitors in the EEC for the attachment of their products to IBM System/370 products and to provide certain Systems Network Architecture (SNA) documents. It also undertook, if requested, to supply in the EEC certain central processing units without main memory or with the minimum strictly necessary for testing.

IBM has submitted to the Commission a comprehensive report of the second year's operation of the undertaking. In this report IBM states that it believes that the undertaking continues to achieve the intended objective of enabling EEC companies to get interface information from IBM in accordance with the terms of the undertaking.

IBM states that it has incorporated the undertaking requirements into its business process where appropriate. New procedures have been established and others modified to facilitate handling requests for information under the undertaking.

Since the last report to the European Commission in July 1985, 8 companies have made 10 inquiries containing 255 individual requests. These requests included two for System Network Architecture (SNA) information and the remainder were for System/370 information. IBM states that it continues to hold discussions with some companies to resolve individual technical questions concerning interface information. IBM reports that a few requests were denied because they were not within the scope of the undertaking.

Since the inception of the undertaking on 1 August 1984, there have been a total of 45 inquiries from 18 competitors covering 475 individual requests.

Two companies have signed the Technical Information Disclosure Agreement (TIDA) and received information under the agreement: a third is in the final process of signing.

IBM has not received any customer request for System/370 Central Processing Units without main memory or with only such capacity as is required for testing.

The Commission itself has monitored closely the effects and the implementation of the undertaking during the last 12 months. It has maintained a wide range of contacts with the computer industry and has examined carefully any questions raised by other parties. Some questions which have arisen on the interpretation of the undertaking are still outstanding but the Commission is confident that the few which remain will be settled shortly.

The Commission's services will continue to monitor the operation of the undertaking and are ready to assist in the resolution of any future problems which may arise. To this end, the Commission has also maintained contact both with IBM and other companies active in the computer industry in order to keep itself fully informed of developments in this sector.

Istituto/IMC and Angus

76. Following a complaint by the Istituto Chemicoterapico Italiano, an Italian pharmaceutical company, about restrictions of competition in the market in aminobutanol (a raw material used in the manufacture of a drug for the treatment of pulmonary tuberculosis), the Commission investigated the practices of two American firms, the International Minerals and Chemicals Corporation (IMC) and Angus Chemical Co. which had taken over IMC's aminobutanol business. [1]

At the relevant time IMC and Angus held a dominant position in the common market for aminobutanol. The Commission found that this positin had been abused in that they had refused to supply the Istituto Chemicoterapico Italiano with aminobutanol unless certain conditions were met which would have been prejudicial to the interests of that company and would, in effect, have closed off the market to new entrants.

Following the intervention of the Commission, IMC and Angus immediately resumed supplies to the Istituto Chemicoterapico Italiano. They terminated the exclusive purchasing agreements and the resale ban for aminobutanol. The new contracts provide for the delivery of fixed amounts of aminobutanol over a period of two years with automatic renewal for one year unless terminated with six months' prior notice. This gives the contracting parties a sufficiently long period for planning production and delivery without unduly excluding the dominant firms' competitors.

This case is in line with the Commission's previous decisions in this area as confirmed by the Court of Justice, [2] the underlying principle of which is that supply contracts concluded by firms in a dominant position must not, either in their terms or their operation, be unduly restrictive.

---

[1] Bull. EC 5-1986, point 2.1.52.
[2] Eleventh Competition Report, points 73-76. Case 85/76 *Hoffman-La Roche & Co. AG v Commission* [1979] ECR 461.

Part II

Application of Articles 65 and 66 of the ECSC Treaty

Application of Article 65

Joint-buying agreement operated by the Northern Ireland Coal Importers' Association (Nicia)

77.   The Commission authorized [1] some 30 Northern Ireland coal wholesalers to operate a joint-buying agreement within the meaning of Article 65 of the ECSC Treaty covering their purchases of solid fuels for household use from the National Coal Board, London (NCB).

The scheme as intially proposed contained certain features making new membership conditional on sponsorship by an existing member and the agreement of one of the two most important associates. Moreover, the latter had concluded bulk contracts with the NCB for nearly all their household solid fuel requirements, which secured them substantial rebates on the NCB list prices. By means of subcontracts, the other Nicia members could obtain a share of these contracts. Against the commitment to purchase almost all of their supplies in this way, the rebate was passed on in full.

When the Commission objected to these features, Nicia made fundamental changes to membership rules. Also, new contracts made by the two leading firms with the NCB no longer provide that they must obtain almost all their requirements from the Board and the subcontracts have been cancelled.

In these circumstances the Commission considered that the agreement proper, concluded within the framework of Nicia and covering joint planning, joint shipping arrangements, the organization of a distribution and allocation scheme and the running of an advisory service jointly with the NCB, satisfies the tests for authorization under Article 65(2). The authorization was, however, made subject to the condition that Nicia, within the framework of the Coal Advisory Service, does not arbitrarily place at a disadvantage Community fuels other than those supplied by the NCB.

---

[1]   Decision of 21 March 1986, Bull. EC 3-1986, point 2.1.64.

Application of Article 66

Stahlcenter Röchling-Possehl

78.   Under Articles 65 and 66 of the ECSC Treaty, the Commission authorized [1] the formation of 'Stahlcenter Röchling-Possehl GmbH & Co. KG', Mannheim, by Röchling Eisenhandel KG, Ludwigshafen (Röchling) and Possehl Eisen- und Stahl GmbH, Mannheim (Possehl), a wholly-owned subsidiary of Saarlux. It also approved the agreement concluded in this connection despite the restrictions of competition it contains. The purpose of the joint venture is to concentrate the sales operations of the two immediate parent companies in the Mannheim Ludwigshafen area on a single depot — that of Possehl in Mannheim — and close Röchling's depot in Ludwigshafen. This will enable the firms concerned, which lately returned lower profits, to increase their efficiency by restructuring their operations.

Scrutiny of the deal under Article 66 showed that the two depots which are to be merged hold an extremely small share of the relevant (i.e. German) market, less than 0.3 % in fact. Even allowing for a group effect in the Federal Republic between the groups indirectly involved (Gebr. Röchling and Sacilor, which operates on this market through Saarlux as well as through Possehl), the two groups' joint share of the German market comes to no more than 4.8 %. Moreover, in that market the parties face keen competition from numerous large steel dealers, both members of groups and independent operators.

Consequently, the Commission decided that the formation of Stahlcenter Röchling-Possehl satisfies the requirements of Article 66(2) and granted its authorization.

The authorization granted under Article 65(2) concerns an additional agreement between the firms forming the joint venture whereby they undertake not to compete with it in its sales territory.

In the Commission's view, the agreement is a necessary accompaniment to the formation of the joint venture and is simply intended to safeguard its viability and prevent its expected beneficial effects from being undermined. It therefore satisfies the tests of Article 65(2) and was accordingly authorized until 31 December 1993. This is the first case involving a joint venture in which the Commission has applied Articles 65 and 66 of the ECSC Treaty simultaneously.

---

[1]   Decision of 5 February 1986, OJ L 39, 14.2.1986.

United Engineering Steels Ltd

79.   Acting under the competition rules of the ECSC Treaty, the Commission authorized [1] a restructuring operation whereby British Steel Coprporation, London (BSC) and Guest Keen & Nettlefolds, Redditch (GKN) are to merge their engineering steel activities in a new joint company called United Engineering Steels Ltd (UES).

The activities in question are the production and sale of engineering steel (semi-finished products and/or bars) at the BSC works in Rotherham, Stockbridge, Sheffield and Wolverhampton and the GKN works in Brymbo (near Wrexham) and Wolverhampton. The GKN forgings business, located in England and Scotland, will also be included in the joint venture (forgings are an EEC Treaty product).

UES is being set up against a background of overcapacity and with the object of rationalizing the UK engineering steels sector, optimizing the investment opportunities available and enabling it to meet international competition.

An assessment of the projected merger under the competition rules showed that UES will rank second among Community producers of engineering steel billets and fourth among Community producers of engineering steel bars. Imports of the relevant products in the UK are substantial, as are exports from the UK to other Member States. Several other Community producers will continue to compete actively with UES. The Commission accordingly concluded that the tests of Article 66(2) of the ECSC Treaty were met in that competition was safeguarded.

Klöckner—Heuvelman

80.   The Commission authorized [2] Klöckner & Co. KG a A, Duisburg (Klöckner) to acquire a majority holding in Heuvelman s'Gravendeel Holding BV, s'Gravendeel (Heuvelman). Klöckner and Heuvelman are both, among other things, scrap merchants.

As a result of the transaction, Klöckner's market share will increase from 23 to 25% in the Federal Republic of Germany, from 2.3 to 16.3% in the Netherlands and from 6 to 8% in the Coal and Steel Community of Ten (data for the Community of Twelve are not yet available). However, Klöckner will

---

[1]   Decision of 18 March 1986, Bull. EC 3-1986, point 2.1.65.
[2]   Decision of 2 April 1986.

not become the market leader in any of these markets and thus competitive conditions will not be radically altered.

The Community market for scrap is characterized by strong competition. In the first instance scrap is interchangeable with pig iron as the primary raw material in steel production, accounting for 40% of supplies. Furthermore, purchasers, mainly iron and steel works, have as a rule their own integrated scrap trading businesses and in many cases cover most of their own scrap requirements. In addition, imports from third countries account for up to 15% of supplies to the Community market.

The scrap market in general is a free market with no restrictions on trade. Market trends are determined by events on the world market, in particular the supply and demand situation, and, owing to the very strong position held by the United States as the biggest scrap exporter, the dollar exchange rate. Scrap prices in the Community therefore tend to reflect world prices.

Notwithstanding, therefore, the merger with Heuvelman, Klöckner will be obliged, if it is to maintain its position on the European market, to sell at prices which take account of conditions on the world market.

Usinor/Creusot-Loire

81. The Commission authorized [1] the acquisition by Usinor, Paris, of the Creusot-Marrel and specialized engineering divisions of Creusot-Loire. The first manufactures heavy steel plate at its Creusot and Châteauneuf works; it also manufactures heavy forgings and castings at Creusot. The second uses steel in the manufacture of arms.

This acquisition can be seen as part of the restructuring of the French steel industry. In July 1984 the Commission had already authorized the transfer of a major part of the steelmaking activities of Creusot-Loire to Usinor and Sacilor (the other large steel company controlled financially by the French State). [2] The present transaction concerns the remainder of these activities, Creusot-Loire itself being in liquidation.

From the point of view of competition, the importance of this merger lies primarily in the fact that Usinor is the main Community producer of heavy steel plate. However, the acquisition of Creusot-Marrel only slightly increases

---

[1] Decision of 26 May 1986, Bull. EC 5-1986, point 2.1.53.
[2] Commission Decision of 23 July 1984 (not published), Bull. EC 7/8-1984, point 2.1.60.

its share in Community production. This is because nine other large or medium-sized firms produce heavy plate in the Community, quite apart from several smaller fabricators. These other producers will continue to compete effectively with Creusot-Marrel, and this — combined with the substantial influence of imports from non-Community countries — will ensure that the acquisition of Creusot-Marrel does not give Usinor the power to determine prices or to define its sales policy without taking into account other producers and the freedom of choice of users on the market.

For these reasons, coupled with the fact that the merger scarcely alters the position with regard to access to supplies and outlets, the Commission concluded that the competition-safeguarding tests of Article 66(2) of the ECSC Treaty were met and authorized the transaction accordingly.

Since forgings and castings fall under the EEC Treaty, the Commission considered whether Article 86 was applicable, because any merger may constitute an abuse of a dominant position for the relevant products in a substantial part of the common market. The Commission's conclusion was that the merger would have no harmful effects.

Ryan Consolidated Ltd

82.   Ryan International plc, Cardiff, a group of companies whose main businesses are the recovery and sale of discarded coal from colliery coal tips in the United Kingdom and Belgium, and Consolidated Gold Fields, plc, London, a group of companies engaged mainly in mining, other than coal-mining, and construction material production, have set up a joint venture. Using recycling methods, it will carry on tip reclamation business, drawing on the skills and experience of the Ryan group in this field and the financial resources and marketing expertise of the Consolidated Gold Fields group.

The coal will mainly be sold to power stations and industrial consumers in Great Britain. Taking account of the supply structure of that market, characterized by the presence of British Coal, the principal supplier of solid fuels, and the limited market share of the parties concerned, the Commission acknowledged that the transaction satisfies the tests for authorization and authorized it accordingly. [1]

---

[1]   Decision of 4 June 1986, Bull. EC 6-1986, point 2.1.88.

Saarstahl-Völklinger

83. By means of a Decision [1] the Commission authorized Völkinger to appoint certain persons from Arbed SA and Dillinger Hüttenwerke to the supervisory board and board of directors of Saarstahl for a period of one year. This Decision derogates from Article 3(a) of the Commission Decision [2] authorizing the merger between Arbed SA, Neunkircher-Eisenwerk AG and SA Métallurgique et Minière de Rodange-Athus and Article 2(1) of the Commission Decision [3] authorizing the merger between Usinor, Sacilor and Société Métallurgique de Normandie. The purpose of the Decision was to enable Saarstahl to benefit from the services of experienced individuals during its restructuring drive.

Coalite Group — Hargreaves Group

84. On 12 November the Commission authorized the acquisition of the Hargreaves Group by the Coalite Group. [4]

Coalite's main activities include solid smokeless fuel manufacture, oil and chemicals processing and fuel distribution. Hargreaves is an industrial holding company whose subsidiaries are likewise engaged in solid and liquid fuel trading, processing and distribution.

The Commission authorized the merger because it will help counterbalance the market strength of British Coal, the leading supplier of solid fuels on the UK market.

Gekanor

85. The Commission authorized Acenor SA, Bilbao (Acenor) and United Engineering Steels Ltd, Rotherham (UES), to set up a new joint venture company to be called Gekanor SA (Madrid) for the purpose of financial participation in certain Spanish companies which make steel drop forgings. [5]

Acenor is a group of five Spanish companies which produce engineering steels. The companies concerned are SA Echevarria, Aceros de Llodio SA, Aceros y

---

[1] Decision of 25 July 1986.
[2] Decision of 6 June 1978, OJ L 164, 21.6.1978; Eighth Competition Report, point 137.
[3] Decision of 2 December 1982, OJ L 139, 19.5.1982; Twelfth Competition Report, point 97.
[4] Bull. EC 11-1986, point 2.1.79.
[5] Decision of 25 November 1986, Bull. EC 11-1986, point 2.1.78.

Fundiciones del Norte Pedro Orbegozo, Forjas Alavesas and Olarra. UES is the main producer of engineering steels in the United Kingdom; it is owned jointly by the British Steel Corporation and GKN plc.

The purpose of Gekanor is to enable progress to be made with rationalization in the Spanish drop forging sector, having first grouped up to six drop forging producers under unified ownership and control. The companies to be included initially in the Gekanor proposals are Forjas de Basauri SA (Vizcaya), which as a subsidiary of Echevarria is already in the Acenor group, Forjas de Asua SA (Vizcaya), currently a subsidiary of Motor Iberia and Forjas de Villalba SA (Forvisa), owned by INI (National Institute of Industry).

The examination of the Gekanor project under the competition rules of the ECSC Treaty was mainly concerned with the question of the supply of steel forging billets and bars (which are ECSC Treaty products) for the manufacture of drop forgings (which are an EEC Treaty product). It was concluded that the creation of Gekanor would not place Acenor and UES in an artificially privileged position involving a substantial advantage in access to supplies or markets for ECSC Treaty products. The Commission's assessment on this point took account of the considerable size of certain other Community producers of engineering steels which are vertically integrated with drop forging companies, such as Finsider/Teksid, Sacilor/Usinor, Thyssen and Krupp/Gerlach.

The Commission concluded, therefore, that the tests of Article 66(2) of the ECSC Treaty were met and authorized the project under Article 66(1).

Since steel drop forgings are an EEC product and since both UES and Gekanor will make drop forgings, the Commission checked on the possible applicability of Article 86 of the EEC Treaty to the concentration of those activities, taking into account that a concentration could in certain circumstances constitute an abuse of a dominant position for the product concerned in a substantial part of the common market. The examination concluded, having regard to the considerable strength of certain Community competitors, that the merger will have no effect of this nature.

Klöckner Stahl — Hellenic Steel

86. The Commission authorized [1] Klöckner Stahl GmbH, Duisburg (Klöckner) to acquire 26.4% of the share capital of Hellenic Steel Co., Athens (Hellenic Steel).

---

[1] Decision of 4 December 1986, Bull. EC 12-1986, point 2.1.108.

Hellenic Steel is controlled jointly by the Hellenic Industrial Development Bank SA, Athens ('ETBA') and the Japanese company C. Itoh & Co. Ltd, Tokyo (Itoh). Following the proposed transaction, Hellenic Steel will be controlled jointly by ETBA, Itoh and Klöckner.

Hellenic Steel produces cold-rolled steel sheets, galvanized sheets and tinplate. Klöckner produces, *inter alia,* cold-rolled sheets but not the other two products concerned. An assessment of the projected merger under the competition rules showed that Klöckner and Hellenic Steel combined will stand in ninth place among Community producers of cold-rolled sheets.

The Commission concluded that the competition-safeguarding tests of Article 66(2) of the ECSC Treaty were met as the parties concerned will not have the power to hinder effective competition for steel products as a result of the merger.

Cogea

87.   The Commission authorized Nuova Italsider SpA to transfer all or part of its shareholding in Consorzio Genovese Acciaio SpA — Cogea to the Leali, Lucchini, Riva, Bellicini, Regis and Sassone groups. [1]

Within the framework of the restructuring of the Community steel industry and at the Commission's request, Nuova Italsider firstly closed down its wide strip mill at Genoa-Cornigliano and, secondly, set up Cogea, to which it contributed the crude steelmaking facilities already deprived of their principal outlet. Cogea's capital was apportioned betwen Nuova Italsider (80%), Dalmine (14%) and Deltasider (6%). All these companies belong to the Finsider group.

For their part, the Leali, Lucchini, Riva, Bellicini, Regis and Sassone groups, which had scrapped crude steel and semis production capacity totalling 2 220 110 tonnes of crude steel, proposed to acquire a shareholding in Cogea in order to exploit the existing complementarity between this enterprise, which had been left without outlets, and their facilities, which were no longer adequately supplied with semis from within their group.

During a transition period of two or three years, which should make it possible to determine the definitive value of Cogea plants, this firm's capital will be allocated between Nuova Italsider (12.4%), Dalmine (14%), Deltasider (6%)

---

[1]   Decision of 19 December 1986, Bull. EC 12-1986, point 2.1.106.

and the groups Leali (22%), Lucchini (9.32%), Riva (17,20%), Bellicini (1.80%), Regis (11.47%) and Sassone (5.80%). At the end of the transition period, the Leali, Lucchini and Riva groups will be entitled to fix their definitive shareholding somewhere between 32.27% and 61%. Nuova Italsider is authorized to transfer, in whole or in part, to other steel companies any residual shareholding it may have at that time.

This transaction will enable all the parties concerned to control Cogea jointly and will lead to a concentration within the meaning of Article 66 between Cogea and each of the parties to the transaction, without there being any concentration between the parties themselves.

The agreement also provides that:
(i)   each party buys from Cogea a quantity of semis (blooms and billets) proportional to its shareholding;
(ii) the selling price will be calculated on the basis of the average price charged by domestic producers on the domestic market;
(iii) each party may transfer, in whole or in part, its quota to the other parties.

Cogea's production capacity will rise during the transitional period to 1 million tonnes a year of semi-finished products, equivalent to 1 170 000 tonnes of crude steel, which represents about 4.92% of Italian and 1.10% of Community crude steel production.

The transaction will produce the following benefits:
(i)   a reduction of 1.4 million tonnes a year of crude steel production capacity;
(ii) better exploitation of Cogea's full cycle;
(iii) considerable economies of scale as a result of the concentration within Cogea of semis production, until now divided among several plants at different sites;
(iv) A significant contribution to the restructuring and competitiveness of the Italian and hence Community steel industry.

The Commission concluded that the proposed transaction satisfied the conditions for authorization laid down in Article 66(2) and granted its authorization.

Chapter III

Main cases decided by the Court of Justice

88. In 1986 the Court delivered eight judgments involving EEC competition law. Of these judgments five were in actions brought by firms against Commission decisions (Article 173 of the EEC Treaty), [1] whereas two contain preliminary rulings requested by Member States' courts (Article 177 of the EEC Treaty). [2] 43 cases are curently still pending before the Court, 31 in Article 173 proceedings and 12 in Article 177 proceedings.

The above-mentioned judgments deal with the following questions:

(i)   application of the competition rules to air transport; [3]

(ii) appraisal of selective distribution systems in the light of Article 85(1) and (3) and Article 86; [4]

(iii) application of Article 85 to franchise agreements; [5]

(iv) appraisal of patent licensing agreements in the light of Article 85(1); [6]

---

[1]   Judgments (not yet reported):
    (a) Case 193/83 *Windsurfing International v Commission*, OJ C 79, 8.4.1986.
    (b) Case 53/85 *AKZO Chemie v Commission and Engineering & Chemical Supplies Ltd*, OJ C 196, 5.8.1986 *(AKZO business secrets)*.
    (c) Case 5/85 *AKZO Chemie v Commission*, OJ C 265, 21.10.1986 *(AKZO investigation)*.
    (d) Case 75/84 *Metro SB Grossmärkte and United Kingdom v Commission, SABA and Federal Republic of Germany*, OJ C 296, 22.11.1986, *(Metro v SABA II)*.
    (e) Case 226/84 *British Leyland v Commission and Merson*, OJ C 318, 11.12.1986.
[2]   Judgments (not yet reported):
    (a) Case 161/84 *Pronuptia v Schillgalis*, OJ C 44, 26.2.1986.
    (b) Joined Cases 209 to 213/84 *Ministère public v Asjes and others*, OJ C 131, 25.9.1986 *('Nouvelles Frontières')*.
    (c) Case 10/86 *VAG France v Magne*, OJ C 23, 30.1.1987.
[3]   *'Nouvelles Frontières'* (footnote 2(b)).
[4]   *Metro v SABA II* (footnote 1(d)).
[5]   *Pronuptia* (footnote 2(a)).
[6]   *Windsurfing International* (footnote 1 (a)).

(v) interpretation of block exemption Regulation (EEC) No 123/85 on vehicle distribution and servicing agreements; [1]

(vi) isolation of national markets as an abuse of a dominant position within the meaning of Article 86; [2]

(vii) anti-trust procedures and legal protection. [3]

---

[1] *VAG v Magne* (footnote 2(c) on p. 97).
[2] *British Leyland* (footnote 1(e) on p. 97).
[3] *AKZO business secrets* (footnote 1(b) on p. 97), *AKZO investigation* (footnote 1(c) on p. 97) and *Metro v SABA II* (footnote 1(d) on p. 97).

§ 1 — Application of the competition rules to air transport

89. Five identically worded references for a preliminary ruling made by the Paris police court afforded the Court of Justice an opportunity to pronounce on the compatibility with the EEC Treaty, and in particular with the competition rules, of the compulsory approval procedure laid down by French law for air tariffs.

90. The French Civil Aviation Code — like the relevant provisions of the other Member States — stipulates that air transport may be provided only by enterprises approved by the Minister for Civil Aviation. These enterprises must submit their tariffs to the Minister for approval. The approval of a tariff renders it binding on all traders selling tickets of the airline concerned in respect of the route specified in the application for approval. In internation air transport, which is governed by a network of bilateral agreements between the interested States, it is normal practice for companies authorized to operate a certain route first of all to negotiate a common tariff within IATA and then to submit it to the authorities of the signatory States for approval. The question referred was raised in criminal proceedings against the executives of airlines and travel agencies who had been prosecuted for marketing air tickets at prices not ministerially approved or different from the approved prices.

91. The Court held that the Treaty's competition rules are equally applicable to the air transport sector. This follows from the very wording of Article 74, the first article in the Title on transport, in which Member States are urged to pursue the objectives of the Treaty, including, therefore, that set out in Article 3(f), namely undistorted competition. It is borne out by other provisions of the Title on transport — Articles 61 and 77 — which presuppose that the competition rules apply to the transport sector whether or not a common transport policy has been established, and by the fact that there is no provision in the Treaty which, along the lines of Article 42 in the Chapter on agriculture, excludes the application of the competition rules to transport or makes it subject to a decision by the Council.

92. The Court considers that Article 84(2) serves merely to suspend the application of Article 74 *et seq.* to sea and air transport pending a Council decision on the subject. These modes of transport will therefore be included in a common transport policy at some time in the future. [1] The argument advanced

---

[1] See Case 167/73 *Commission v France* [1974] ECR 359; Case 156/77 *Commission v Belgium* [1978] ECR 1881.

even in recent years by several Member States that the competition rules do not for the time being apply to air transport has thus been definitively refuted.

93.   As the *Asjes* judgment expressly states, Member States are obliged, under Article 5(2) in conjunction with Articles 3(f) and 85, not to adopt or maintain in force any measures which could deprive those provisions of their effectiveness in the field of air transport. [1]

In the Court's opinion, the approval procedures for air tariffs applied so far by Member States may infringe Article 5(2) read in conjunction with Articles 3(f) and 85(1) as they require or favour the adoption of prohibited agreements, decisions or concerted practices or reinforce their effects. Such an infringement is committed where, for example, national authorities require airlines to submit to them only tariffs they have agreed upon between themselves and refuse to approve tariffs submitted independently. The Court considers, however, that it does not automatically render the relevant national provisions invalid as, in the current state of Community law in the air transport field, the prohibition contained in Article 85(1) has no direct legal consequences.

94.   The Court was not prepared to acknowledge that the ban on restrictive practices has direct effect with regard to this branch of the economy also. It based its view on considerations of legal certainty. Since the Council has yet to adopt the measures giving effect to Articles 85 and 86 referred to in Article 87, Articles 88 and 89 continue to apply. Article 88 provides that the authorities in Member States must apply Article 85, in particular paragraph 3, and Article 86 in accordance with the law of their country. Article 89 empowers the Commission to investigate cases of suspected infringement of the principles laid down by Articles 85 and 86, formally record any infringements and propose measures to bring them to an end. However, this system is too fragmentary to ensure a complete application of Article 85 because, firstly, national authorities determine the admissibility of only those restrictive practices which are submitted to them for approval under the applicable national competition law and, secondly, the Commission can grant no exemptions under Article 85(3). It would nevertheless be contrary to the principle of legal certainty, which in the Court's opinion is in the nature of a general rule of law, if a restrictive practice falling within the ambit of Article 85 were to be considered prohibited and void under civil law even before it was possible to ascertain whether Article 85 as a whole was applicable.

---

[1]   General legal principle, see Case 14/68 *Walt Wilhelm v Bundeskartellamt* [1969] ECR 1; Case 13/77 *INNO v ATAB* [1977] ECR 2115; Case 229/83 *Association des Centres Edouard Leclerc v Au Blé Vert*, not yet reported — see in this connection Fifteenth Competition Report (1985), points 91 to 93.

95.   Restrictive practices in the air transport sector, including tariff agreements between airlines, must therefore be regarded as void within the meaning of Article 85(2) only in so far as they fall under the prohibition in paragraph 1 and either the competent national authority has decided they do not qualify for exemption from that prohibition under Article 85(3), or the Commission has formally recorded that they constitute infringements of Article 85, which ultimately amounts to the same thing. The Court adopted the same attitude towards other restrictives practices during the period leading up to the entry into force of Regulation No 17.[1] That attitude predetermines at the same time the answer to the question referred. Any assessment of the compatibility of national provisions concerning approval of air tariffs with Community law depends on the nature of the approved tariffs and their appraisal in the light of Article 85: 'Where a decision has been taken by the competent national authorities under Article 88 or by the Commission under Article 89(2) ruling that the concerted action leading to the establishment of the air tariffs was incompatible with Article 85, it is contrary to the obligations of the Member States in the field of competition to approve such tariffs and thus to reinforce their effects'.

96.   The Commission's response to the air tariffs judgment has been twofold. First, it has redoubled its efforts to achieve early adoption of its proposal for a Regulation on the details of the application of Articles 85 and 86 to air transport. It has amended its original proposals to assist the Council in reaching a decision.[2] Secondly, it has sent letters under the third setence of Article 89(1) to 10 European airlines stating that Article 85 has been infringed and proposing measures to bring the infringements to an end.[3] The Commission will not hesitate, once the appropriate decisions have been adopted, to take action against the tariff approval policies of the Member States should the latter refuse to bring them into line with the Community's competition policy or unduly protract the alignment process.

---

[1]   See Case 13/61 *Bosch v Van Rijn* [1962] ECR 45.
[2]   See above point 36.
[3]   See above point 37.

§ 2 — Appraisal of selective distribution systems in the light of Article 85(1) and (3) and Article 86

97. In its judgment of 22 October the Court dismissed in its entirety the action brought by Metro SB Grossmärkte GmbH [1] against the renewed exemption of the selective distribution system operated by SABA GmbH. [2] The Commission's original exemption decision [3] had already been unsuccessfully challenged by the same applicant. [4]

The Court's new judgment contains statements on the assessment of selective distribution systems in the light of Article 85(1) and (3) and on the applicability of Article 86 whose significance reaches far beyond the confines of this case.

98. As far as the application of Article 85(1) is concerned, the Court reaffirmed, and at the same time greatly clarified, its findings in *Metro v SABA I* as regards qualitative selective distribution systems. These systems, which are based on purely qualitative dealer selection criteria, are capable of constituting an aspect of competition compatible with Article 85(1). They may nevertheless have the effect of restricting or eliminating competition. In the Court's view, this is the case 'where the existence of a certain number of such systems does not leave any room for other forms of distribution based on a different type of competition policy or results in a rigidity in price structure which is not counterbalanced by other aspects of competition between products of the same brand and by the existence of effective competition between different brands'.

99. The Court thus makes clear that qualitative selective distribution systems may be caught by Article 85(1). On the other hand, the existence of a large number of qualitative selective distribution systems does not in itself permit the conclusion that competition is restricted or distorted. The decisive factor is, rather, the effect such systems actually have on the competitive situation in the market concerned. Not only the question of the appreciable restriction of competition within the meaning of Article 85(1), but also that of the exempta-

---

[1] *Metro v SABA II,* footnote 1(d), p. 97.
[2] Decision of 21 December 1983, *SABA's EEC distribution system II,* OJ L 376, 31.12.1983.
[3] Decision of 15 December 1975, *SABA I,* OJ L 28, 3.2.1976.
[4] Case 26/76 *Metro v SABA I* [1977] ECR 1875.

bility of the distribution system under Article 85(3), is judged according to this criterion. Like the Commission, the Court therefore adopts an economic approach when assessing individual cases.

100. The increase in the number of qualitative selective distribution systems said by the applicant to have taken place after the first exemption was granted did not have to be taken into consideration by the Commission when renewing the exemption because it did not endanger the maintenance of workable competition. Nor was the effect on the market of other types of selective distribution system containing restrictions of competition so marked that a different assessment was called for. Lastly, following the proliferation of selective distribution systems of all types, no increase in the rigidity of the price structure could be identified by the Court. Some limitation of price competition within the system had to be tolerated if it was counterbalanced by an improvement in the services provided to customers.

101. The judgment rejects, moreover, the applicant's argument that the restrictions of competition inherent in the SABA distribution system could not be regarded as indispensable within the meaning of Article 85(3)(a) owing to the nature of the products in question, only a small part of which required an after-sales service. The existence of a variety of channels of distribution adapted to the individual characteristics of the various producers and to the requirements of the various categories of consumer is justified in a sector where a relatively small number of large and medium-scale producers offer a varied range of consumer durables which are readily interchangeable and which are technically advanced and of high quality. The need regularly arises in this sector for the establishment of a specialized sales and after-sales service, which is feasible only within the framework of a selective distribution system. [1]

This also applies to colour television sets owing to the complexity of the product and the many different ways in which it may be used.

102. The applicant's contention that the SABA distribution system tended to eliminate competition entirely in respect of a substantial part of the products in question and therefore ran counter to Article 85(3)(b) was likewise rejected. The Court observed that competition could not be eliminated if the selective distribution systems of certain producers continued to exist side by side with

---

[1] A similar view was expressed in *Metro v SABA I,* footnote 4, p. 102.

other methods of distribution based on a different market strategy. The applicant had not proved that the self-service wholesale trade was being squeezed from the consumer electronics market. Metro itself and other self-service wholesalers were perfectly able to obtain the equipment they wanted, including colour television sets, from producers other than SABA.

103.   A general statement made by the Court in this connection is of considerable practical importance: if a distribution system is identical in all essential respects to a system previously in operation which was the subject of an exemption decision, the Commission may assume, in the absence of evidence to the contrary, that the new system also fulfils the conditions of Article 85(3). This finding will greatly simplify the examination of applications for an extension in the future.

104.   The applicant submitted lastly that firms in the Thomson-Brandt group, of which SABA is a member, constitute a single economic unit which has a dominant position on the market in consumer electronics in general, and colour television sets and video recorders in particular, in a substantial part of the common market. SABA's refusal to supply Metro constituted an abuse of that dominant position.

The judgment rejects this contention, too. To substantiate the argument of economic unity, Metro would have had to furnish evidence that, not only were the individual firms in the Thomson-Brandt group linked at the level of capital, but they also pursued a coordinated marketing strategy in accordance with the directions of their parent company or with a plan agreed among themselves. In the absence of such evidence, it had to be assumed that as far as the distribution of its products was concerned SABA was independent of its parent and fellow group members. But with a market share of less than 10% in its principal market, the German market in colour television sets, SABA by itself was far too weak to be considered a dominant enterprise, especially since technically complex or readily interchangeable products offered by 18 other producers were involved.

105.   The build-up of concentration in the consumer electronics industry, which had led to the formation of two big European groups (Thomson-Brandt and Grundig-Philips) did not alter the position. An increase in the degree of concentration was of importance only if it affected the structure of competition on the relevant market. Such an effect did not always occur where the trend towards concentration was at the level of production and

not at that of distribution, which was what the Commission was concerned with here. In such a case it had to be proved that the company mergers in question helped to eliminate price competition at the marketing stage or to oust other channels of distribution. Such proof had not been adduced by the applicant.

106. The Commission considers that the *Metro v SABA II* judgment endorses the policy it has pursued for many years now in the field of selective distribution systems, especially in the consumer electronics sector.

It will continue to pursue this policy in future, making whatever adjustments are necessary in the light of changing economic circumstances.

§ 3 — Application of Article 85 to franchise agreements

107.   In its *Pronuptia* judgment of 28 January, [1] the Court took a stand for the first time on the appraisal of franchise agreements in the light of competition law. The judgment is concerned exclusively with distribution franchising. Agreements on service franchising and production franchising will be assessed later.

108.   In a distribution franchise system an enterprise which has established itself on a given market and thus developed certain business methods grants independent traders, for a fee, the right to establish themselves in other markets using its business name and the business methods which have made it successful. In addition to being a method of distribution, it is a way for an enterprise to derive financial benefit from its expertise without investing its own capital. Moreover, the system gives traders who do not have the necessary experience access to methods which they could not have learned otherwise or until much later and allows them to benefit from the reputation of the franchisor's business name. Franchise agreements for the distribution of goods differ in that regard from dealerships or contracts which incorporate approved retailers into a selective distribution system, which do not involve the use of a single business name, the application of uniform business methods or the payment of royalties in return for the benefits granted.

109.   In the Court's opinion, such a system, which allows the franchisor to profit from his success, does not in itself interfere with competition. The same applies to all the contractual obligations which are objectively necessary in order for the franchise system to work. The Court distinguishes in this respect between two categories of contractual clause, neither of which is caught by the prohibition contained in Article 85(1), namely:

1. Provisions which are essential in order to ensure that the know-how and assistance provided by the franchisor do not benefit competitors. In the Court's view, these provisions include:

   (a) the clause prohibiting the franchisee, during the lifetime of the agreement and for a reasonable period after its expiry, from opening a shop of the same or a similar nature in an area where he may compete with a member of the network;

---

[1]   Footnote 2(a), p. 97.

(b) the franchisee's obligation not to transfer his shop to another party without the prior approval of the franchisor.

2. Provisions which establish the means of control strictly necessary for the purpose of maintaining the identity and reputation of the network bearing the franchisor's business name or symbol. In the Court's view, these include:

(a) the franchisee's obligation to apply the business methods developed by the franchisor and to use the know-how provided;

(b) the franchisee's obligation to sell the goods covered by the agreement only in premises laid out and decorated according to the franchisor's instructions, the aim being to ensure uniform presentation in conformity with certain requirements;

(c) the franchisee's obligation not to transfer his shop to another location without the franchisor's approval;

(d) the franchisee's obligation not to assign his rights and obligations under the agreement to third parties without the franchisor's approval;

(e) the franchisee's obligation to sell only products supplied by the franchisor or by suppliers selected by him where this is the only technically feasible or economically justifiable method of ensuring the quality of the goods offered for sale or safeguarding the reputation of the distribution network; such a provision may not, however, have the effect of preventing the franchisee from obtaining those goods from other franchisees.

(f) the franchisee's obligation to obtain the franchisor's approval for all advertising; this requirement may concern only the nature of the advertising.

110. On the other hand, the Court regards as restrictions of competition within the meaning of Article 85(1) provisions sharing markets between the franchisor and the franchisees or between franchisees, and in particular territorial protection clauses in exclusive agreements. The same goes for exclusive purchasing obligations in so far as they prevent the franchisee from buying the goods covered by the agreement from other franchisees. Provisions which prevent franchisees from engaging in price competition with each other also fall in principle under Article 85(1). However, if the franchisor simply provides franchisees with price guidelines, this does not constitute a restriction of competition so long as there is no concerted practice between the franchisor and the franchisees or between the franchisees themselves for the actual application of such prices. In the Court's opinion, the block exemption Regulations for exclusive distribution and exclusive purchasing agreements are not applicable to franchise agreements because the latter constitute a distinct type of contract.

111.   Owing to the large number of franchise agreements, the economic importance of which is constantly increasing, the Commission considers it necessary to make such agreements subject to a general set of rules stating clearly the preconditions for the application of Article 85(3). To prepare the ground for this new block exemption Regulation, during the period under review the first individual decisions were taken in the field of franchising. [1]

---

[1]   *Yves Rocher* and *Pronuptia,* 17.12.1986, OJ L 8, 10.7.1987 and OJ L 13, 5.1.1987; see also above, point 53.

§ 4 — Appraisal of patent licensing agreements in the light of Article 85(1)

112. The *Windsurfing International (WSI)* judgment of 25 February [1] confirms in all essential respects the Commission decision [2] adopted in the same case. In this decision the Commission had found that a number of clauses which the enterprise concerned included in its patent licensing agreements until 1982 infringed Article 85(1). The licensor was fined accordingly.

113. Although in Germany WSI enjoyed patent protection only for a 'rig for a sailboard', in practice it also claimed patent protection for the sailboard as such. On the strength of this WSI imposed the following conditions on its German licensees:

(i)   The licence was restricted to certain types of board which had been given WSI's approval. New models had to be approved by WSI.

(ii)   The separate sale of components, in particular the patented rig, was prohibited.

(iii) The licensee was obliged to affix to boards offered for sale a notice stating that they were licensed by WSI.

(IV)   The licensee was prohibited from starting production in areas not covered by a patent.

Some licensees were also prohibited from challenging either the patents covered by the licensing agreement or the validity of the trade marks 'Windsurfer' and 'Windsurfing' used by WSI in Europe. The Commission regarded these prohibitions as restrictions of competition which clearly went further than the protection that could be laid claim to under the patent.

114. The Court endorsed the Commission's assessment of the above-mentioned clauses in the light of competition law:

(i)   The licensee's obligation to use the patented rig only for attachment to certain boards specified in the licensing agreement and to submit new types of sailboard to the licensor for approval exceeds, in the Court's view, the scope of the patent and cannot be justified on grounds of quality and safety control. Such controls must be effected according to objective criteria agreed upon in advance, they may not be left to the discretion of

---

[1]   Footnote 1(a), p. 97.
[2]   Decision of 11 July 1983, OJ L 229, 20.8.1983.

the licensor as he might otherwise impose his own selection of models upon licensees, which would be contrary to Article 85.

(ii) The Court regarded the obligation to sell only complete sailboards although the rig alone was patented as an arbitrary restriction of the licensee's economic freedom. It took a similar view of the licensee's obligation to affix a notice even on sailboards not covered by the patent. On the other hand, it considered that the obligation on the licensee to pay royalties on sales of components on the basis of the net selling price of a complete sailboard, to which the Commission had objected in the same context, did not, on factual grounds, constitute a restriction of competition within the meaning of Article 85(1).

(iii) Lastly, the Court held that the obligation on licensees not to manufacture the products concerned in other countries in which there was no patent protection, and the obligation not to challenge the validity of the patentee's trade mark or of the licensed patents themselves, did not fall within the specific subject-matter of the patents. Such clauses therefore always constitute restrictions of competition within the meaning of Article 85(1). The same reasoning underlies Regulation (EEC) No 2349/84 on the block exemption of patent licensing agreements.

115.   The Court's remarks on the Commission's powers in cases in which there is disagreement over the validity or scope of a patent are worthy of note.

Although the Commission is not competent to determine the scope of a patent, it cannot refrain entirely from making an assessment in this regard if such scope is relevant for the purpose of determining whether there has been an infringement of Articles 85 or 86 of the Treaty. Even in cases where the actual scope of a patent is the subject of proceedings before a national court, the Commission must be able to exercise its powers in accordance with the provisions of Regulation No 17 under the supervision of the Court of Justice.

116.   The Court's remarks on the criterion of effect on trade between Member States in Article 85(1) are also of general interest. That article does not require that each separate clause of an agreement should be capable of affecting trade. The question is, rather, whether the agreement as a whole is capable of affecting trade between Member States. If so, it only remains to be examined which clauses of the agreement, taken in isolation, have as their object or effect a restriction or distortion of competition.

§ 5 — Interpretation of block exemption Regulation (EEC) No 123/85 on vehicle distribution and servicing agreements

117.   In its judgment in *VAG v Magne* the Court had to interpret Article 5(2) point 2 of Regulation (EEC) No 123/85. This provision makes block exemption conditional on the agreement concerned being concluded either for a period of at least four years or for an indefinite period, in which case there must be a period of notice of at least one year. The court making the reference had asked whether the provision contained binding rules which directly affected the validity or content of the agreement as a whole or of certain of its clauses, or which obliged the parties to adapt the content of their agreement to bring it into line with the Regulation. The defendant in the main action, a dealer in cars supplied by the applicant, VAG France, had suggested that the latter was obliged under the Regulation to offer to conclude with him a new four-year dealer agreement. The offer of an agreement of indeterminate duration with a one-year period of notice, such as the plaintiff had made, was unsatisfactory as the old agreement, which had to be brought into line with the Regulation, was for a fixed, and not an indefinite, period.

118.   In answering the question referred, the Court drew attention to the common thread running through Article 85(1) and (3), Council Regulation No 19/65/EEC empowering the Commission to adopt block exemption regulations and Commission Regulation (EEC) No 123/85 adopted pursuant to that Regulation. In the Court's opinion, block exemption regulations, and individual exemption decisions based on Regulation No 17, are simply a particular form of the declaration of inapplicability provided for in Article 85(3). They afford enterprises an opportunity to ensure that their agreements, even where they contain restrictive clauses within the meaning of Article 85(1), escape the prohibition on restrictive practices. They do not, however, compel enterprises to avail themselves of this opportunity. Nor does a block exemption regulation have the effect of modifying the content of an agreement or of rendering it void where it does not fulfil all the conditions of the regulation. In the latter event, the parties may either apply for an individual exemption from the prohibition on restrictive practices or establish that the conditions of another block exemption regulation are fulfilled, or, failing that, demonstrate that, for other reasons, the agreement in question is not caught by the prohibition in Article 85(1).

The Court accordingly answered the question referred in the negative and found that Article 5(2) point 2 of Regulation (EEC) No 123/85 has no direct, peremptory effects. The judgment confirms the Commission's thinking both on what the outcome of the case should be and on the reasons for it.

§ 6 — Isolation of national markets as an infringement of Article 86

119.   The *British Leyland (BL)* [1] judgment of 11 November, which upholds the Commission decision [2] in the same case, underlines a general principle of competition policy whereby measures taken by a dominant enterprise having as their object or effect the shielding of the territory of a Member State from parallel imports from other parts of the Community constitute serious infringements of Article 86 and are therefore punishable by a fine.

120.   In the present case the British car manufacturer BL abused its dominant position by deciding to allow national type approval for left-hand-drive (LHD) Metros to lapse in 1981 and by refusing to provide trade importers with certificates of conformity, which are necessary if individual vehicles are to be registered. Furthermore, when BL issued certificates of conformity for individual vehicles, it charged excessive fees. As a result of these practices traders and users were impeded or deterred from importing LHD Metros, which can easily be converted to right hand drive, into the UK. There was a considerable demand for such vehicles because of significant pre-tax price differences for new Metros in the UK and in other Member States and because right-hand-drive Metros were not at that time readily available for export from other Member States.

121.   The Court's comments on the relevant market, the concept of dominant position and the nature of the abuse are of general importance going beyond the confines of this case.

The judgment states that the relevant market is not the car market but a separate, ancillary market for services which are indispensable for traders who wish to sell the vehicles manufactured by BL in a specific geographical area. In this separate market for services BL occupies a dominant position because it has been granted an administrative monopoly in respect of the issue of certificates of conformity. Traders are therefore placed *vis-à-vis* that firm in a position of economic dependence which is characteristic of a dominant position. These pronouncements constitute a further development of the existing case-law on Article 86. [3] They will enable the Commission in future to assume in certain cases that there is market dominance restricted to the relationship between manufacturer and retailer. [4]

---

[1]   Footnote 1(e), p. 97.
[2]   Decision of 2 July 1984, OJ L 207, 2.8.1984; Fourteenth Competition Report, point 96.
[3]   See Case 26/75 *General Motors* [1975] ECR 1367.
[4]   See also in this connection the study on the relevant market discussed in Part Four.

122.   With regard to the concept of abuse, the judgment states that a manufacturer cannot justify the prevention of parallel imports on the ground that it has to save its selective distribution network, which has been accepted as permissible by the Commission, from destruction. An abuse may consist not only in acts such as the withholding of certificates of conformity or the charging of excessive fees for parallel-imported vehicles, but also in omissions, especially where they are clearly aimed at partitioning a national market from the other markets in the Community. BL's decision to let the type approval certificate required for left-hand-drive vehicles of the Metro type expire and not to renew it, so as to put an end to parallel imports of such vehicles, was therefore rightly viewed by the Commission as an infringement of Article 86.

§ 7 — Anti-trust procedures and legal protection

123.   Finally, the Court shed light on a number of procedural questions and in so doing gave the Commission pointers on how to develop its administrative practice in this field.

124.   The *Windsurfing* judgment [1] states with regard to Article 4(2)(2)(b) of Regulation No 17 that patent licensing agreements must be notified where they contain clauses which exceed the scope of the patent. In *Metro v SABA II* [2] the Court points out that form A/B must be used only for the first notification of an agreement pursuant to Articles 4, 5 and 25 of Regulation No 17. When applying for the extension or renewal of an exemption within the meaning of Article 8(2) of Regulation No 17, a mere letter detailing any amendments to the original agreement is sufficient, provided the agreement remains basically unchanged.

125.   As the Court explains in the *AKZO investigation* judgment, [3] Article 14(3) of Regulation No 17 is intended to enable the Commission to carry out quickly and without notice investigations into enterprises suspected of having committed infringements. Consequently, the obligation to consult the competent national authorities beforehand may not be interpreted in such a way as to jeopardize the speedy adoption of the necessary decision ordering the investigation. Informal contacts, including those established by telephone, therefore suffice. No record need be kept of them.

In the same judgment the Court stresses once more [4] that Article 14(3) of Regulation No 17 is compatible with Article 8 of the European Convention on Human Rights. It confirms, moreover, the lawfulness of the system of delegation of powers operated within the Commission. In the Court's opinion, the empowering of individual Members of the Commission as provided for in Article 27 of the Commission's provisional rules of procedure [5] accords fully with the principle of collegiate responsibility enshrined in Article 17 of the Merger Treaty.

What is more, such delegation of powers is necessary to enable the Commission to carry out its functions. The empowering of the Member of the Commission

---

1   Footnote 1(a), p. 97.
2   Footnote 1(d), p. 97.
3   Footnote 1(c), p. 97.
4   See also Case 136/79 *National Panasonic (UK) Ltd* [1980] ECR 2033, 2056 *et seq.;* Tenth Competition Report (1980), points 42 and 43.
5   OJ No 147, 11.7.1967.

responsible for competition matters to take decisions ordering investigations cannot therefore be objected to on legal grounds.

126.   The comments contained in the *AKZO business secrets* judgment [1] concerning the principle of *audi alterem partem* and legal protection against Commission measures which might affect firms' legitimate interests in the preservation of their business secrets deserve particular attention. When communicating business documents to a third party, especially a complainant, the Commission must exercise particular care. Before transmitting documents containing information whose confidentiality is in dispute, the Commission must give the firm concerned an opportunity to state its views and appeal to the Court. In this way the firm is afforded an opportunity to obtain preventive legal protection in a particularly sensitive field. However, the Commission's power to decide itself, under the supervision of the Court, on the secret nature of certain facts and on whether or not they are worthy of protection is not affected.

---

[1]   Footnote 1(b), p. 97.

Chapter IV

Application of national and Community competition law in the Member States

Belgium

127. The law of 27 May 1960 on the protection against abuse of economic power was not amended in 1986.

128. New legislative proposals concerning competition were placed before the Senate on 31 July.

The objectives of the proposed law are to safeguard and promote the Belgian economy and to move progressively from a pricing policy towards a competition policy. To this end, the Bill prohibits conduct on the part of undertakings and public bodies which prevents, restricts or distorts competition. The law will not apply to certain classes of agreements, notably agreements of minor importance or to banks, credit institutions, savings banks and other financial or insurance undertakings. Exemptions will be available for agreements on ground similar to those set out in Article 85(3).

In order to further the realization of the objectives to the Act it is planned to entrust its execution to a body of officials experienced in the competition field and to reinforce the number of judges in the Council and to appoint special office officials to assist them.

The Crown has been charged with determining which sectors, categories of products or products should no longer be subject to the system of maximum prices and to price increase declarations.

129. The Council for Economic Disputes concluded that there had been an abuse of economic power by a manufacturer of phototypesetting equipment. The Council found that the relevant market consisted of maintenance and repairs of second-hand equipment of that manufacturer. Since the latter had a monopoly in respect of spare parts and software for its machines, it was held to occupy a dominant independent position *vis-à-vis* independent companies mending original spare parts. That dominance was compounded by the fact that the manufacturer's technicians had build up particular expertise in the maintenance of the equipment.

The Council went on to find that the manufacturer abused its position, and hence acted against the public interest, by arbitrarily differentiating amongst its customers. For the same service (access to technical service), its conditions varied widely and were in many respects unfair. The Council noted that the public interest was severely affected by jeopardizing the continued healthy existence of these companies.

The Minister for Economic Affairs, however, ruled against the Council's opinion. He indicated that the Council should have examined whether reconditioned or new spare parts were available from other sources and whether other companies could maintain or repair the equipment involved. He noted that discrimination itself is not objectionable when it is objectively justified. The Minister found that the manufacturer had in fact not committed an abuse. He further held that the discrimination in question affected private interests only and that these are not protected by the law unless they extend to collective interests, i.e. consumers' interests, which was not established in the case under review.

130.   The four companies acting under the name 'Fruitbeurs', to whom a recommendation for terminating an abuse had been addressed, [1] applied for the withdrawal of that ruling. The Council for Economic Disputes accepted this application in view of the favourable evolution of the market for exotic fruits and the resulting disappearance of the abuse.

Denmark

131.   In the course of 1986 there was only one change in the legislation of the Monopolies Control Authority. That was the repeal of the law relating to the list prices to be respected in the steel trade and the relevant implementing measures concerning the publication of the price lists of the steel trade. The steel trade is henceforth subject to the rules applied by the Monopolies Control Authority.

---

[1]   Ninth Competition report, point 47.

132.   A group of experts set up in 1985 reported in July 1986 on the updating of the existing competition legislation. A Bill is expected to be submitted in 1987.

133.   The Monopolies Control Authority published a survey on mergers and take-overs in 'Danish Industry 1985' and a report on the situation in the food can industry and the situation in the physiotherapy profession as well as a report on the developments in prices and costs in 1985.

134.   The Monopolies Appeal Tribunal annulled a decision by the Monopolies Control Authority requiring notification and regulation of United International Pictures ApS which held a dominant position in the film hire sector. The Tribunal upheld a decision requiring registration of Rockwool A/S and Superfos Glasuld A/S as being in a dominant position in the production and sale of high performance heating insulation materials and soft insulation materials.

135.   The Monopolies Control Authority has furthermore required Skandina-visk Kaffekompagni A/S, which is a company set up as a result of a merger between the Danish subsidiary of General Foods Northern Europe Ltd and Karat Koffe A/S, to be registered as a supplier of roasted coffee; the merger agreement as such was not subject to registration.

136.   Since the Commission has abandoned its plan to adopt a Community framework for book prices, the Monopolies Control Authority, in the light of the developments in the Danish book market, is reconsidering the temporary permission granted to fix book prices.

137.   Furthermore, the Monopolies Control Authority has dealt with a large number of complaints of refusal to supply and disruption of deliveries. In most cases the Authority has found that the conditions for granting an injunction were not satisfied. The Monopolies Appeal Tribunal, has, *inter alia,* upheld a decision by the Monopolies Control Authority refusing to compel Lancôme SA to supply Bilka with cosmetics. Bilka has appealed the decision to the Court of Appeal.

138.   A decision by the Monopolies Control Authority refusing to intervene in a rearrangement of the distribution to hospitals of industrially produced drugs, which was subsequently upheld by the Monopolies Appeal Tribunal and by the Court of Appeal, was referred by the Association of Local Authorities Council to the Supreme Court.

139. The Monopolies Control Authority has, after the annulment of the pricing system for oil products, required the fining companies to report any price changes related to the sale of certain given oil products. This reporting obligation has also been imposed on certain companies operating in the coal sector and the anti-rust products sector.

140. The Monopolies Control Authority has according to the relevant Commission directive amended the implementing measures relating to the price labelling of foodstuffs.

141. Finally, the Monopolies Tribunal has established that Metro self-service wholesalers are subject to the provisions on retail price labelling as set out in the Law on Price Labelling.

142. There have been no cases involving the application of Community competition law by the Danish Court.

Federal Republic of Germany

143. The law against unfair competition was amended in the course of the year to restrict certain types of advertising.

144. The Monopolies Commission published in its Sixth Report on the current state of corporate concentration. Concentration is increasing slowly but is not appreciably affecting the economy nor is it expected to do so in the foreseeable future. In 1986 the Cartel Office prohibited one merger and 11 planned mergers did not take place after intervention by the Office.

The Federal Cartel Office did not prohibit the acquisition by Daimler Benz AG of a majority holding in AEG. Even though, following this merger, Daimler Benz became the largest German enterprise with an annual turnover in excess of DM 60 000 million, since the fields of activities of the two merged firms did not overlap. Daimler Benz is primarily a manufacturer of cars and trucks while AEG is an electrical goods manufacturer. Under German merger control law size alone cannot be a ground for prohibiting a merger. The Cartel Office therefore, proceeded to examine the individual markets affected by the merger to see whether, as a result of it, dominant positions were either created or reinforced as a result of transfer of financial or technical resources. It found that they were not. The Monopolies Commission, on the occasion of the authorization of this merger, called for stricter control of large conglomerate mergers. In its view an analysis of the effect of a merger from the point of view of individual markets is insufficient to overcome the risks inherent in such mergers from the point of view of competition and social policy.

145.   The Federal Supreme Court has given judgment in the Philip Morris Inc./Rothmans Tobacco Holdings Ltd merger case. [1] It held that the question of the first prohibition order of the Cartel Office was now settled since the original merger no longer existed. It did not pronounce upon the problem of the application of domestic law to foreign mergers and dominance in the domestic cigarette market. With respect to the second prohibition of the Cartel Office the Federal Supreme Court held that the present holdership arrangements did not infringe competition law.

146.   The Cartel Office prohibited the planned acquisition by Linde AG, Wiesbaden of Agefko Kohlensaüare Industrie Gmbh Düsseldorf. The merger would have led to a strengthening of dominant positions in the markets for carbon dioxide and industrial gas. The takeover of Agefko by l'Air Liquide SA, Paris was, however, permitted. L'Air Liquide has marketed industrial gases in collaboration with the Swedish producer AGA AB through a joint subsidiary AGA Gas, Hamburg. This joint subsidiary has been declared to be a sales cartel by the Cartel Office and will be dismantled on 1 January 1987.

147.   With respect to newspapers, the Federal Supreme Court upheld the prohibition of the merger of the *Süddeutsche Zeitung* with the *Donau Kurier*. The Court of Appeal upheld the prohibition of the Gruner & Jahr (Bertelsmann)/Zeitverlag merger. The companies in question have lodged an appeal with the Federal Supreme Court.

148.   The Federal Supreme Court held that the Telefunken distribution system did not infringe the ban on resale price maintenance. The ban on vertical price fixing was held not to extend to the right of an enterprise to give instructions to its agents.

149.   In a test case, the Cartel Office prohibited two regional associations of building contractors from reporting on bids received for tenders. This decision has been upheld by the Federal Supreme Court.

150.   Concentration in the food distribution sector continued to attract attention. The Metro-Kaufhof merger, which was prohibited by the Cartel Office

---

[1]   Twelfth Competition Report, point 120. Thirteenth Competition Report, point 184.

has been referred back to the Court of Appeal by the Federal Supreme Court for a rehearing. In the Co-op/Wandmaker case, the Court of Appeal set aside the Cartel Office's prohibition.

151. Since concentration can be achieved not only by mergers but also by cooperations between legally independent enterprises in the matter of purchasing, the Cartel Office is currently examining the interests held by large distributors in purchasing associations of small and medium-sized enterprises. The Court of Appeal has upheld the Cartel Office decision that in its present form the Selex & Tania purchasing association infringes the ban on restrictive practices. Selex & Tania group together with a number of firms some with turnovers in excess of DM 1 000 million. The firms concerned have appealed against the decision to the Federal Supreme Court.

152. German courts directly apply the Community competition rules. During the first half of the year, they dealt with 10 cases involving vertical distribution agreements.

Greece

153. No amendments or additions were made in 1986 to existing competition legislation (Act No 703/77).

154. The Competition Committee investigated a number of cases, involving cosmetics, car paints, clothing and petroleum products.

155. Following complaints from petrol retailers the committee began an investigation under Regulation No 1984/83 of agreements made by oil companies with retailers.

156. The Minister for Commerce issued a total of 14 decisions. The Minister decided that there was no ground for intervention under Articles 1 and 2 of Act No 703/77 in the case of the purchase by a UK petroleum company of the whole of the shares of a Greek petroleum company through the intermediary of a foreign parent company.

157. Following a complaint of abuse of a dominant position which consisted in the refusal of an undertaking established in another Member State to supply car paints to a Greek importer on the Greek market, the Minister for Commerce, for the first time applied Article 32 of the Act and ordered the abuse in question to cease.

Spain

158.   Under the 1978 Constitution, which gave full recognition to economic freedom, competition law plays an increasingly important role in Spain.

159.   The Restraints of Competition Act No 110 of 20 July 1963 is based upon the principles set out in Articles 85 and 86. It aims at ensuring a reasonable level of competition whilst permitting such cooperation and mergers as are necessary for the rational use of resources and the development of new technology.

The Act applies throughout Spain and to all sectors of the economy except agriculture.

Article 1 of the Act prohibits restrictions on competition arising from agreements, amalgamations of enterprises or conscious parallel behaviour by businesses.

The agreements giving rise to such restraints are void. It is to be noted that the agreements themselves are not prohibited but only the practices arising out of them. This situation is not deemed to be satisfactory and an amendment to the Act on this point is being considered.

Agreements and practices may be exempted from the prohibition provided they fulfil conditions similar to those set out in Article 85(3). There is no system of block exemptions.

Abuse of a dominant position is prohibited by Article 2 of the Act. Mergers, in which the newly created entity will hold 30% or more of the domestic market for particular goods or services, are required to be notified.

The authorities responsible for the administration of the Act are:

(a) The Directorate-General for Competition, which is attached to the Department of State for Trade, is responsible for investigating cases of suspected restrictive agreements or abuse of dominant positions and for considering applications for exemption from the provisions of the Act. After completing its investigations the Director-General hands over the cases to the Competition Court for a decision with a recommendation as to which course of action it considers suitable.

(b) The Competition Court, although administratively part of the Department of State for Trade is a totally independent body. It is composed of a President and eight judges appointed for life. It sits as a full court or in chambers. An Appeal against its decision lies to the Court of Appeal and from there to the Spanish Supreme Court.

Since taking up its duties in 1964 the Competition Court has handed down more than 300 decisions. Ten decisions were adopted in 1986.

Spain's entry into the EEC has led to an increased awareness of the importance of maintaining competition. Consequently, several amendments to the Restraints of Competition Act are being considered so as to make its enforcement more effective.

160.   In order to improve the enforcement of Community competition law in Spain, a new Royal Decree No 1882/1986 of 29 August 1986, was issued. It specifies that among national authorities, the Competition Court is responsible for enforcing Articles 85 and 86. This is without prejudice to the right of the ordinary courts to annul agreements on the basis of Article 85(2). The Decree assigns to the Director-General for Competition the responsibility for ensuring cooperation between the Spanish Administration and the EEC Commission in enforcing the Community competition rules in particular with regard to on the spot investigations of companies carried out by the Commission under Article 14 of Regulation No 17. Similar provision is made for the enforcement of the procedure regulation for transport, Council Regulation No 1017/1968.

France

161.   In December 1986 the French Government adopted an entirely new Order on freedom of prices and competition. The Order repeals the Orders of 30 June 1945 and establishes the general principles of freedom to determine prices. Henceforth prices may be controlled only by way of exception: either in sectors where price competition is limited by law or regulation or by the existence of monopolies, or temporarily in the event of a crisis or sudden upset in the market accompanied by excessive price rises in a given sector. Government measures relating to prices must now be taken by decree of the Conseil d'Etat and may be of not more than six months' duration.

162.   An autonomous body, the Conseil de concurrence (Competition Council), is set up. Its constitution, the status of its members and its powers are such that it acts independently of the public authorities. The Competition

Council has extensive jurisdiction, including the power to consult and take decisions. Appeal from its decisions lies to the Conseil d'Etat. It sits in place of the Minister for Economic Affairs and his department in cases involving anti-competitive activities.

163.   The safeguards intended to protect the interests of business people are made more effective. Procedures are introduced which enhance the supervisory role of the courts:

(i)   the investigations needed to seek out and establish the nature of restrictions of competition which involve searches and the seizure of documents may not take place without the prior authorization of a judge;

(ii)   proceedings before the Competition Council will be entirely adversary, thereby strengthening the rights of the defence. At every stage of the proceedings, the firms concerned will have access to all the information on file and will be entitled to submit observations;

(iii)   as regards penalties, the authorities' power of settlement is abolished.

164.   The definition of anti-competitive practices is brought up to date and clarified. The new Order codifies the rules on anti-competitive practices and unfair trading. The basic aim is to punish abuses. Moreover, the system of penalties has been remodelled along largely non-criminal lines.

165.   In the mergers sphere, the Minister retains his decision-making powers. He may carry out a review where the firms' turnover exceeds FF 7 000 million or where one of them has a market share of more than 25%.

166.   The monitoring of individual restrictive practices (tie-in, sale with free gifts, discrimination, resale price maintenance, refusal to sell, etc.) remained active during the first half of 1986: 1 116 checks were carried out, 103 of which resulted in warnings and 89 in reports.

167.   With regard to collective restrictive practices, the Minister for Economic Affairs, Finance and Privatization took, between November 1985 and November 1986 13 decisions based on the opinion of the Competition Commission. Fines totalling FF 17 892 000 were imposed. Of these decisions, the most significant are those which concern the competitive situation in the lift and hoist industry, cut-flower delivery and free newspapers ('free-sheets'). In the lift and hoist case, the Competition Commission was called upon to give a ruling on a set of anti-competitive practices involving prices and the sharing of markets. Aggravating circumstances added to the responsibility of the members of the cartel, including

that of the four largest companies in the industry, which had taken part in all the above-mentioned practices. The behaviour of the participating firms was punished by a fine of FF 15.7 million.

In the cut-flower delivery case, the Minister addressed injunctions and recommendations to two firms in the sector (Interflora and Telefleurs), asking them to modify certain restrictive practices (clause concerning membership of only one network and fixing of minimum order scales) so as to give the consumer a wider choice.

In relation to free newspapers, the Commission established the existence of an arrangement between two groups of enterprises aimed at partitioning the market and of an abuse of a dominant position by one of the groups aimed at eliminating competitors by artificially lowering prices. The firms concerned were fined and ordered to stop the offences.

Ireland

168.   The basic legislation covering merger and take-over activities is the Mergers, Take-overs and Monopolies (Control) Act, 1978. The number of proposed mergers or take-overs which was notified under the Act to the Minister was 75. One proposal was referred to the Examiner of Restrictive Practices under Section 8 of the Act. The Minister having considered the examiner's report and taking into consideration all of the information before him decided that the proposal be allowed to proceed.

169.   Two reports of the Restrictive Practices Commission were published. The first was a report of their public enquiry into the policies of building societies in regard to insurance related to mortgaged properties and valuation reports on properties [1] and the second was a report of their study into cable television systems in the greater Dublin area. [2]

170.   The Minister published the Restrictive Practices (Amendment) Bill, 1986 which will have the effect of revising the institutional arrangements relating to competition, price control and consumer protection and extending the scope of competition legislation to a number of services previously excluded.

---

[1]   PL 3505.
[2]   PL 4295.

Italy

171.   There was no change in Italian competition legislation during the report period.

Luxembourg

172.   No amendments were made to legislation on restrictive trade practices during the course of 1986 (Law of 17 June 1970).

173.   The Prices Office issued a number of Grand-Ducal Regulations, ministerial Regulations and ministerial Decrees on prices.

174.   The Law of 27 November 1986 regulating certain commercial practices and sanctioning unfair competition was enacted mainly to check various abuses concerned with liquidation and sales.

175.   A proposal for legislation to implement Directive 84/450[1] on unfair advertising was placed before the Council of State.

176.   No new cases were referred to the Restrictive Practices Commission.

The Netherlands

177.   The Resale Price Maintenance Bill was passed by the Lower House of Parliament on 11 November and is now before the Upper House. The Bill provides for a general prohibition of collective resale price maintenance. Exemptions are envisaged but subject to stringent conditions. A possibility for the enactment of regulations prohibiting individual resale price maintenance is also provided for in the Bill. An amendment to the Bill would, if accepted, allow the Minister for Economic Affairs discretion to set minimum prices in the public interest or in the interests of a particular sector of the economy.

178.   A Bill to extend the Competition Act to the liberal profession was introduced in the Lower House in February.

[1]   OJ L 250, 19.9.1984.

179.   A regulation to prohibit rules in the building sector whereby tenderers must add a certain sum on to their bid which, in the event of the bid being accepted, will be distributed among the unsuccessful tenderers (the Opzeit system) is being prepared.

180.   In July, the conditions for admission applied by the breakdown services division of Bovag, an association of garage operators and firms in allied trades were condemned as being contrary to the competition rules. Similarly, in November, the equalization and scrapping fund in the sand filled sector in the waters of South Holland and Zeeland was condemned. In December the Competition Board decided to quash a restriction on the location of new shops in the Breukelen shopping centre.

In December the Competition Board was asked to pronounce on the legality of the conduct of a company considered to hold a dominant position in the Dutch market for strip cartoon albums.

181.   No judgments enforcing the Community competition rules were reported in the period covering July 1985 to June 1986. Details of litigation during the last six months of 1986 were unavailable.

Portugal

182.   Decree law No 422/83 of 3 December 1983, which entered into force on 1 June 1984, lays down the competition rules applicable within Portugal. The aim of the law, as set out in Article 1, is to safeguard competition in the general interests of economic and social development and the protection of the consumer as well as to improve the international competitiveness of Portuguese industry.

183.   Agreements and concerted practices between firms or associations of firms which have as their objective or effect the prevention, distortion or restriction of competition on all or part of the national market are prohibited (Article 13).

184.   Abuse of a dominant position is also prohibited (Article 14). Article 15 (1) of the Decree law sets out the circumstances in which exemptions will be granted to the above-mentioned rules.

185.   Articles 3-12 prohibit firms unilaterally to fix minimum prices, pursue discriminatory pricing and sales policy and to refuse to sell. The ban on

minimum prices does not apply to the sales of books, newspapers or periodicals, or to goods and services which are subject to special legislation laying down minimum or fixed prices. Exceptions to the provisions on refusal to sell or the practices of discriminatory pricing and sales policies as set out in the Decree law can be made by legislation. Further derogations from Articles 3-12 can be obtained from the Competition Council.

The Decree law applies to the public and private sectors with the exception of:

(i)   national, regional and local administrations;

(ii)   the production, transfer and distribution of water and electricity, gas and post and telecommunications;

(iii) any other sector in which restrictions on competition are permitted by law or regulation.

186.   The competition rules are applied by the following bodies:

(i)   Competition Council, an independent decision-making body presided over by a judge or lawyer and composed of four experts;

(ii)   the Advisory Committee which administers the Competition Council and which is made up of representatives of industry, commerce and agriculture;

(iii) the Directorate-General for Competition and Prices which monitors the operation of markets continuously with a view to detecting restrictive practices and taking the action necessary to bring them to an end.

187.   In 1986 nine cases were investigated by the Directorate-General for Competition and sent to the Competition Council for opinion. Three requests for a ruling on the compatibility of commercial practices with the competition rules were made.

188.   The Competition Court adopted two decisions.

United Kingdom

189.   The Gas Act 1986 established a Director-General of Gas Supply who, following the privatization of British Gas, is responsible for operating a regulatory regime for the supply of gas. For supply to customers who take only small quantities, the regime includes a system of price control. Supply to larger customers is not subject to the same degree of regulation but the Act enables the Director-General of Fair Trading (DGFT) to refer this market to the

Monopolies and Mergers Commission (MMC) for investigation under the Fair Trading Act 1973 (FTA).

190.   The Airports Act 1986 brings within the DGFT's responsibilities under the competition legislation the non-aeronautical operations of airports and gives the Civil Aviation Authority a role in regulating the aeronautical operations of major airports, including powers to deal with anti-competitive practices.

191.   The provisions of the Financial Services Act 1986 are expected to be implemented by the end of 1987. The Act applies a special competition regime to the rules and regulations of the self-regulatory system for the conduct of investment business. The exemption from the Restrictive Trade Practices Act 1976 (RTPA) for the provision of banking services in Northern Ireland has been withdrawn, thus extending the provisions of the Act to banking services throughout the UK.

192.   The DGFT made two monopoly references to the MMC under the FTA concerning the supply of pest control services and the supply of beer for retail sale on licensed premises. Five monopoly reports were published by the MMC on: the supply of tampons; [1] the supply, maintenance and repair of postal franking machines; [2] the supply of white salt; [3] the management of greyhound racing tracks; [4] and the supply of agency services by travel agents for tour operators. [5] In each case the MMC found that a monopoly situation existed and, in four, identified detriments to the public interest. In the case of tampons the MMC found that the prices charged did not operate against the public interest and the companies were released from undertakings given after an earlier MMC report. On advice from the DGFT, the Minister for Corporate and Consumer Affairs decided to make an order under the FTA against the practice of tour operators prohibiting travel agents from allowing discounts on the price of foreign package holidays. In the three other cases the Minister asked the DGFT to seek appropriate undertakings from the parties concerned.

193.   The Restrictive Practices Court accepted undertakings from, and in one case made orders against, parties to price fixing agreements for a number of concrete, ferrous and polyethylene products used mainly in the construction

---

[1]   Cmnd 9705 January 1986.
[2]   Cmnd 9747 March 1986.
[3]   Cmnd 9778 June 1986.
[4]   Cmnd 9834 July 1986.
[5]   Cmnd 9879 September 1986.

industry. Undertakings were also accepted in relation to the arranged closure of betting shops and aerodrome landing charges.

194.   On an appeal by the Royal Institution of Chartered Surveyors the Court of Appeal determined that possession of a Royal Charter does not give immunity from the RTPA.

195.   The DGFT initiated three investigations under the Competition Act 1980 into: the refusal by two publishers of trade newspapers for the amusement industry to accept for publication advertisements containing certain price information; and the conduct of Sealink Harbours Ltd in determining and applying the charges for customers clearance services and for the grant of port exit permits at two harbours in the UK.

196.   The DGFT give advice to the Secretary of State on 293 mergers and prospective mergers and the Secretary of State referred 13 cases to the MMC. Of these, six have lapsed after the mergers were abandoned. The MMC reported on six cases: British Telecom plc/Mitel Corporation,[1] BET plc/SGB Group plc,[2] General Electric Co. plc ('GEC')/The Plessey Co. plc,[3] Elders IXL Ltd/ Allied Lyons plc,[4] Norton Opax plc/McCorquodale plc[5] and Peninsular and Oriental Steam Navigation Group ('Pand 0')/European Ferries Group plc.[6] In two cases, BT/Mitel and GEC/Plessey, the MMC concluded that the mergers might be expected to operate against the public interest.

197.   After completing a programme of reviews on restrictions in the professions undertaken at the request of ministers, the DGFT published four reports on: advertising and charging rules of the professions serving the construction industry;[7] restrictions on the kind of organization through which members of professions may offer their services;[8] restrictions on the patent agents profession;[9] and remaining significant advertising restrictions.[10] The DGFT has been asked by ministers to discuss with the professional bodies concerned a number of the recommended changes to their rules.

---

[1]   Cmnd 9715 January 1986.
[2]   Cmnd 9795 May 1986.
[3]   Cmnd 9897 August 1986.
[4]   Cmnd 9892 September 1986.
[5]   Cmnd 9904 September 1986.
[6]   Cmnd 31 December 1986.
[7]   Published 26 March.
[8]   Published 27 August.
[9]   Published 25 September.
[10]   Published 2 October.

198.   Following a report by the MMC,[1] and subsequent negotiations, the DGFT has now accepted undertakings from the Ford Motor Co. Ltd that it will grant licences to independent firms allowing them to manufacture and/or supply in the UK replacement body parts for Ford vehicles, which are protected by registered design.

199.   In *Cutsforth v Mansfield Inns*[2] an injunction was granted following a breach of Article 85 EEC. After Mansfield Inns had acquired a number of tied public houses which the plaintiff had previously supplied with amusement machines, it introduced a new approved list of suppliers on which it refused to include the plaintiff. The judge held that the High Court was entitled to grant injunctive relief if there was a violation of Article 85 or Article 86; that the agreements between the defendant and its tied houses were covered by Article 85(1); that the restriction on supply of machines was outside the block exemption in Regulation 1984/83 by virtue of Article 8(1)(b) of that Regulation; and that Article 86 did not apply because the area affected was not a substantial part of the common market.

200.   In *Argyll Group plc & Others v Distillers Company plc*[3] an injunction was sought against a merger alleged to be contrary to Article 86 EEC. The injunction was refused on grounds of uncertainty and convenience.

---

[1]   Fifteenth Competition Report, point 164.
[2]   1986 1 CMLR 1.
[3]   1986 1 CMLR 764.

Part Three

Competition policy and government assistance to enterprises

Chapter I

State aids

§ 1 — General policy problems and developments

201. The Community's efforts to complete a single unified internal market by 1992, mapped out in the Commission's 1985 White Paper, lend added weight and importance to the enforcement of the competition rules, and in particular the rules on State aid.

202. The general lines of Commission policy in this area and their application are well established and have been described in previous competition reports. Notable developments in 1986 were the implementation of the new rules on aid to the steel industry (Decision No 3484/85/ECSC) [1] and the coal industry, the publication and implementation of the Community framework on State aids for research and development, [2]   the adoption by the Council on 22 December of a new (sixth) directive on State aids for shipbuilding, and the extension of the Community framework on State aids for environmental protection. A start was also made on assessing the existing aid schemes in Spain and Portugal under Article 93(1) of the EEC Treaty.

203. The Commission continued its policy of systematically ordering the recovery of aid granted illegally by Member States and found to be incompatible with the common market and reaffirmed its intention of gradually applying the same principle also to aid that is illegal only for procedural reasons, i.e. disregard by Member States of the obligation to give prior notification of aid proposals. Instances of the application of this policy are reported in the relevant section of this chapter.

204. A synopsis of the Commission's activity in applying the State aid rules is given in the table below showing the number of aid cases notified by the

---

[1]   OJ C 340, 18.12.1985.
[2]   OJ C 83, 11.4.1986.

Member States and the number of cases determined by the Commission during the year, compared with previous years.

TABLE 1

Activity in the control of State aids
(excluding aids to agriculture and fisheries and transport)

| Year | No of proposals notified | Action taken by the Commission[1] | | | | Proposals notified and later withdrawn by Member States |
		To raise no objection	Open the procedure of Art. 93(2) EEC or Art. 8(3) of Decision 2320/81/ECSC	Decisions to close the procedure Art. 93(2) or Art. 8(3) of Decision 2320/81/ ECSC[2]	Final decision Art. 93(2) or Art. 8(3) of Decision 2320/81/ ECSC[3]	
1981	92 (of which steel = 16)	79 (of which steel = 11)	30 (of which steel = 9)	19 (of which steel = 4)	14	
1982	200 (of which steel = 81)	104 (of which steel = 25)	86 (of which steel = 56)	30 (of which steel = 13)	13 (of which steel = 1)	
1983	173 (of which steel = 4)	101 (of which steel = 18)[4]	55	18	21 (of which steel = 9)	9
1984	162 (of which steel = 10)	201 (of which steel = 66)[4]	58 (of which steel = 1)	34	21[5]	6
1985	133 (of which steel = 7)	102 (of which steel = 21)[4]	38 (of which steel = 1)	31	7	11
1986	124	98	47	26	10	5

NB   The figures in the first column do not total with those of the next four columns on account of carry-overs from one year to the next and because if the procedure of Article 93(2) EEC or Article 8(3) of Decision No 2320/81/ECSC is initiated the Commission has to take two decisions, firstly to open the procedure and then a final decision terminating it.

[1]   For details, see the Annex to this Report. Actions in steel include both EEC and ECSC steel products, and because of the tranche system the number of actions exceeds the number of notifications.

[2]   In most cases after amendments negotiated during the procedure to remove those aspects which *a priori* made the proposal incompatible with the common market.

[3]   Published in the *Official Journal*.

[4]   Including tranches of aid released under decisions of 29 June 1983.

[5]   Excludes the 'conditional' decision on French investment aids (see Fourteenth Competition Report, point 253).

A full list of the cases determined in 1986, broken down by the type of decision and Member State and providing details of subject matter, is given in the Annex. The absolute figures in the table show that, in comparison to the previous year, there was no significant change in the number of Commission decision on State aids nor in the type of decision taken.

The number of notifications continued the downward trend observable in previous years. While these figures should be interpreted with caution as a decrease in the number of notifications of course does not necessarily mean a decrease in the volume of aid they represent, the fall may, as the Commission surmised in last year's Report, [1] reflect the changing climate of opinion in Member States about the utility of certain types of aid, especially support for industries or firms in chronic decline.

In last year's Report the Commission drew attention to the steps it was taking to obtain notification of State aids as required by Article 93(3) of the EEC Treaty, [2] to give wider information on final decisions, in particular to interested third parties, [2] and to prepare an inventory [3] of aid measures in Member States.

In 1986 the task force set up to draw up the inventory has been preparing standardized data on the aid measures existing in the Community. The data being assembled cover, in particular, the basic objectives of the aid measures, the activities and expenditure eligible for aid, the precise terms of the assistance, regional or sectoral restrictions, and limits on the size of awards or of qualifying enterprises. In addition, details of the financial resources associated with the implementation of the aid instruments are being collected.

---

[1] Fifteenth Competition Report, point 168.
[2] Fifteenth Competition Report, point 171.
[3] Fifteenth Competition Report, point 172.

§ 2 — Sectoral and investment aids

General aid schemes

205.   Most Member States have legislation giving their governments general powers of intervention in industry. Such powers are mainly directed at supporting investment or the restructuring of individual companies or sectors and at rescuing companies in difficulties. When examining proposals for such general aid schemes the Commission may require the prior notification of significant individual awards pursuant to Article 93(3) of the EEC Treaty. Authorization of a scheme does not, moreover, mean that the Commission will exercise a general presumption in favour of individual awards or groups of awards under the scheme.

In 1986 the Commission took four decisions on such general aid schemes, one each in Belgium and Greece and two introduced by states of the Federal Republic of Germany.

Belgium

1984 Economic Recovery Act

206.   In November 1986 the Commission decided not to object to the general aid provisions of this Act, and to open the procedure laid down by Article 93(2) of the EEC Treaty in respect of its aid provisions having a regional application. [1] The provisions not contested by the Commission were a partial relief from corporation tax for six years for companies which before 31 December 1987 reduce their weekly working hours by at least 8 % and correspondingly increase their workforce, and a partial relief from corporation tax for 10 years for 'innovative' companies employing less than 100 people engaged in the exploitation of new high technologies.

The Commission raised no objection to the implementation of these parts of the Act, because they were in line with stated Commission policy to encourage employment by reducing working hours and to promote small and medium-sized enterprises, particularly in high-technology sectors.

---

[1]   See point 272 of this Report.

Federal Republic of Germany

Baden-Württemberg — Aid to firms in difficulties

207.   In December 1986 the Commission opened the Article 93(2) procedure against aid to firms in difficulties under the Baden-Württemberg state economic development programme

The Commission had authorized this programme in 1984 after the German authorities had agreed to prior notification of awards to firms in difficulties employing more than 300, except in the textiles, clothing and footwear industries where a threshold of 50 was to apply. In addition, the Commission codes for aid to certain sectors (steel, textiles and clothing, synthetic fibres and shipbuilding) were to be observed. After differences of opinion had emerged as to the interpretation of this obligation, the Commission recommended the German Government to notify such awards as an 'appropriate measure' under Article 93(1) of the EEC Treaty. The German Government did not agree, stating that it considered notification justified only in cases where the part of the firm's production exported to other Member States was so significant that it threatened to distort competition and trade between Member States.

The EEC Treaty empowers the Commission to keep under constant review all systems of aid existing in the Community. Under the machinery for the control of State aid it is the Commission, and not the State granting aid, that is responsible for determining the compatibility of the aid with the common market. The Commission has examined a number of similar schemes in the past [1] and has come to the conclusion that aid to companies of a certain size that are in danger of going out of business should be strictly monitored. Without prior notification, the Commission would be unable to ascertain in individual cases that such rescues do not adversely affect trading conditions to an extent contrary to the common interest.

Lower Saxony — Loan guarantees

208.   In April 1986 the Commission closed the Article 93(2) procedure against a general loan guarantee scheme in the state of Lower Saxony. Under the scheme, the state may guarantee, for a premium, loans to creditworthy firms

---

[1]   See also point 208 of this Report.

to enable them to carry out measures designed to promote general economic development, and loans to firms in difficulties which serve to bring about a lasting improvement in their financial and economic situation and are accompanied by a comprehensive reorganization plan.

In assessing this scheme the Commission distinguished between the general loan guarantees and those on loans to firms in difficulties. General guarantees may be granted when firms are unable to provide sufficient security to meet bank requirements, a well-known predicament of small and medium-sized companies. Such aid can facilitate the development of certain economic areas and so qualify for exemption under Article 92(3)(c) of the EEC Treaty. The guarantees on loans to firms in difficulties, however, although only provided where the firm has submitted a coherent reorganization plan likely to permanently restore its competitiveness, could by keeping the firms in business prevent the normal operation of the market and threaten the survival of other firms that would otherwise be economically viable. The Commission is therefore of the opinion that aid in such cases must be strictly monitored to ascertain if it qualifies for any of the exemptions in Article 92(3).

The Commission closed the procedure after the Federal Government had agreed to notify in advance significant awards (i.e., guarantees on loans exceeding 0.5 million ECU for firms employing more than 300, or more than 50 in sensitive sectors such as textiles, clothing and fibres) and to observe the special rules for aid to certain industries (shipbuilding, steel and synthetic fibres).

Greece

Act 1386/1983 — Business reconstruction organization

209. In October 1986 the Commission opened the Article 93(2) procedure with respect to Act 1386/1983 which had been put into effect by the Greek Government in 1983 without prior notification to the Commission. The Act gives the Government general powers both for the reconstruction of companies in financial difficulties and for selective assistance. It is not specific as to the possible types of assistance, nor does it lay down budgets, specific types of grants, loans, etc. Under the Act an organization for the financial reconstruction of companies which operates under the name of the Business Reconstruction Organization has been set up. The objects of the BRO are expressed as to contribute to the social and economic development of the country through

financial rejuvenation of businesses pursuant to the provisions of the Act, i.e. rescuing companies that have got into financial difficulties, the importation and application of foreign technology and the development of Greek-based technology, and the establishment and operation of publicly-owned or mixed publicly and privately-owned undertakings. The BRO has a registered capital of DR 5 000 million provided by the State and can draw on funds from the national budget and obtain loans from banks on the strength of its special status. The aid given by the BRO in rescue cases is primarily in the form of conversion of debt (wich in Greece costs the company 20% or more in annual interest) into equity capital carrying no fixed costs. In addition it can provide loans and other forms of finance. The Commission understands that since the beginning of its operations the BRO has intervened in 45 cases of companies in difficulty, notably in the textile and clothing sectors.

Given the nature of the BRO's operations and past Commission decisions in similar cases, and in the light of the Commission's communication to Member States of 17 September 1984 on the application of Articles 92 and 93 of the EEC Treaty to government provisions of capital to companies, Act 1386/1983 clearly falls within Article 92.

Steel

210.   The Commission ensured that the new rules for aid to the steel industry [1] which came into force on 1 January 1986 were strictly applied.

The Commission submitted a report to the Council [2] on the application of the steel aid code in 1984 and 1985. The report contains an updated table of all aid payments to the industry since 1980, which is reproduced below.

211.   In 1986 the Commission also carried out an assessment with the Spanish and Portuguese Governments of the viability prospects of Spanish and Portuguese steel companies, as required by the terms of accession. [3]

---

[1] Fifteenth Competition Report, point 181.
[2] COM(86) 235 final of 6 August 1986.
[3] Protocols Nos 10 and 20 to the Act of Accession.

TABLE 2

Total aid[1] to the Community steel industry cleared for payment since 1.2.1980 shown by objective

million ECU

	Investment	Research and development	Closures	Continued operation	Emergency	Total
Belgium	719	—	118	3 408	12	4 257
Denmark	13	—	—	68	—	81
FR of Germany	1 120	163	619	1 942	—	3 844
Greece	—	—	—	—	—	—
France	3 039	—	302	5 111	689	9 141
Ireland	—	—	—	264	—	264
Italy	1 791	54	1 053	9 171	—	12 068
Luxembourg	440	—	15	176	—	631
Netherlands	234	—	—	222	—	456
United Kingdom	1 788	49	1 036	2 767	—	5 640
Total EEC	9 144	266	3 143	23 129	701	36 381

[1] The aid totals shown in this table include aid in all forms, e.g. grants, interest relief, loans at low interest, guarantees etc.

TABLE 3

Aid disbursed by Member States 1.1.1981-31.12.1985 shown by aid purpose

million ECU

	Investment	Research and development	Closures	Continued operation	Emergency	Total
Belgium	1 030	9	166	2 110	142	3 457
Denmark	13	—	—	68	—	81
FR of Germany	1 090	44	294	1 143	—	2 571
Greece	—	—	—	—	—	—
France	2 174	—	—	6 742	164	9 080
Ireland	—	—	—	264	—	264
Italy	1 814	43	876	7 288	—	10 021
Luxembourg	83	—	7	315	—	405
Netherlands	135	—	—	227	—	362
United Kingdom	496	—	589	4 083	—	5 169
Total EEC	6 835	96	1 932	22 240	306	31 410

Following this assessment, made with the help of outside consultants, the Commission proposed additions to the industries' restructuring plans to ensure that the viability of the companies would be restored by the end of the transitional period provided for in Articles 52 and 212 of the Act of Accession (end of 1988 for Spain and end of 1990 for Portugal).

Coal industry

212. A new set of Community rules on aid to the coal industry replacing those in Commission Decision No 528/76/ECSC was adopted on 30 June 1986 to cover the period from 1 July 1986 to 31 December 1993. [1] Under the new rules, aid provided directly or indirectly by Member States may only be considered as Community aid and therefore compatible with the proper functioning of the common market if it serves at least one of the following objectives:

(i)   improvement of the competitivity of the coal industry;

(ii)   the creation of new, economically viable capacity;

(iii)   the solution of the social and regional problems related to developments in the coal industry.

The new Decision provides that Member States must, in seeking authorization by the Commission under Article 95 of the ECSC Treaty for aid which they intend to grant, give details of the aid proposed, which must be sent at least three months before the measures are to take effect. They were also obliged to provide by October 1986 a statement of intentions and objectives for the industry for the period 1987 to 1993.

Although investment aid may be considered compatible with the common market and thus receive authorization, the new Decision provides that such aid may not exceed 50% of the costs of the investment project and the Commission must have delivered a favourable opinion on the project.

The new Decision also extends to aid to coking coal and coke supplied to the Community iron and steel industry under long-term contract, thus replacing the previous Decision 73/287/ECSC in this area.

---

[1]   Commission Decision No 2064/86/ECSC, OJ L 177, 1.7.1986.

TABLE 4

State aids to the coal industry:

Aid not relating to current production[1]

million ECU

	Social security measures pursuant to Art. 4 of Decision No 528/76			Aids to cover inherited liabilities pursuant to Art. 5 of Decision No 528/76		
	Total		Infringements of Article 4 (1985)	Total		Infringements of Article 5 (1985)
	1984	1985		1984	1985	
FR of Germany	2 953.6	3 058.3	228.3	123.0	70.2	—
Belgium	943.3	958.9	—	—	—	—
France	1 482.6	1 467.5	—	322.4	394.9	—
United Kingdom[1]	102.8	110.8	—	446.3	1 117.6	—
Total for the Community	5 482.3	5 595.5	228.3	891.7	1 582.7	—

[1] The United Kingdom has an integrated social security system. The figure shown in this column covers only the special miner's pension fund, which exists side-by-side with the general social security system.

TABLE 5

State aids to the coal industry:

Aid for current production in 1985[1]

	Unit	FR of Germany	France	Belgium	United Kingdom	Community
A. Aid under Decision 528/76						
1. Infringement of:						
Article 4	Mio ECU	(228.3)	—	—	—	(228.3)
Article 5	Mio ECU	—	—	—	—	—
Total	Mio ECU	(228.3)	—	—	—	(228.3)
per tonne of production	ECU	(2.68)	—	—	—	(1.09)
2. Indirect aid	Mio ECU	15.7	16.9	12.2	—	44.8
per tonne of production	ECU	0.18	1.10	1.85	—	0.21

	Unit	FR of Germany	France	Belgium	United Kingdom	Community
3. Direct aid						
Article 7	Mio ECU	92.1	—	13.2	—	105.3
Article 8	Mio ECU	85.2	—	0.3	35.6	121.1
Article 9	Mio ECU	—	—	—	—	—
Article 10	Mio ECU	60.5	—	—	—	60.5
Article 11	Mio ECU	—	—	—	—	—
Article 12	Mio ECU	—	550.9	107.3	245.8	904.0
Total	Mio ECU	237.8	550.9	120.8	281.4	1 190.9
per tonne of production	ECU	2.79	35.77	18.30	2.75	5.69
B. Coking coal aid (Decision 73/287)	Mio ECU	583.0	—	98.2	—	681.2
per tonne of production	ECU	6.83	—	14.88	—	3.25
C. Total (A + B)	Mio ECU	836.5	567.8	231.2	281.4	1 916.9
per tonne of production	ECU	9.80	36.87	35.03	2.75	9.15
		(1 064.8)[2]	—	—	—	(2 145.2)[3]
		(12.48)[2]	—	—	—	(10.24)[3]

[1] Planned figures.
[2] Including aid in excess of the limits laid down by Article 4 of Decision No 528/76/ECSC. Aids totalling DM 2 100 million (941.7 million ECU) was granted under the Third Electricity-from-coal Law. If this were added, the German aid for current production would total 2 006.5 million ECU or 23.52 ECU/t.
[3] Including aid granted by Germany in excess of the limits laid down by Article 4. If the aid granted under the Third Electricity-from-coal Law were added, the average would be 14.74 ECU/t.

Shipbuilding and ship-repair

National aid schemes

France

213.   The Commission decided in June 1986 to close the Article 93(2) procedure initiated in July 1985 against an aid scheme for the French shipbuilding and ship-repair industry. [1]

During the procedure, the French Government had substantially altered the scheme by reducing the level of production aid to 20 % for large shipyards and to 10 % for smaller and medium-sized yards, as in the previous 1983/84

---

[1]   Fifteenth Competition Report, point 189.

scheme. Individual exceptions were to be subject to prior notification to the Commission. The Commission also noted that the aid would be linked to restructuring measures entailing an accelerated decrease of capacity in ship-building and ship-repair. Under these circumstances, the Commission concluded that the aid measures were compatible with the criteria set out in Articles 5 and 6 of the Fifth Directive.

Italy

214.   In July 1986[1] the Commission opened the Article 93(2) procedure against part of the provisions of Act 111/85 which had introduced an aid scheme for shipbuilding for the period 1984/86. When the Commission approved the aid scheme in 1985,[2] it had reserved its position on Article 10 of the Act. The implementing regulations made under this article allow large shipyards to receive grants of 12.5 % of the value of certain stocks of inputs. The Commission considered that such aid, apparently for current operations, could well slow down the necessary restructuring.

Aid to shipbuilding after 1986

215.   The Fifth Council Directive on aid to shipbuilding expired at the end of 1986.

It had become clear that the ever-deepening structural crisis in the shipbuilding industry could no longer be appropriately met by the aid policy embodied in the Fifth Directive, if the long-term future of the industry and the jobs depending on it were to be secured. While the market outlook made further rationalization indispensable, budgetary constraints were leading most Member States to reappraise their support of the industry. Furthermore, the lack of transparency in the various forms of aid with which shipbuilding was being supported in the various Member States had virtually eliminated intra-Community competition in recent years.

In order to meet the situation the Commission decided on a new selective aid strategy, designed to steer Community shipbuilding towards the market segments where it remains most competitive and where the links with subcontractors and supply industries are closest, so as to spur further restructuring, provide the necessary aid transparency and revive intra-Community competition. This

---

[1]   OJ C 317, 10.12.1986.
[2]   Fourteenth Competition Report, point 223, and Fifteenth Competition Report, point 186.

aid strategy was set out in the Commission's orientation paper on a future aid strategy for shipbuilding sent to the Council in August 1986,[1] and the resulting aid rules were put into legal form in its proposal for a new Sixth Directive on aid to shipbuilding which the Council approved on 22 December 1986.[2]

The main features of the new Directive, which is to apply for four years, are as follows:

(i)   All production aid, including that granted to third parties for construction of ships, is subject to a common aid ceiling, set as a percentage of contract value before aid in the case of contract-related aid and of turnover in merchant shipbuilding in the case of other operating aid.

(ii) The ceiling which initially has been set at 28 % will be subject to annual reviews.

(iii) In addition, aid can be granted for genuine restructuring purposes for both shipbuilding and ship-repair.

(iv) Transitional arrangements are provided for Spain and Portugal under specific conditions.

(v)   Rules on notification, monitoring and reporting will ensure full aid transparency.

The Commission has set out a number of objectives for social, regional and industrial measures which, partly with the assistance of necessary additional budgetary resources to be obtained through the Council, should accompany restructuring effort within the sector.

In the context of the new aid rules the Council, the Parliament and the Commission have all stressed the importance of exerting the Community's full influence to secure from international competitors an equitable contribution to the structural adjustment of the industry necessary to create a worldwide equilibrium between supply and demand.

Textiles and clothing

Belgium

216.   In September 1986 the Commission initiated the Article 93(2) procedure against an aid scheme for the Belgian textiles and clothing industries.[3] Under the scheme, the sums allocated by private firms for the repurchase of their

---

[1]   Bull. EC 7/8-1986, point 2.1.82.
[2]   OJ L 69, 12.3.1987.
[3]   OJ C 312, 6.12.1986; see also point 241 of this Report.

own shares which in previous years had been acquired by public investment corporations would be exempt from Article 117 of the Belgian Income Tax Code and thus from normal corporation tax at the rate of 45 % in 1986 and 43 % thereafter and 37 % throughout the period for small companies. The proposed exemption would apply until the end of 1990 and would be limited in each accounting year to the repurchase of a block of shares not exceeding 20 % of the public holding. It would apply to non-voting shares held by public corporations in textiles and clothing firms totalling some BFR 7 200 million.

The Commission considered that by exempting the repurchase of the non-voting shares from corporation tax, the aid would artificially lower the tax burden on companies in the industries and thus weaken the competitive position of other producers in the EEC. As a large proportion of Belgian production of textiles and clothing is exported to other Member States and demand is only increasing slowly, trading conditions would be seriously affected by the proposed aid.

France

217.   In April 1986,[1] the Commission initiated the Article 93(2) procedure against two new aid schemes financed by levies for the French textiles and clothing industry. The proceeds of the levies, which could amount to FF 300 million in 1986, would be spent by the Comité de développement et de promotion du textile et de l'habillement primarily on subsidizing modernization investments and promoting applied research and exports.

The schemes would succeed earlier programmes which the Commission had declared incompatible with the common market in 1983[2] and 1985.[3] In opening the procedure the Commission considered that there were no substantial differences between the old and the new schemes and that the latter were therefore equally unlikely to meet the criteria for exemption from the general incompatibility of such permanent forms of aid.

Italy

218.   In January 1986 the Commission initiated the Article 93(2) procedure against two awards under Act 675/77 to companies in the publicly-owned textiles and clothing group Eni-Lanerossi.[4] The aid would take the form of a

---

[1]   OJ C 177, 15.7.1986.
[2]   Thirteenth Competition Report, point 254.
[3]   Fifteenth Competition Report, point 193.
[4]   OJ C 132, 30.5.1986.

40 % interest subsidy on 10-year loans covering half of the cost of investments. In one of the two cases the Commission found that the aid would apparently be used for normal modernization investment.

In the other it established that restructuring aid had previously been granted to the same company and that the Italian Government had stated in 1983 that the restructuring was about to be completed. Neither of the two awards would consequently appear eligible for any of the exemptions under Article 92.

Synthetic fibres

219. Having been asked to clarify its position on whether texturizing is covered by the synthetic fibre and yarn aid code, [1] the Commission confirmed in July 1986 by letter to Member States that aid for texturizing is fully subject to the code and must be notified to it in advance in all cases. The Commission took the view that, like the actual production of yarn, texturizing too was faced with problems of overcapacity so that the objective of reducing or at least controlling overcapacity in synthetic fibre and yarn justifies the application of the aid code in this business. In common with aid for actual yarn production, subsidies for texturizing would, in general, merely lead to the artificial preservation of uneconomic capacity.

Federal Republic of Germany

220. In May 1986 the Commission concluded its scrutiny of aids (a grant of DM 6.12 million and a low-interest loan of DM 11 million) provided by the Federal and the Bavarian state Governments to Textilwerke Deggendorf GmbH, a producer of polyamide and polyester yarn based at Deggendorf. Noting that the assistance had been provided illegally in violation of the procedural provisions of Article 93(3) EEC and was incompatible with the common market, [2] the Commission ordered the Federal Government to recover the aid.

The aid breached the synthetic fibre and yarn aid code, as the investment for which it was granted, amounting to DM 61.2 million, was intended for modernization and rationalization of the production facility and not for any

---

[1]   OJ C 171, 10.7.1985 and Fifteenth Competition Report, point 196.
[2]   OJ L 300, 24.10.1986.

of the changes required by the code, and also considerably increased the company's net production capacity in both polyamide and polyester yarn.

On 6 October 1986 the Federal Government informed the Commission that it had commenced proceedings for the recovery of the federal aid and had asked the Bavarian state government to recover its part of the aid.

Italy

221.   In February 1986 the Commission concluded its scrutiny of the Italian Government's proposal to grant financial assistance to Anicfibre SpA, the State-owned producer of man-made fibres and yarn with production facilities at Pisticci, Ottana and Porto Torres, and decided to withdraw its reservations and to close the procedure with it had initiated in 1985,[1] following several modifications to the initial aid proposal.

Under the amended proposal only investment projects relating to conversion to polyester non-woven products, to general services directly linked to this conversion and to R&D activities also outside the traditional synthetic fibre and yarn field are to be aided. The Italian Government completely withdrew its initial proposal to aid investments in this traditional field and will not grant the aid originally proposed for this purpose amounting to LIT 33 020 million in low-interest loans and LIT 13 219 million in direct grants.

The Commission therefore considered that the amended proposal conformed to the Community synthetic fibre and yarn aid code and that the LIT 17 375 million in low-interest loans and LIT 6 939 million in grants for the remaining projects, representing 9.5% net grant equivalent ([2]) of total investment costs of LIT 100 700 million, qualified for exemption under Article 92(3)(c) as compatible with the common market.

---

[1]   OJ C 105, 26.4.1985, and Fifteenth Competition Report, point 199.
[2]   In the accounts of the individual aid cases in this Report an attempt has been made to give the intensity of the aid in terms of net grant equivalent, whenever this could be calculated and was important for the assessment of the aid's compatibility with the common market. The chief merit of the net grant equivalent measure—which gives the net (i.e., after tax, assuming normal tax liability) value of the aid relative to the investment cost or the number of jobs created—is that it permits a comparison of the intensity of aid provided in different forms and subject to different tax treatments in different countries. However, a calculation of net grant equivalent is not always feasible or meaningful, particularly because of the nature of the operations supported (e.g., restructuring) or the type of aid measure (e.g., capital injections). Certainly, net grant equivalent is only a very rough guide to the effect an aid award has on competition.

United Kingdom

222.   In October 1986 the Commission initiated the Article 93(2) procedure against a British proposal to award a grant of UKL 0.5 million to Crimpfil Ltd, a synthetic yarn texturizing firm at Abargoed. [1]

The Commission took the view that the proposed aid for the purpose of paying off part of the company's debts would be against the synthetic fibre and yarn aid code. The aid would not facilitate any restructuring or conversion nor lead to a reduction in capacity. Furthermore, several of the conditions laid down by the Commission for rescue aid were not fulfilled. In a situation where there was considerable trade in textured yarn in the EEC and competition was very keen, the proposed assistance was liable to affect trade and distort or threaten to distort competition and was not considered to serve any of the objectives set out in Article 92(3) EEC Treaty.

Chemical and pharmaceutical industries

Belgium

223.   In July 1986 [2] the Commission opened the Article 93(2) procedure against an aid scheme for Belgian pharmaceutical companies. The aid takes the form of so-called 'planning agreements' under which pharmaceutical companies may increase the prices of medicines (which are reimbursed in part by the social security scheme) in return for an undertaking that they will step up laboratory research, investment and employment in Belgium and make a special effort to promote Belgian products abroad. As the aid measures had not been notified in advance, they were illegal under Community law. The Commission took the view that the measures did not qualify for any of the exemptions under Article 92.

France

224.   In May 1986, [3] the Commission opened the Article 93(2) procedure against aid to the chemical company CDF-Chimie. The Commission considered that subscriptions of FF 6 365 million of new capital by public authorities and public enterprises were likely to contain elements of State aid. As the aid had

---

[1]   OJ C 332, 24.12.1986.
[2]   OJ C 312, 6.12.1986.
[3]   OJ C 311, 5.12.1986.

not been notified in advance, the Commission concluded that it was illegal under Community law. From the information available the Commission also considered the view that the measures would not qualify for any of the exemptions provided for in Article 92 EEC.

Motor, automotive parts and engineering industries

France

225.   In July 1986 the Commission opened the Article 93(2) procedure against FF 3 000 million of new equity capital provided by the French Government in 1986 to the volume car and car parts manufacturer, Renault. [1] In view of the financial difficulties of the group the capital injection could not be considered as a provision of risk capital according with standard investment practice in a market economy and therefore included an element of aid falling within Article 92(1). On the information available the Commission also believed the aid did not qualify for any of the exceptions provided for by Article 92(3).

In March 1986 the Commission also opened the procedure against aid the French Government had provided or intended to provide in support of a FF 340 million restructuring plan by Kleber, mainly in its agricultural tyres business. [2] The aid involved a grant of FF 60 million and a low-interest FDES loan of FF 140 million. From the information available, the aid measures did not seem to be compatible with the common market on the basis of Article 92.

In July 1986 the procedure was also opened against unnotified aid of FF 21 million that the French Government had provided in the form of a capital injection in the company Trailor which produces trailers and semi-trailers. [3] As the French authorities had not notified the aid or provided any information on it, the Commission concluded that it was illegal. The Commission also noted that, given the serious overcapacity problems in the industry, the aid was probably incompatible with the common market and unlikely to qualify for any of the exceptions provided for by Article 92(3).

The Article 93(2) procedure was opened in January 1986 [4] agains a FIM loan of FF 160 million to the Valeo electrical car equipment manufacturer for an

---

[1]   OJ C 269, 25.10.1986. In 1985, the procedure was also opened against both capital and loans from the Industrial Modernization Fund (FIM) to Renault; the procedure is still pending in this case: Fifteenth Competition Report, point 203.
[2]   OJ C 165, 3.7.1986
[3]   OJ C 276, 1.11.1986.
[4]   OJ C 128, 27.5.1986.

investment programme costing FF 227.5 million. The Commission considered that most of the investments involved straightforward modernization. Also, from the information supplied by the French Government it could not identify aspects that might justify an exemption.

In February 1986 [1] the Commission also opened the Article 93(2) procedure against a proposal notified by the French Government to grant assistance for the restructuring by Tenneco of the agricultural machinery business International Harvester-France. The aid consists of a FF 135 million loan at a variable, reduced interest rate and a grant of FF 40 million for investments of FF 1 200 million planned over the period of 1986-89. The information so far supplied by the French Government has not revealed any factors that might allow the Commission to consider any of the exemptions of Article 92 applicable.

In July 1986 the Commission closed the Article 93(2) procedure initiated in 1983 against a French plan for the machine tool industry. [2] It has opened the procedure because it had insufficient information to decide whether any of the exemptions of Article 92 might be applicable.

In deciding to close the procedure, the Commission noted, *inter alia,* that the plan, which had expired on 31 December 1985, had brought about a thorough restructuring of the French industry, leading to a reduction in production of 30%. It concluded that the exception provided for in Article 92(3) (c) could be considered applicable to the aid, which had involved FF 1 000 million of grants and advances and FF 1 600 million of equity loans over the period 1982-85.

Italy

226.   In April 1986 the Commission opened the Article 93(2) procedure against a plan notified by the Italian Government to grant investment aid under Act 675/77 to PAI-DEMM SpA, which mainly produces commercial vehicle components. [3] The aid with a net grant equivalent of 17% consists of a low-interest loan of LIT 2 300 million and interest relief on LIT 7 700 million of bank loans in support of a LIT 20 000 million investment programme. On the information available, the Commission felt that the aid did not conform to the conditions the Italian Government had accepted for application of Act 675/77 and did not qualify for any of the exceptions provided for in Article 92(3).

---

[1]   OJ C 128, 27.5.1986.
[2]   OJ C 107, 21.4.1983.
[3]   OJ C 203, 12.8.1986.

United Kingdom

227.   In December 1986 the Commission opened the Article 93(2) procedure against the UK Government's proposal to provide new equity capital of an unspecified amount to the Rover Group to support the restructuring of its two commercial vehicle subsidiaries, which produce buses, trucks and their parts. [1] The capital injection, which will be used for debt write-offs and restructuring costs for both subsidiaries after privatization, could not be considered as a provision of risk capital according with standard investment practice in a market economy because of the financial difficulties of the group, and the Commission therefore felt that it involved aid falling within Article 92(1). From the limited information available the Commission also thought the aid would be incompatible with the common market and that more detailed information was needed about the forthcoming privatizations and the restructuring of both industries.

Belgium

228.   In October 1986 [2] the Commission decided that an aid scheme for the brewery equipment industry administered by the financing corporation Technibra was incompatible with the common market and must consequently be abolished. It also decided that the rescue aid that had been provided under the scheme in the form of a subscription of BFR 50 million of new capital by Technibra in Meura of Tournai, which is currently in bankruptcy proceedings, must be recovered as far as the proceeds of the liquidation allowed. The Commission had initiated the Article 93(2) procedure in January 1986 [3] as neither the scheme nor its first and only application had been notified in accordance with Article 93(3).

In its final decision the Commission held that the constitution of Technibra contained nothing to suggest that any of the exemptions might be applicable. With regard to the aid to Meura, the Commission noted that on 17 April 1984 it had taken a final negative decision [4] on earlier aid to the same company and considered that the new aid had kept the firm going artificially until its bankruptcy in January 1986 and hence constituted rescue aid. The Belgian Government was required to inform the Commission of the measures taken to comply with the Decision before 4 February 1987.

---

[1]   OJ C 24, 31.1.1987.
[2]   OJ L 20, 22.1.1987.
[3]   OJ C 76, 4.4.1986.
[4]   Fourteenth Competition Report, point 252; see also point 313 of this Report.

Non-ferrous metals

Federal Republic of Germany

229. In January 1986 the Commission opened the Article 93(2) procedure against a grant of DM 2 million provided by the Baden-Württemberg state government to Bug-Alutechnik GmbH, a producer of semi-finished and finished aluminium products.[1] The Commission considered that the aid was granted illegally, as it had not been notified, and appeared from the information available to constitute a rescue aid which was not eligible for any of the exemptions provided for by Article 92(3).

Belgium

230. In February 1986 the Commission closed the procedure initiated in October 1983[2] in respect of aid of BFR 600 million that the Belgian public authorities had planned to provided to Sidal NV, a producer of semi-finished aluminium products. From the information supplied the Commission concluded that the subscription of BFR 250 million of capital in the firm by the Flemish Regional Authorities, instead of the BFR 600 million initially planned, did not contain an aid element because in view of the company's good financial performance since 1982 the subscription could be considered as the provision of risk capital according with standard investment practice in a market economy. This view was confirmed by the fact that the public shareholding had been sold to the private shareholder in 1985 at a significant profit.

Italy

231. In December 1986 the Commission closed the procedure initiated in December 1984[3] and November 1985[4] concerning aid to the Italian State-owned aluminium industry controlled by the State-holding company EFIM. The LIT 1 445 000 million of aid provided since 1983 or still to be provided in the form of capital, grants and low-interest loans was considered eligible for exemption under Article 92(3) (c) because the restructuring of the Italian State-owned aluminium industry contributed to the restructuring of the aluminium

---

[1] OJ C 77, 5.4.1986.
[2] Thirteenth Competition Report, point 265.
[3] Fourteenth Competition Report, point 248.
[4] Fifteenth Competition Report, point 208.

industry in the Community as a whole, without adversely affecting trading conditions to an extent contrary to the common interest. Under the EFIM restructuring plan, capacity would be reduced in the most sensitive sectors (primary and extrusions), where there is proven overcapacity at EEC level, frozen in the less sensitive sectors (rolled semis and foil) which still face a small degree of overcapacity and expanded in the growth sectors (special aluminium and newly developed finished products), all of which can be considered favourable to the development of the aluminium industry in the Community.

United Kingdom

232.   The Commission decided in November 1986 not to object to aid in the form of loans and loan guarantees of up to UKL 25 million notified by the UK Government for Carnon Consolidated Ltd, which operates the two remaining tin mines in Cornwall. The aid is to assist the modernization of the two mines and the mineral processing plant, at a cost of UKL 31 million. The Commission concluded that the aid was eligible for exemption under Article 92(3) (c), taking into account the restructuring already carried out in the UK tin mining industry, the Community interest in maintaining the last large tin mines in the Community, and the possibility of higher tin prices within five years when the company should start to repay the aid.

France

233.   The Commission decided in November 1986 to close the Article 93(2) procedure against aid in the form of a FF 35 million grant and FF 50 million in equity loans, with a net grant equivalent of 14%, to Compagnie Royale Asturienne des Mines and its subsidiary Asturienne-France, a zinc foundry. The Commission had initiated the procedure[1] because no information had been made available that might justify the aid. During the procedure the French Government provided details of a restructuring of the companies entailing reductions and transfers of production capacity which enabled the Commission to consider the exemption provided for in Article 92(3) (c) as applicable.

In July 1986, the Commission opened the Article 93(2) procedure against awards under the Electronics Industry Scheme,[2] involving several aid measures of

---

[1]   Thirteenth Competition Report, point 264.
[2]   See also point 234 of this Report.

unspecified nature and intensity for FF 206 million of investment in Eurocel, a company manufacturing copper foil for printed circuit boards. [1]

Information technologies, consumer electronics and household appliances

France

234.   In February 1986[2] the Commission opened the Article 93(2) procedure against a proposed FIM loan of FF 250 million with a net grant equivalent of 5.2%, which the French Government had notified for the telecommunications equipment manufacturer Thomson Telecommunications. The Commission considered that most of the planned investments involved straightfoward modernization, and from the information supplied by the French Government the project did not appear to have any features that might justify aid.

In November 1986, the Commission closed the procedure against the French scheme to assist the microelectronic industry[3] and decided to raise no objection to its successor, the Electronics Industry Scheme. After having been informed of the Electronics Industry Scheme, the Commission had linked the further investigation of the microelectronics scheme to its examination of the whole sector.

The Electronics Industry Scheme comprises measures to develop the electronic components, consumer electronics, data processing, software and services sectors, the aerospace industry and specific applications, and aims to improve the use of electronic products and services by industry. The measures consist mainly of research contracts totalling FF 4 550 million in 1985 and grants and repayable loans totalling FF 540 million. The scheme also supports training, notably for engineers and senior technicians, from an annual budget of FF 120 million.

In view of the Community interest in having a viable high-technology industry, and taking into account the market situation in electronics, the Commission decided that the exemption provided for in Article 92(3) (c) was applicable to the scheme.

In December 1986 the Commission closed the procedure initiated in December 1985[4] with respect to the granting of an FIM loan of FF 200 million, with a

---

[1]   OJ C 293, 19.11.1986.
[2]   OJ C 159, 26.6.1986.
[3]   Thirteenth Competition Report, point 260.
[4]   Fifteenth Competition Report, point 205.

net grant equivalent of 9%, by the French Government to Bull, the computer and auxiliary equipment manufacturer. The Commission considered that the aid was intended to develop genuinely innovative electronic products and that the exemption provided for in Article 92(3) (c) was therefore applicable to this aid.

For similar reasons, also in December 1986, the Commission decided to close the procedure initiated in December 1985 with respect to a FIM loan of FF 150 million, with a net grant equivalent of 8.3%, granted by the French Government to the semiconductor electronic components manufacturer Matra-Harris.

In July 1986 the Commission opened the Article 93(2) procedure against various aid the French Government wanted to provide for restructuring at the household appliance manufacturer Electrolux-Arthur Martin. [1] The aid consists of grants of FF 53 million, a FIM loan of FF 145 million and a freeze on local business tax. On the basis of the limited information available at that stage the Commission concluded that, considering the present overcapacity problems in the industry at a Community level, the aid was not compatible with the common market.

In November 1986 the Commission closed the procedure initiated in December 1985 in respect of an FIM loan of FF 86 million that the French Government had provided to La Radiotechnique, a company mainly producing television sets. [2] The French authorities had explained that the loan, with a net grant equivalent of 5%, was for development of genuinely innovative products, such as flat screen TV tubes, which would replace Japanese imports into the Community. The new investments would also not increase capacity. The Commission concluded that the aid qualified for exemption under Article 92(3) (c).

Italy

235.   In March 1986 the Commission closed the procedure opened in September 1985 [3] against aid that the Friuli Venezia-Giulia region proposed to provide for the restructuring of the Zanussi household appliances business. The Commission concluded that the LIT 75 000 million aid package consisting of a subscription of share capital, a shareholder's loan and an investment loan contained certain aid elements, but that these could be considered eligible for the exemption of Article 92(3) (c), because of the significant reduction in

[1]   OJ C 310, 4.12.1986.
[2]   Fifteenth Competition Report, point 207.
[3]   Fifteenth Competition Report, points 206 and 237.

production capacity for white goods effected by the restructuring plan at a time when there was overcapacity in the Community.

Film industry

France/Italy

236.   In January 1986 the Commission opened the Article 93(2) procedure against aid schemes for the film industry in France and in Italy. [1] The schemes provide for tax relief of up to 25 % for individuals and up to 50 % for companies in France and up to 70 % for companies in Italy, if the money is invested in the production of films and other audio-visual works.

The Commission considered that the two schemes, neither of which has been notified in advance under Article 93(3), contained conditions which excluded nationals of other Member States from participating in the aided audio-visual works. The conditions would therefore infringe Articles 48, 52 and 59 of the Treaty on free movement of workers, freedom of establishment and the freedom to provide services within the Community.

Federal Republic of Germany

237.   The Commission decided in December 1986 to close the Article 93(2) procedure against an aid scheme for the German film industry. The Commission had opened the procedure in November 1985, as the notified draft scheme contained nationality restrictions which would have been incompatible with Articles 48, 52 and 59 of the Treaty.

During the procedure the German Government substantially altered the draft, thereby immediately eliminating all but one of the restrictions and setting a timetable for the abolition of the remaining infringing clause. In view of these changes, the Commission considered that the scheme would be compatible with the common market.

---

[1]   French Act No 85 of 11.7.1985 and Italian Act No 163 of 30.4.1985.

Glass, ceramics, wood, paper and construction materials

Flat glass

Belgium

238.   In July 1986 the Commission decided that a proposal to grant aid for investments costing BFR 2 044 million by the flat glass producer Glaceries Saint Roch at Auvelais could not be implemented. [1] The aid, under the 1959 Economic Expansion Act, was for the renovation of two float glass lines leading to reductions in energy consumption.

The Commission had initiated the Article 93(2) procedure in September 1984 [2] on the grounds that the renovation of a float line was in principle a normal replacement and modernization investment not eligible for exemption from the State aid rules. During the procedure the Belgian Government had amended its original notification by limiting the aid to an interest subsidy of 4% for five years on BFR 625 million, which represented the extra cost of the technological innovation incorporated in the investment, and a corresponding exemption from land tax, giving a net grant equivalent of 2.5% of the total investment.

The Commission however considered that the company itself would be the first to gain from any reduction in energy consumption and hence production costs. Investment for this purpose would therefore be undertaken normally at the time of the periodic renovation of float lines without the need for incentives in the form of State aid. Consequently, even the amended proposal did not satisfy the conditions necessary for the application of one of the exceptions of Article 92(3).

In December 1986 the Commission also decided that a proposal to grant aid for investment effected by the flat glass producer Glaverbel at Moustier could not be implemented. [3] The aid, likewise under the 1959 Economic Expansion Act, was to be granted in the form of an interest subsidy or capital grant of 4% for six years on two-thirds of the investment and an exemption from land tax, giving a net grant equivalent of 5.8% of the BFR 1 200 million investment.

The Commission had initiated the procedure against this proposal in January 1986 [4] on the grounds that the investment in question, involving renovation

[1]   OJ L 342, 5.12.1986.
[2]   Fourteenth Competition Report, point 249.
[3]   OJ L 77, 19.3.1987.
[4]   OJ C 17, 25.1.1986.

and modernization of two float lines, would not be eligible for an exemption. During the procedure the Belgian Government emphasized that the investment would make it possible to produce coloured and coated flat glass directly on the float line.

The Commission based its final decision on the fact that the renovation of a float is in principle a normal replacement and modernization investment and that the part of the aid relating to the production of coated flat glass would affect trading conditions to an extent contrary to the common interest, given the clear overcapacity situation in the Community for toughened and coated glass.

Glass containers

France

239. In November 1986 the Commission closed the Article 93(2) procedure against a grant of FF 30 million to the bottle manufacturer Verrerie Ouvrière D'Albi. The Commission had opened the procedure in February 1986[1] because of the failure of the French Government to notify the aid. During the procedure the French Government stated that the company was reducing its workforce by 35%, decreasing its production, mainly of standard wine bottles, by 20%, and improving its quality control and its organization with the object of regaining competitivity. The Government also emphasized that the company is situated in a redevelopment area, that it would receive no other form of aid for its restructuring and that its exports account for only 5% of its production. Under these circumstances the Commission considered the exception provided for in Article 92(3) (c) applicable.

Bottled mineral waters

240. In December 1985 the Commission opened the Article 93(2) procedure against a FF 70 million loan from the Industrial Modernization Fund (FIM) to a company in the mineral water sector (Société générale des grandes sources d'eau minérale française) to part-finance investment costing FF 266 million. The investment was to automate the company's production and increase its production capacity for glass bottles.

---

[1] OJ C 135, 3.6.1986.

In November 1986 the Commission took a final negative decision in the case, principally on the grounds that the investment involved straightforward modernization, that contrary to the claims that had been made it did not contain a major element of innovation and that there was no necessity for the aid as the company had ample own resources, was profitable and the investment was in its own commercial interests. The Commission also considered that the aid would affect trade and competition to an extent contrary to the common interest in an industry in which there was substantial trade between Member States and that the aid did not serve any of the Community objectives set out in Article 92(3) of the EEC Treaty. In its letter to the French Government of 28 November 1986, the Commission recalled that in 1982 it had taken three negative decisions against proposals by the Belgian Government to grant aid to companies in the same sector.

Belgium

241. In September 1986 the Commission initiated the Article 93(2) procedure against an aid scheme for the Belgian glass container industry. [1] Under the scheme, the sums allocated by private firms for the repurchase of their own shares which in previous years had been acquired by public investment corporations would be exempt from normal corporation tax at the rate of 45% in 1986 and 43% thereafter and 37% throughout the period for small companies. The proposed exemption would apply until the end of 1990 and would be limited in each accounting year to the repurchase of a block of shares not exceeding 20% of the public holding.

The Commission considered that by exempting the repurchase of the non-voting shares from corporation tax the aid would artificially lower the tax burden on companies in the industry. As a large proportion of the output of Belgian glass container manufacturers is exported to other Member States and demand is falling, trading conditions would be seriously affected by the proposed aid.

Ceramics

Belgium

242. In June 1986 the Commission decided that a proposal to grant aid in the form of a subscription of BFR 295 million of new capital in Boch SA, a manufacturer of crockery and ceramic sanitaryware situated at La Louvière

---

[1] OJ C 312, 6.12.1986; see also point 216 of this Report.

and currently in liquidation, was incompatible with the common market and that an advance of BFR 104 million unlawfully paid in 1984 must be recovered as far as the proceeds of the liquidation allowed. [1]

The Commission had initiated the Article 93(2) procedure in August 1984 [2] on the grounds that the financial support was aid falling within Article 92(1) and did not appear to satisfy the conditions necessary for application of any of the exemptions provided for in Article 92. During the procedure the Belgian Government announced that the regional authorities had decided to wind up the firm and that as a result the BFR 295 million capital increase had not taken place.

The Commission, however, discovered that an advance of BFR 104 million had in fact been paid to the firm in 1984. The Commission considered that this advance payment amounted to a rescue and that the firm had been kept in business artificially for a number of years before that by repeated injections of aid. [3] Such aid does not qualify for application of any of the exemptions provided for in Article 92(3).

Subsequently the Belgian Government informed the Commission of its intention to comply with the decision by calling upon the liquidators of the company to refund the aid.

Wood and paper

France

243. In February 1986 the Commission closed the Article 93(2) procedure against financial assistance to Chapelle Darblay, the biggest French manufacturer of newsprint and light-weight coated paper, based at Rouen.

The Commission had initiated the procedure [4] against FF 2 300 million in grants and interest-free loans, which had not been notified.

During the procedure the French Government altered its proposal, substantially reducing the amount and the intensity of the aid to a net grant equivalent to 20%. In its decision to close the procedure the Commission also took into account the significant capacity reduction taking place and the fact that around

---

[1]   OJ L 223, 9.8.1986.
[2]   Fourteenth Competition Report, point 250.
[3]   Fifteenth Competition Report, point 211.
[4]   Fourteenth Competition Report, point 251.

FF 700 million worth of the FF 3 200 million of investment were directly in the Community interest. In these circumstances the Commission felt that the exemption provided for in Article 92(3) (c) could be considered applicable to the revised aid proposal.

In April 1986 the Commission also closed the Article 93(2) procedure against grants totalling FF 31 million, with a net grant equivalent of 19%, awarded to the pulp manufacturer Cellulose de Strasbourg. The plant had been shut down following the bankruptcy of its parent company and had only been able to restart production as an independent company in March 1983 with the help of the aid.

The Commission had initiated the procedure in May 1983,[1] following the failure of the French Government to notify the aid. In deciding to close the procedure the Commission considered that the restructuring taking place and the limited trade in Community-produced pulp warranted an exemption under Article 92(3) (c).

In November 1986, the Commission opened the Article 93(2) procedure against a package of grants, equity loans and tax breaks to the wood-processing firm Isoroy.[2] The Commission took its decision following the failure of the French Government to notify additional grants totalling FF 200 million and FF 50 million in equity loans. The company had already received FF 80 million in grants and FF 180 million in equity loans and had enjoyed tax breaks worth FF 150 million since 1983, none of which had been notified to the Commission. The Commission also noted that Isoroy exports 20% of its production to other Member States.

Netherlands

244. In December 1986 the Commission opened the Article 93(2) procedure against investment aid to the solid board industry.[3] The Commission noted that this sector exports half its output and that the proposed aid in the form of grants totalling HFL 7.4 million would be provided for investment totalling HFL 23.3 million which would increase production and capacity. It therefore considered that the aid was likely to distort competition and affect trade between Member States, and none of the exceptions provided for in Article 92 appeared applicable.

---

[1] OJ C 153, 11.6.1986.
[2] OJ C 9, 14.1.1987.
[3] OJ C 78, 25.3.1987.

Construction materials

France

245.   In July 1986 the Commission opened the Article 93(2) against FF 46.8 million in grants and FF 14.5 million of equity loans reportedly provided or planned to the plaster-board manufacturer Escogypse based at Anzin.[1] The Commission took its decision in view of the failure of the French Government to reply to its request for information.

In November 1986 the Commission also opened the Article 93(2) procedure against a new aid scheme financed by levies for the French construction materials industry.[2] The proceeds of the levies, which could amount to FF 60 million in 1986, would be made available to technical centres serving the industry. In opening the procedure, the Commission noted that products imported from other Member States were not explicitly excluded from the levy, that the use of the levy was likely to involve aid falling under Article 92(1) EEC but the purposes to which it would be put were unclear, and that the scheme had not been notified in advance.

Furniture, leather and rubber

France

246.   The Commission decided in July 1986 to open the Article 93(2) procedure against a new aid scheme financed by levies for the French furniture industry.[3] The proceeds of the levies, which could amount to FF 80 million in 1986, would be made available to the French Furniture Industry Development Committee and the Technical Centre for Wood. In opening the procedure, the Commission noted that the use of the levy was likely to involve aid falling under Article 92(1) EEC, but the objectives of the five-year scheme were unclear, that it did not continue the degressivity of a previous scheme in the industry and that products imported from other Member States were not excluded from the levy. Furthermore, the scheme had not been notified in advance.

---

[1]   OJ C 261, 18.10.1986.
[2]   OJ C 13, 17.1.1987.
[3]   OJ C 272, 28.10.1986.

In July 1986 the Commission also opened the Article 93(2) procedure against a new aid scheme financed by levies for the French leather and footwear industry. [1] The proceeds of the levies, which could amount to FF 80 million in 1986, would be made available to a technical centre for the industry and to the Leather and Footwear Industry Development Committee (Cidic). In opening the procedure, the Commission noted that the new scheme was likely to involve aid falling under Article 92(1) EEC, but that the Commission could not measure the effect of the aid on competition as the French Government had neglected to submit yearly reports on the results obtained under the former scheme. Furthermore, the new scheme had not been notified in advance.

In December 1986 the Commission closed the procedure initiated in December 1985 [2] against a FIM loan of FF 65 million to the rubber goods manufacturer Hutchinson. The Commission considered that the aid, with a net grant equivalent of 4.4%, was intended to promote genuinely innovative products as part of a large restructuring programme. The Commission therefore decided that the exemption provided for in Article 92(3) (c) was applicable.

---

[1] OJ C 261, 18.10.1986.
[2] Fifteenth Competition report, point 217.

§ 3 — Horizontal aids

Aids for research and development

Application of the Community framework on state aids for research and development

247.   In 1985, the Commission adopted a Community framework setting out its policy on State aid for research and development. [1] In its Resolution on the Fifteenth Competition Report the European Parliament placed the effects of R&D aid among the most significant distortions of competition. [2] 1986 saw the first steps to implement and follow up the framework.

When preparing its framework the Commission had noted that aid for R&D had become one of the largest, and in many Member States *the* largest, form of government support for industry. Moreover, experience had shown that in many cases Member States questioned the necessity of notifying such aid. After completion of the framework the Commission therefore undertook a detailed review of known R&D aid schemes operating in Member States and in November 1986 wrote to all Member States requesting them to notify formally both a list of aid schemes operating within their boundaries and significant individual awards under such schemes, 'significant awards' being defined as multinational R&D projects where the total project cost exceeds 20 million ECU, even if the part of the project that is executed in a single Member State falls below that threshold.

In examining the R&D schemes and projects notified to it, the Commission will exercise a general presumption in favour of such aid because of the contribution that R&D aid can make towards achieving Community goals as set out in Article 2 of the EEC Treaty, because of the risks attached to R&D and the long pay-back periods which may be involved so that the activity would often not take place without aid, and finally because of the fact that aid for R&D by its nature may be less prone to distort trade between Member States than aid for investment which has a direct impact on production capacity and output. Furthermore, the Commission is aware that R&D is necessary to

---

[1]   OJ C 83, 11.4.1986; Fifteenth Competition Report, point 218.
[2]   Resolution on the Fifteenth Report on Competition Policy, adopted on 14 November 1986, point 4(V) of the general conclusions.

provide a constant stream of new products so as to sustain the growth, prosperity and worldwide competitiveness of Community industry and that State aids may have a role to play in this process. On the other hand, the Commission is also deeply conscious of the fact that aid for R&D may be used as a cover for granting aid for activities which should normally be carried out by the beneficiary enterprises with their own resources, and that such aid, if not analysed and monitored on the basis of recognized principles, could become the equivalent of simple aids for modernization or even operating aid.

Belgium

248.   In May 1986[1] the Commission opened the Article 93(2) procedure against research grants totalling BFR 310 million awarded by the Belgian Government to five pharmaceutical companies: Janssen, Smith-Kline-RIT, UCB, Omnichem and Labaz-Sanofi. The grants would cover 50% of the costs of research personnel. As the aid had not been notified in advance, it was illegal under Community law. From the information available the Commission also believed that the aid was not eligible for any of the exemptions under Article 92 EEC.

In September 1986 the Commission decided not to object to aid which the Belgian Government had granted for a data-processing development project by the Swift organization concerning the second generation of a telecommunications system through which firms exchange private and confidential messages, notably international payments, previously sent by post. The aid worth BFR 204.16 million consists of a low-interest loan for an investment costing BFR 1 914 million (net grant equivalent = 5.24%). The firm is the sole supplier of this information technology service and there is no other public or private body within the EEC currently providing such a service or even in a position to do so.

Italy

Awards under Act 46/82 to promote innovation

249.   In April 1985 the Commission had opened the Article 93(2) procedure against two proposed awards to the chemical company Enichemica.[2] The first concerned a programme of research, development and experimentation for new

---

[1]   OJ C 181, 19.7.1986.
[2]   Fifteenth Competition Report, Annex 'Aid cases in which the Commission decided to open the Article 93(2) EEC procedure'.

proceesses and products in the field of industrial auxiliaries, intermediates and pesticides. The total programme costs amounted to LIT 30 400 million. The aid was to take the form of a low-interest loan of LIT 13 000 million representing 42.6 % of the programme cost and a net grant equivalent of approximately 11 %. The research programme involved new industrial auxiliaries, new processes for industrial intermediates and new technologies for producing pesticides. The Italian Government, in putting forward the programme, argued that it would help to widen the Community's technological base, that the products in question were now imported from outside the Community, that the programme was outside the company's normal sphere of activity as it carried particularly high technical and commercial risks and that there was little or no intra-Community trade in the field.

The Commission however concluded that the degree of technical innovation involved was not sufficiently high to justify aid on these grounds, that the company was in intense competition with other chemical companies in the Community, as it exported up to 40 % of its output of various product categories to other Member States, that the R&D programme was in its normal commercial interests and that consequently the proposal did not qualify for any of the exemptions provided for in Article 92(3), in particular Article 92(3)(c). The Commission took a decision in April 1986 prohibiting the Italian Government from granting the aid.

The second project involved a six-year research programme in the field of polycarbonates, modified polyphenylene oxides, pre-impregnated composite materials and polymer blends which would be capable of replacing traditional engineering materials in applications requiring high standards of performance and stability in the aerospace, motor, electrical, telecommunications and other industries. The research programme was intended to develop the basic and applied technology necessary to produce new tailor-made materials. The total programme cost amounted to LIT 39 000 million. The aid consisted of a low-interest loan of LIT 21 700 million covering 55.7 % of the programme cost and having an aid intensity of approximately 14 % net grant equivalent.

After intensive investigation the Commission concluded that the programme covered entirely new product areas, was not linked to any existing production plant and was in a field in which there was no production within the Community, all such materials being in fact imported from outside the Community, and in which there was little evidence of trade and competition within the Community. The Commission concluded that the project could qualify for exemption under Article 92(3)(c).

In February 1986 the Italian Government notified a proposed aid award for an R&D and innovation programme being undertaken by the lorry manufacturer Iveco Fiat SpA. It should be noted that there is a situation of overcapacity in this sector and that Iveco is the second largest producer in Europe. The programme concerned various activities of product and process innovation and the development of a standard product range. The aid was to be given in the form of a grant of LIT 41 2000 million and a soft loan of LIT 96 200 million towards total project costs of LIT 350 000 million. It represented a net grant equivalent of 12%.

The case raised issues of aid for innovation, on the one hand, and of safeguarding competition, on the other. The Commission did not adopt a definitive position in this case within the time limit of 30 working days which it has set for its initial scrutiny of aid proposals.

Netherlands

250. The Dutch Government notified seven cases of aid for R&D by companies in the chemical (Dow: HFL 12 million; AKZO: HFL 30 million; DSM: HFL 18.4 million), biotechnology (Unilever: HFL 3.275 million), medical engineering (Medtronic: HFL 15 million) and electronics sectors (Philips: HFL 50 million; ASM: HFL 38.6 million). The aid intensity after tax varied but never exceeded 26%. The cases were analysed against the R&D framework. It was found that the projects represented additional research activities and in some cases the aid was necessary for the project to be undertaken. The real research activities were situated far from the market place and were risky for the companies concerned given the basic nature of the project and the amount of money involved. Moreover, in several cases the projects were complementary to research actions directly supported by the Commission. Under these circumstances the Commission decided not to object to the aid.

The Dutch Government also notified aid for research into wind turbines and for the installation of such. The aid intensity after tax was 40% for the research part and a maximum of 17% for the installation. (The installation grants were to decrease over time and to be abolished by 1991). A budget of HFL 37 million was allocated for the research and HFL 68.5 million for the installation part of the scheme.

The research part of the scheme was found to comply with the framework criteria except that the aid intensity was higher than the normal limit. However, in October 1986 the Commission decided not to object because of the following specific considerations in the case: wind energy as an alternative renewable and environmentally accptable energy source was very attractive and actions to promote its use were encouraged by the Commission; the research risks were high and the beneficiary firms small compared to other firms in the energy sector.

The installation part was also accepted as intra-Community trade, was unlikely to be significantly affected because the subsidy was also available for the installation of wind turbines produced in other Member States, the installation of wind turbines was desirable from the point of view of diversification of energy sources and involved economic risks, and because the aid intensity quickly decreased over time.

Netherlands/Federal Republic of Germany

251.   In May 1986, the Commission decided not to object to aid of HFL 190 million and DM 320 million which the Dutch and German Governments proposed to grant to Philips and Siemens respectively for a collaborative R&D project costing them HFL 475 million and DM 800 million on the development of electronic memories. This bilateral project was set up to develop submicron C-MOS technology and the technology for producing the tools for designing integrated circuits incorporating memories of a complexity equal to or greater than one megabit. The project is considered of great importance for the future development of the electronics industry, notably in the computer and telecommunication fields. The Commission considered that the exemption provided for in Article 92(3)(c) was applicable to the aid.

United Kingdom

Aid for R&D activities by small and medium-sized firms

252.   In May 1986 the British Government informed the Commission of its intention to introduce the Smart programme (Smart = Small firms merit award for research and technology). The Smart programme is a pilot scheme aimed at encouraging innovative and original R&D projects by firms starting up in business or existing firms of up to 200 employees. The programme is divided into two stages. During stage I, aimed at carrying out necessary feasibility studies, beneficiaries may obtain a public grant of up to UKL 37 500. Support may continue if the final report on stage I indicates favourable technical and commercial prospects. At both stages awards will be allocated on a competitive

basis. Stage II aid is limited to UKL 100 000. The aid intensities will be 50 % of the project costs during the first year of stage II and 25 % during the remaining two years. The total budget provisions for the Smart programme will amount to UKL 1 300 000.

The programme was scrutinized by the Commission, which concluded that the scheme qualified for exemption under Article 92(3)(c). Therefore the Commission decided in July to raise no objection to the scheme.

Aid to stimulate employment

253.   The Commission's general policy on aid to stimulate employment has been described in previous reports. [1] The general lines of this policy are that such aid which simply has the effect of reducing labour costs without meeting special needs or furthering Community policies is to be regarded as operating aid and is in principle incompatible with the common market. On the other hand, where it can be shown that temporary employment aid leads to the creation of new and additional jobs and/or is intimately bound up with restructuring, and especially if the new jobs are to be filled by particularly disadvantaged groups, for example the young or long-term unemployed, who have special training needs, the Commission may decide to allow such measures.

Italy

254.   In February 1986 the Italian Government notified an aid scheme under Act No 49 of 27 February 1985 to support cooperatives. Act 49 set up two funds, 'Foncooper', a permanent revolving fund for promoting and extending the cooperative movement, and a four-year 'Special Fund' to assist cooperatives set up to preserve endangered jobs. Foncooper provides low-interest loans to non-profit-making cooperatives for projects aiming to increase labour productivity or employment by expanding and modernizing the enterprise's production facilities or to restructure the facilities or switch to a different product. A budget of LIT 184 000 million has been provided. For the first type of project assistance is available only to cooperatives with an invested capital of less than LIT 500 million and the maximum loan is LIT 200 million. For the second category, all other cooperatives are eligible and loans of up to LIT 2 000 million are possible. The Special Fund is intended to assist the formation of cooperatives

---

[1]   Seventh Competition Report, point 223 et seq.

by workers who are on short-time working or laid off and in receipt of income supplements from the 'Cassa Integrazione', or who are employed by firms that have filed for bankruptcy, or who have been made redundant by firms that have ceased trading or reduced their workforce. Grants from the Fund are available to cooperatives which acquire, lease or take over the management of such businesses or parts of them or start up an alternative enterprise and thereby preserve jobs. In practice the total grant payable to an individual cooperative should not exceed LIT 1 200 million. Grants will normally only be awarded to cooperatives with a maximum of 100 members. Proposed exceptional awards to cooperatives with over 100 members will be individually notified under Article 93(3). Such projects must have special features in terms of employment or technology making them particularly worthy of support. Under both funds, awards will mainly and as a matter of priority go to industrial sectors. Many industries are excluded from the scheme.

In view of the acute problems of unemployment which the cooperatives are designed to counter, the limited effects on intra-Community trade because of the lack of trading infrastructure that obliges them to operate almost exclusively in the local market, and, finally, the exclusion of sensitive industries, the Commission decided in December not to oppose the implementation of the scheme.

Netherlands

Aid for re-employment of long-term unemployed

255.   In September 1986 the Dutch Government notified an aid scheme for the employment of the long-term unemployed, defined as those who had been out of work for three years or more. Employers taking on such people in jobs additional to their existing workforce before 31 December 1987 will be eligible for a reduction in their social security charges equal to 15% of the new employees' salaries for four years. The scheme also offers a one-off grant of HFL 4 000 to employers or associations of employers who establish retraining programmes for the long-term unemployed.

The Commission, in examining this proposal, was concerned that the period over which the subsidy was to be paid was exceptionally long and that the total subsidy was relatively high. However, in view of the mounting problem of long-term unemployment in the Community, the Commission's declared policy in this field, and the strict conditions laid down for the Dutch scheme, in particular the link to new job creation, and the effect of the incentive in keeping the long-term unemployed in their new jobs, it decided in December not to raise any objection to the scheme.

United Kingdom

New Workers' Scheme

256.   In 1982 the Commission raised no objection to the implementation of an aid scheme called the Young Workers' Scheme designed to encourage the employment of young people by reducing their employment costs through a direct payment to employers. This scheme has been extended annually since that time. [1] In July 1986 the British Government notified a minor modification of this scheme, which has been renamed the New Workers' Scheme. In view of the scale of youth unemployment (in the UK young people in the 16-to-25 age group account for over 35 % of the unemployment total of over 3 million) and the conditions and objectives of the scheme, the Commission decided in September to raise no objection to the implementation of the amended scheme.

Aid for exports within the Community

General

257.   The Commission, supported by judgments of the European Court of Justice has always held and applied a policy that aids for exports within the Community are basically incompatible with the internal market and do not qualify for any of the exceptions provided for in Article 92(3). The steps taken to enforce this policy have been reported in many past competition reports. 1986 saw no change in this approach. In the early months of 1986 the Commission became aware of allegations that some Member States might be circumventing their Community obligations under this policy by establishing dummy companies in third countries to which the restrictions on subsidized export credits do not apply, and using these to re-export into the Community. It was alleged that in practice these dummy companies only handled the paperwork and that in fact the goods in question went directly from one Member State to another. In April 1986 therefore the Commission wrote to all Member States requesting them to confirm that where they granted subsidized

---

[1]   Fifteenth Competition Report, point 226.

export credits their systems were so structured that they could give an assurance that the goods benefiting from such subsidized credits did not re-enter the Community. Member States were asked to provide both assurances and, where necessary, documentation to show how their systems worked. The Commission received the requested assurances and therefore took no further action.

Greece

258. The Commission reported in 1985 on the steps it had taken to secure the abolition of the system of Greek export aids paid under Currency Committee Decision 1574/70 and its subsequent amendments. [1] It also reported that in view of the serious general economic situation in Greece it had taken Decision No 85/594/EEC under Article 108(3) EEC Treaty allowing Greece to take certain safeguard measures including the continuation in total of the system of export aids until 31 December 1986. The Greek economic situation has been kept under continuous review, and while it has improved steadily the improvement has not been considered sufficient to allow the full abolition of the export aids. The Commission has therefore taken a new Decision under which the Greek Government has to reduce the export subsidy to 60% of its original value by the introduction of VAT and then abolish the remaining subsidy in four equal steps on 1 January 1987, 1988, 1989 and 1990. [2] The Commission, well aware of the high number of complaints received, has specified that it could vary or withdraw its decision in the light of changes in the initial situation or in the effects of the decision itself.

Aid for environmental protection

Community framework on State aids for environmental protection measures

259. Up to now the Commission's scrutiny of aid proposals for environmental protection measures has been based on the criteria laid down in the 'Community approach to State aids in environmental matters'. This framework was first adopted in 1974. [3] In 1980 it was decided to extend it with slightly modified criteria for a further six years. [4]

---

[1] Fifteenth Competition Report, points 227 and 228.
[2] OJ L 357, 18.12.186.
[3] Fourth Competition Report, points 175-183.
[4] Tenth Competition Report, points 222-226.

Under these criteria environmental aid schemes qualify for exemption under Article 92(3)(b) if the following conditions are fulfilled:

(i) The aid is intended to facilitate the implementation of new environmental standards.

(ii) It does not exceed 15% net grant equivalent of the value of the aided investment.

(iii) Only firms having installations in operation for at least two years before entry into force of the standards in question may quality for aid.

(iv) The eligible firm must bear the entire cost of normal replacement investments and operating costs.

Aid proposals not meeting these criteria may be authorized under the other exemptions provided for in Article 92(3)(a) and (c). These exemptions are restricted to special circumstances (e.g. to support R&D in this field). The approach represents a compromise aimed at reconciling the generally recognized need for acceleration of urgent pollution-control investment with the requirements of undistorted competition in a unified market. In 1974 it was considered as a transitional measure mainly aimed at catching up on the substantial backlog of investments necessary in this field. At the time it was expected the backlog could be eliminated within a certain limited period.

However, developments in the years since 1974 have changed the context of environmental policy. This process has culminated in the environmental provisions of the Single European Act, which states that: 'Action by the Community relating to the environment shall be based on the principles that preventive action should be taken, that environmental damage should as a priority be rectified at source, and that the polluter should pay. Environmental protection requirements shall be a component of the Community's other policies' (Article 130 R (2)). These developments call into question the concept of a purely transitional approach since it is now clear that improvement in the environment and the need to avoid distortions of competition caused by national measures in this field will remain a major task for an indefinite period.

In view of the changed context of environmental policy as outlined above the Commission has begun a review of the application of the 'polluter pays' principle. The work will be undertaken on the basis of a detailed analysis of the current situation and an assessment of foreseeable future developments. Pending this review, the Commission decided on 17 December 1986 to continue to apply for the period covered by the fourth environmental action programme (1987-92) the existing Community framework on State aids for the environment using the same criteria as are set out in the Commission's 1980 memorandum for the period 1980-86. However, the Commission reserves the right to alter its criteria before the expiry date of the environmental action programme if the outcome of its review suggests the necessity and urgency of modifications on environmental or competition policy grounds.

Federal Republic of Germany

Aid for meeting stricter air pollution standards

260.   In September 1986 the Federal Government notified to the Commission a scheme by the State of Baden-Württemberg to encourage air pollution control measures going further than current statutory standards. The aid is to be available either in the form of a direct grant of 20 % of the cost or in the form of 10-year loans at an interest rate 4.5 percentage points below market rates. In both cases only additional investment costs exceeding the costs of plans merely fulfilling statutory obligations would be eligible for aid. The annual budget provided for the scheme will be 4.7 million ECU.

Mainly because of its restriction to additional investment costs directly attributable to the wish to go further than statutory requirements, the Commission concluded in November that the proposed scheme did not raise any problem with regard to possible distortions of competition. It therefore raised no objection to the scheme.

Amendments to the Effluent Discharges Levy Act

261.   In March 1986 the Federal Government notified its intention to introduce certain amendments to the Effluent Discharges Levy Act (Abwasserabgabenge-setz). The changes to the legislation mainly concern liability to the levy. With regard to aid aspects, the abolition of the discretion to waive the levy for economic reasons (hardship clause) improves the compatibility of the legislation with the requirements of an undistorted internal market. A new clause providing for a partial relief from the levy of 20 % of the normal rate if particularly dangerous substances are reduced below certain limits was carefully scrutinized by the Commission. It concluded that the amended legislation would not affect trading conditions to an extent contrary to the common interest. The Commission therefore decided in June not to raise objections to implementation of the amendments.

§4 — Regional aids

General developments

262.   In 1986, apart from the ongoing work of scrutinizing national aid schemes and individual awards under such schemes (see below), the Commission concentrated its attention on issues that had become a matter of priority as a result of Spanish and Portuguese accession and the Council's adoption of the Single European Act in December 1985.

The entry of Spain and Portugal, coming after that of Greece, has made it necessary for the Commission to refine its methods and criteria for assessing regional aid in the so-called 'peripheral' regions of the Community, which as well as in the countries mentioned also occur in Ireland and Italy.

The economic and social problems of these areas, which are predominantly agricultural, industrially underdeveloped and have widespread underemployment, call for a certain rethinking of the Commission's policy towards regional aid.

Similar issues have been raised by the amendments to the Treaties made in Title II of the Single European Act. The new Title V of Part Three of the EEC Treaty, Article 130A, requires the Community to 'develop and pursue its actions leading to the strengthening of its economic and social cohesion' and, in particular, to aim at 'reducing disparities between the various regions and the backwardness of the least-favoured regions'.

Determinations on certain national aid schemes and individual awards under such schemes

Denmark

263.   In December 1986 the Commission opened the procedure laid down in Article 93(2) of the EEC Treaty in respect of some of the changes notified by the Danish Government to its regional aid scheme which were due to take effect on 1 January 1987.

The changes adapt the area coverage of the scheme to developments in the regions' economic and social situation since the last review in 1981. They would reduce the percentage of the country's population living in assisted areas from 24.1% to 20.7%. The proposals also make changes in the classification of assisted areas as ordinary or special development areas, the overall effect of which would be to reduce the proportion of the population in the latter areas from 15.5% to 11.1.%.

The Commission accepted the majority of the changes. However, on the basis of the economic and social data available it had doubts about the justification for the retention of certain parts of the countries of North Jutland, Viborg, Ringkøbing and South Jutland as ordinary or special development areas.

Portugal

264. The Commission decided in October 1986 not to raise any objection to implementation until the end of 1986 of a general aid scheme to promote the development and modernization of Portuguese industry. Major awards are to be notified to the Commission in advance.

The scheme provides grants for investment in mining, manufacturing and research and development which are likely to reduce regional disparities, create jobs or lead to innovation and modernization in industry. The maximum rates of grant are 15% net grant equivalent of the investment cost for projects helping to reduce regional disparities, ESC 200 000 to 300 000 per job subject to a limit of 10% net grant equivalent of the investment cost for projects creating new jobs, and 20% net grant equivalent of the investment cost for projects fostering innovation and modernization. The total aid package for any project may not exceed 33% net grant equivalent of the investment.

France

Special Employment Premium Scheme

265. In February 1986 the Commission approved part of an aid scheme to attract new job-creating investment to the Nord-Pas-de-Calais region. The scheme, called the 'Special Employment Premium' scheme, is intended to alleviate the effects on employment of rationalization in the steel, coal and shipbuilding industries. Under the scheme, the Government will pay for three years a declining part of the wage costs associated with jobs created between 1 January 1986 and 30 June 1987 in the worst-hit areas. Firms in the industrial sector, except for certain industries suffering from overcapacity (steel, man-

made fibres, textiles and clothing, shipbuilding, flat glass, the milk powder and butter sectors of the dairy industry, sugar and isoglucose), are eligible for assistance.

Ten areas in different employment districts were proposed by the French Government for inclusion in the scheme. The Commission has accepted six and part of a seventh. In the other areas (the Insee Category B areas Roubaix-Tourcoing, Douai, Bruay and Boulogne) it considered that it had not been established that the problems on the local labour market were linked to rationalization in declining industries. It therefore opened the Article 93(2) procedure with respect to inclusion of these areas in the scheme.

Regional Planning Grants Scheme

266.   In February and April 1986 the French Government asked the Commission for authorization to retain in the Regional Planning Grants (PAT) scheme all the areas listed in Article 1 of its Decision of 10 October 1984 on the PAT scheme. The areas concerned are in Franche-Comté, Upper Normandy and the department of Sarthe.

In its 1984 Decision the Commission had held that the economic and social situation of these areas did not justify assisted status, but had allowed them to remain within the scheme until the end of 1985.

After reviewing the situation in each of the areas, the Commission felt that their situation relative to other parts of France had not changed and that assisted status would still be incompatible with the common market under Article 92. In June 1986 it therefore opened the Article 93(2) procedure with respect to the retention within the PAT scheme of any of the areas listed in Article 1 of the Decision.

European Development Zone

267.   In February 1986 the French, Belgian and Luxembourg Governments jointly notified to the Commission a proposal to establish a 'European Development Zone' in an area straddling the three countries' frontiers around Longwy, Aubange and Rodange. At the centre of the zone it is planned to set up a 408 ha business park, in which investment will attract national and Community aid of up to a total of 30 % net grant equivalent and special customs arrangements, involving the free warehouse ('magasin franc') system and simplified procedures for inward processing, will be applicable. The plan also includes

programmes to improve road and rail links in the area, develop research and educational facilities in high technology, and reclaim derelict land.

After a detailed examination of the areas concerned in the project, the Commission agreed that they faced special problems of industrial redevelopment and that a joint, coordinated response that would help solve the economic problems of the region held definite advantages from the point of view of European integration. In November the Commission decided that an exception could be made for the higher-than-normal aid ceiling of 30 % net grant equivalent (including ERDF grants, if appropriate) and authorized the scheme.

Any projects for which the three Member States feel it necessary to give aid in excess of the ceiling are to be individually notified to the Commission.

Italy

Aid in the centre and north of Italy

268.   The Commission decided in July 1986 not to raise any objection to Act No 710 of 28 November 1985 which amended Decree No 902 of 9 November 1976 providing for aid in the form of soft loans to industry in the centre and north of Italy.

The main purpose of the amending legislation was to allocate LIT 400 000 million of new funding to the Decree 902 scheme. Article 1 of the Act states that this is the final allocation and the Italian authorities have informed the Commission that they expect it to be used up at the latest by the end of 1987. More restrictive criteria will be applied for the soft loans by abolishing the tax concessions previously available.

United Kingdom

Extension of existing regional aid schemes

269.   The Commission approved the extension of a number of existing regional aid schemes to further areas. In April, it approved the extension of the Investment Aid scheme to Blackpool and those parts of Hull and Grimsby not already covered by the scheme, whilst in June it agreed to the extension of a slightly modified version of the Business Improvement Services package of schemes of assistance for small enterprises to the Penzance and St Ives Travel-to-Work-

Area. Blackpool, Hull and Grimsby are areas which have suffered under the sharp decline in their fishing industries whilst the Penzance and St Ives TTWA, an area already experiencing a high rate of unemployment, has been seriously affected by the collapse of the market price for tin.

At the end of July, the Commission raised no objection to the inclusion of the areas of Forres and Upper Moray within the area eligible for aid from the Highlands and Islands Development Board. The analysis of the Commission showed that the Forres and Upper Moray areas exhibit social and economic characteristics of fragile rural communities similar to those which justified the existing derogation granted to the Highlands and Islands Development Board.

Cumulation of aids

270. Finally, in September the Commission agreed to the derogation requested by the UK authorities to permit the cumulation of the 15% Investment Aid scheme grant under the Business Improvement Services package with the award of Regional Development Grant. Such a derogation was requested because in certain circumstances the absolute ceiling of 40% net grant equivalent of initial investment could be exceeded. In reaching this decision the Commission took into account, *inter alia*: the limited number of areas in which the derogation could apply, that the Investment Aid grant is only available to small enterprises with a maximum of 25 employees and that the maximum grant is only UKL 15 000.

Ireland

271. In September the Commission raised no objection to the Irish Government's intention to introduce a scheme of incentives to promote development and reconstruction in certain Irish inner-city areas. In arriving at this position the Commission took account of the general decay and dereliction in the inner cities concerned and in particular of the high percentage of land covered by derelict sites or buildings as well as the age and quality of the housing stock. The Irish Government confirmed that the totality of aids provided under the scheme of incentives notified and other existing aid systems would observe the ceilings of aid intensity in the coordination principles (mainly 75% net grant equivalent of initial investment).

Belgium

272. In November 1986 the Commission opened the Article 93(2) procedure in respect of Articles 50-62 of the Belgian Economic Recovery Act of 31 July 1984. The Act allows the government to take temporary equity stakes in new

companies setting up in development areas or to grant the partial relief from corporation tax on distributed profits. Each of these forms of assistance would be available in addition to other types of regional aid. As the Act did not provide any procedure for limiting the aid intensity of such packages, the Commission had doubts whether the aid ceilings applicable in Belgium would always be observed.[1]

Germany

Joint Federal/state regional aid programme (14th General Plan)

273. In March 1986 the Commission opened the Article 93(2) procedure against the 14th General Plan of the joint Federal/state regional aid programme ('Improvement of regional economic structures' — 'Gemeinschaftsaufgabe') notified by the Federal Government. It did so firstly because there was a danger that the changed grants for highly-graded jobs might exceed the maximum rate which it had authorized for assisted areas in Germany and the aid ceilings for central areas of the Community laid down in the principles for the coordination of regional aids.[2]

Secondly, the Commission opened the procedure because the Federal Government opposed the notification rules proposed under Article 93(1) for significant cases of cumulation[3] between regional aids under the joint programme and aid under 33 general schemes available in addition to regional aid. Without such notification there was a lack of transparency, preventing proper assessment of the compatibility with the common market of such aid packages. The Commission also opened the Article 93(2) procedure in December against the cumulation of regional and research investment allowances, energy and research allowances and the latter two with other cumulable aids.

However, the Commission decided not to raise any objection to the extension of assistance under the 14th General Plan to new service industries, intangible assets, expansion of young businesses not involving job creation, and to firms previously ineligible which sell at least 50 % of their output outside their region, thus helping to reinforce the indigenous potential of the region.

---

[1]   OJ L 312, 9.11.1982.
[2]   OJ C 31, 3.2.1979.
[3]   Fourteenth Competition Report, point 199.

Joint programme aid in Landsberg and Miesbach

274. In February the Commission took a final negative decision under Article 92(1) prohibiting regional aid under the joint Federal/state programme ('Gemeinschaftsaufgabe') in the Labour market regions of Landsberg and Miesbach. The assessment in the procedure opened in January 1985 [1] showed that neither were particularly disadvantaged. The decision does not affect assistance for tourism and infrastructure projects.

Bavarian state regional aid programmes

275. In April 1986 the Commission opened the Article 93(2) procedure against the rules of the Bavarian state regional aid programmes because of the same two elements as had been challenged in the 14th General Plan of the joint Federal/State programme. The Commission also had doubts about the compatibility with the common market of State grants in the parts of the intermediate zone (Mittelbereich) of Landsberg where joint programme aid had been prohibited. [2]

Aid by the state of Rheinland-Pfalz

276. In July 1986 the Commission decided that two regional aid awards by the state of Rheinland-Pfalz, to Lignotock Fasertechnik GmbH und Co. Produktions KG and Schäferwerke KG and Fritz Schäfer KG, against which the Commission had opened the procedure in the autumn of 1985, [3] were incompatible with the common market and could not be granted. Its decision was based on the fact that the area in which both firms are located and which is not an assisted area does not show severe social and economic disparities.

Aid to a textile producer in Lower Saxony

277. In July the Commission decided not to raise any objection to a DM 1 022 million grant proposed by the Federal Government under the 14th General Plan of the joint Federal/state regional aid programme to the household textiles manufacturer ADO-Gardinenwerke of Papenburg-Aschendorf.

---

[1]   Fifteenth Competition Report, point 231.
[2]   See point 274 of this Report.
[3]   Fifteenth Competition Report, point 234.

During the proceedings the German Government amended its initial proposal by withdrawing the part of the aid originally planned for synthetic yarn production. Noting that after this modification the proposal no longer fell under the synthetic fibre and yarn aid code [1] and that it was not likely to affect trade to an extent contrary to the common interest, the Commission decided that the exemption provided for in Article 92(3) (c) was applicable.

Aid to Daimler-Benz AG

278. In October the Commission, in the light of the submissions made by the Federal Government, closed the procedure [2] against an investment grant covering 8.31 % net grant equivalent of the cost of extensions at a Bremen car plant of Daimler-Benz AG. This grant, under the joint Federal/state regional aid programme's special Bremen Scheme, will help create much-needed jobs in Bremen which is an area of high unemployment.

At the same time the Commission was informed of aid planned by Baden-Württemberg state and Rastatt local authority for a new Daimler-Benz car plant at Rastatt. The State and local authorities propose to sell a site which has been cleared and prepared for building work and to connect it to essential services such as water, electricity, telephones, etc., at a price which appears to be subsidized. Rastatt is an area which has a generally high level of economic development compared both to other regions of Germany and to other Member States. Furthermore, any State aid in the Community car industry must be carefully examined. The Commission therefore decided to open the Article 93(2) procedure to enable it to examine the proposed aid in more detail.

Netherlands

279. In June 1986 the Commission agreed to a number of minor changes to the Regional Investment Premium (IPR) scheme. The changes notified by the Netherlands Government tighten up some of the definitions of eligible investment costs and also confirm the devolution of decisions on aid for investments of under HFL 2 million to the provinces. The Commission has reserved final judgment on the devolution, however, until notification of the provinces' award procedures.

The other changes are as follows:

---

[1]   OJ C 171, 10.7.1985; Fifteenth Competition Report, point 196.
[2]   Fifteenth Competition Report, point 233.

(i) Extension investments will henceforth only be eligible if they increase production capacity or total jobs by at least 20%, instead of 10% as previously.

(ii) All new investment undertaken in a 10 km radius of an existing establishment belonging to the same firm or group will in future count as extension investment.

(iii) Assistance will normally no longer be available for takeovers of existing businesses or acquisitions of assets not permanently remaining within the firm.

§ 5 — Aid in the transport sector

280. The year 1986 was marked by the joint efforts of the Commission and the Council to formulate the legislative provisions necessary to achieve increased competition for all modes of transport.

Land and inland waterway transport

281. In the areas of land transport it is of particular interest to note the proposals relating to the carriage of goods by road and by inland waterway [1] whose implementation will contribute to the furtherance of competition in the market. This development should be accompanied by the harmonization of competition conditions. To this end, the Commission, following a recommendation by the Council, presented to the latter, in December 1986, a report on the elimination of distortion of competition with respect to fiscal provisions relating to the road haulage.

Inland waterway transport by small barges has not shown any signs of recovery and certain Member States are continuing to offer aids for the scrapping of ageing vessels so as to reduce the chronic structural overcapacity which persists in this sector.

The Commission approved a Dutch programme of scrapping and a French programme of scrapping accompanied by improved pre-retirement schemes to encourage certain boatmen to leave the industry. A the same time provision was made for aid to enable 40 young boatmen to join the industry. The Commission approved this part of the aid scheme on condition that it respected the reduction of the overall capacity of the small barge fleet. This will in fact occur since the new boatmen are to be assigned to boats bought up and put back into service by the National Office of Navigation.

It was not yet possible to assess the results of these initiatives at the meeting of the Consultative Committee for transport aid held at the end of the year.

---

[1]   (a) Proposal for a Council Regulation laying down the conditions under which non-resident carriers may operate national road haulage transport services within a Member State. (Cabotage)
(b) Proposal for a Council Regulation laying down the conditions under which non-resident carriers may operate national road passenger transport services within a Member State.
(c) Proposal for a Council Regulation laying down the conditions under which non-resident carriers may transport goods or passengers by inland waterway within a Member State.
(d) Proposal for a Council Regulation on access to the market for the carriage of goods by road between Member States.
(e) Proposal for a Council Regulation setting out common rules for the international carriage of passengers by coach and bus.

Air and sea transport

282.   With respect to maritime transport, the Commission conducted a survey into the different aid schemes for shipowners in each Member State. The Commission started to examine certain aids granted by the Italian and United Kingdom Governments to ports, the main aim of which was to reduce excess personnel by means of early retirement. Article 93(2) [1] proceedings were opened in December 1986 with respect to these aids. Consideration is being given to means of improving the transparency of financial relations between public bodies and ports and to obtain a better means of comparing the amounting system in this sector.

Concerning air transport, the Commission is pursuing, in conjunction with the Members States and in accordance with the guidelines laid down in Memorandum No 2, [2] its review of aids granted in this sector.

The Commission was informed of a plan for British Airways to supply financial assistance to various independent airlines for up to 15 new routes between the United Kingdom and the Continent. The Commission raised no objections to this plan. In this context, the Commission also examined the direct application of this plan with regard to 13 specific cases and decided not to raise objections under Article 92(3) of the EEC Treaty. The main aims of this measure are to reorganize and increase the competitiveness of United Kingdom aviation as well as to develop services from regional airports.

---

[1]   OJ C 78, 25.3.1987; OJ C 96, 9.4.1987.
[2]   Civil aviation — Memorandum No 2 — Progress towards the development of a Community air transport policy (COM(84) 72 Final).

§ 6 — Aid in the agriculture sector

Applicability of Articles 92 to 94 of the EEC Treaty to products listed in Annex II to the Treaty

283. The framework for policy on national aids to agriculture is set by Article 42 of the Treaty, which states that 'The provisions of the chapter relating to rules on competition shall apply to production of and trade in agricultural products only to the extent determined by the Council within the framework of Article 43(2) and (3) and in accordance with the procedure laid down therein, account being taken of the objectives set out in Article 39'.

It was when the EEC market organizations were set up that the Treaty provisions on competition were declared applicable to agricultural production and trade in agricultural products, as well. Since that time, agriculture has also normally been subject to the provisions of the EEC Treaty on State aids. [1]

However, the applicability of these Treaty articles on competition is not unconditional. Under Article 42 of the Treaty, they cannot prevail over relevant provisions of secondary agricultural legislation.

The market organizations

284. The market organizations have their own rules governing or prohibiting national aids, as regards specific areas of agricultural production; in any case, the Member States must refrain from any action liable to derogate from or encroach upon the regulations establishing a market organization. Any interference by the Member State in market mechanisms other than action expressly provided for by the Community regulations, notably the payment of additional or different aids, in an area clearly covered by a market organization, would be liable both to hamper the operation of the organization and to distort competition by favouring certain undertakings or certain types of production to the detriment of others.

---

[1] For the few products not yet covered by EEC market organizations (alcohol and alcohol vinegar, honey, bananas, fresh pineapples, coffee, chicory root, cork, horsemeat and potatoes except for starch-making), the rules of competition are applicable under Article 4 of Regulation 26 of 4 April 1962, which states, however, that only 'The provisions of Article 93(1) and of the first sentence of Article 93(3) of the Treaty shall apply to aids granted for production of or trade in the products listed in Annex II to the Treaty'.

Policy on structures

285. The application of Articles 92 to 94 to agricultural production is also subject to the instruments governing the policy on agricultural structures. Regulation (EEC) No 797/85 on improving the efficiency of agricultural structures [1] contains a code of aids for the creation or modernization of viable farms qualifying for Community co-financing, a code of aids for farms not meeting the criteria which would make them eligible for such financing, and a code of aids for the financing of various parallel schemes.

A group of structural schemes has also been set up in connection with the market organizations. The relevant regulations contain rules on national aids. These include the regulations on producers' groups, milk non-marketing and dairy herd conversion premiums, a conversion scheme for wine growers, the improvement of the production and marketing of Community citrus fruit, and the abandonment of certain areas under vines and the renunciation of replanting rights.

In connection with the implementation of Regulation (EEC) No 355/77 on common measures to improve the conditions under which agricultural products are processed and marketed, [2] a set of implementing criteria has been agreed; these are also referred to when aids granted in this context at national level are examined.

Implementation of a competition policy in agriculture

Objectives

286. In view of the fundamental approach provided by the Treaty itself, the policy on national aids for agriculture has never been separated from the general agricultural policy. The main objectives of the policy on competition in this field are:

(i) to underpin the effective operation of the market organizations by preventing the payment of national aids supplementing or differing from those provided for under the market organizations;

(ii) to support the policy on structures in respect of actual farms pursued by the Community, by authorizing aids strengthening this action;

---

[1]   OJ L 93, 30.3.1985.
[2]   OJ L 51, 23.2.1977.

(iii) to step up modernization of processing and marketing facilities in close relation with the requirements of the policy on markets and prices, while facilitating the development of this sector in regions where there are deficits and to reduce and rationalize the capacity for production of surplus products;

(iv) to avoid hampering the national policies supporting schemes for the improvement of the quality of products, technical progress and the conservation of the environment and the rescue of farms which have short-term difficulties to contend with.

In the pursuit of these objectives, the Commission, using its discretionary powers, has worked out over the years appropriate measures in respect of individual products under Article 93(1) of the Treaty, which it has supplemented when expressing its views as regards new aids introduced by the Member States and notified to the Commission under Article 93(3) of the Treaty. [1]

Application of the rules of competition in 1986

287. In 1986, the Commission received 157 notifications [2] concerning the introduction of national agricultural aids or amendments to existing schemes.

In most cases, there was no conflict with the specific rules framed by the Commission (See Annex).

As regards certain schemes, the Commission rendered favourable opinions after eliciting from the national authorities further information on the objectives and having asked them to alter the arrangements either to adapt them to the specific rules of competition or to impose, in certain cases, conditions rendering them compatible with the common market.

A number of aid schemes come under arrangements notified under Regulation (EEC) No 797/85 on improving the efficiency of agricultural structures. The Commission endorsed these measures as regards national aids supplementing investments, granted for farms whose development projects are eligible for Community financing. The Commission also endorsed other aids related to this Regulation for which the Member States have retained the right to take additional action with payment terms or procedures differing from those laid

---

[1] All the comments made by the Commission on agricultural aids are mentioned in the monthly *Bulletin of the European Communities*.

[2] This number includes notifications under Article 93(3) of the Treaty, either aids concerning agricultural products only, or general aids including agricultural products; it also includes aids notified only after the Commission has asked for such notifications.

down by the Regulation or the amounts of which exceed the ceilings set in the Regulation. These cases were mainly aid schemes for training and the setting up of recognized groups for the purpose of mutual assistance between farms or the setting up of agricultural associations with the aim of creating replacement services. The Commission also approved aids for the environment, aids for the qualitative improvement of products, aids for quality control, for breeding, for the purchase of officially-registered pure-bred male reproducing stock and aids for fundamental and applied agricultural research.

It also adopted opinions on aids to income or current cash flow necessitated for the survival of certain farms. These farms had had to face a number of constraints: mounting interest rates just as they were undergoing modernization, more expensive input costs (largely a matter of inflation), the freezing of their revenues because of the administrative restriction of production (milk quotas) and the freezing of agricultural Community prices imposed by budgetary restrictions.

The Commission ensured that the aids did not exceed certain ceilings which it generally applies for investment-related aids; support already granted for such investments has been included in the calculation. The Commission also demanded that the beneficiaries of such aid show that their financial situation justified support. For farms whose debts were partly due to the high costs of operation, the Commission requests that aids should be confined to holdings which will be able in the long term to discharge their financial obligations and to farms submitting restructuring or adaptation plans related to the new conditions on the market. The Commission felt, too, that cash aids could also be granted where the farms could not realize assets or draw on reserves without encroaching on the profitability of the farm. This case arose, in particular, where there was a need to maintain the farm as a basis of subsistence for the family of the farmer and to safeguard employment, or where the aim was to avoid recourse to public welfare facilities, which, in certain Member States, require farmers to realize their assets.

The Commission initiated the procedure provided for in Article 93(2) of the Treaty in respect of the following measures:

Operating aids:

(i)   action to reduce social security costs for the employment of occasional labour for certain types of agricultural work, in France;

(ii) a scheme taking the form of a currency exchange guarantee in Ireland, the effect of which was to reduce the rate of interest on operating credit over four years;

(iii) aids for the sterilization of land, or subsidies for cooperatives not having qualified, during one or more preceding marketing years, for management loans in the region of Sicily;

(iv) aids for the purchase of cattle feed and the purchase of male poultry reproduction animals in Abruzzi;

(v) action supporting the distillation of table wine and aids for the storage of quality wines in Italy, granted following the 'methanol' scandal, these being measures infringing the rules of the market organization,

(vi) reduced-rate loans over 12 months granted for the purchase of store cattle in the region of Trento (Italy);

(vii) subsidies for the transport of milk granted in the same region;

(viii) aids to dealers in sugar in store granted in Italy;

(ix) payment of part of social security contributions for dairy farmers in France.

Export aids:

(i) measures adopted in Italy relating to the export of cattle and beef/veal to non-member countries;

(ii) reduced rate discount of medium- and long-term loans in connection with the export of food products to non-member countries from Ireland.

Income aids granted in the Province of Trento in Italy for the alpine pasturing of cattle.

Aids exceeding the ceilings or not matching the criteria:

(i) aids related to the loss of cattle as a result of disease and the payment of costs of disease control in the *Land* of Lower Saxony;

(ii) aids to nurserymen and fruit-growers as a result of frost damage in 1984/85, the grant of aid not having been related to a minimum rate of loss due to frost, paid in Belgium;

(iii) aids to investment in the processing and marketing of agricultural products at a rate exceeding the Commission's usual maximum, planned in Luxembourg;

(iv) aids financed by 'parafiscal' charges (Produktschappen in the Netherlands).

Aids to investments in the dairy sector:

(i) aids for the purchase, construction, or extension of the structures required for the transport and preservation of milk planned by the Province of Trento in Italy;

(ii) an aid for the modernization and extension of a starch factory in France.

Under the third subparagraph of Article 93(2), the Council authorized the aid, mentioned above, for the distillation of table wines and aids for the storage of quality wines granted in Italy following the 'methanol' scandal, a national aid in the form of an advanced payment against the Community ewe premium in France and the payment by certain Member States of an aid to the private short-term storage of tables wines and musts.

Special arrangements for existing aids in Spain and Portugal

288. Under Council Regulations (EEC) Nos 3773/85 and 3774/85 [1] respectively, Spain and Portugal have been authorized to maintain provisionally national aid schemes incompatible with the common market. These schemes concern mainly cereals, olive oil and seeds and propagating material in Spain, and sugar, vegetable oils and seeds in Portugal.

This arrangement requires the new Member States to phase out the schemes over a period from 1991 to 1996, at rates laid down in the Regulations themselves.

Where the effect of aid schemes listed in the Regulations is to modify appreciably on the Spanish or Portuguese market the conditions of competition between the products deriving from the other Member States and products produced at home, the Council is to adopt. according to the procedure laid down in Article 89(14) of the Act of Accession, special procedures to ensure equal access to the Spanish and Portuguese markets.

Outlook

289. As a result of policy analysis work carried out by the Commission,[2] essential priorities for agricultural policy in the next 10 years have been established. The action taken by the Member States themselves, within their own areas of responsibility, must be consistent with, and not serve to distort the policies pursued at Community level. To qualify for the waivers conceded in the rules of competition of the Treaty, national aid schemes must therefore

---

[1] OJ L 362, 31.12.1985.
[2] 'A future for European agriculture'. The 'Green Paper' and the Commission guidelines published in *Newsflash, Green Europe*, Nos 33 and 34.

contribute to the implementation of the new approach of the agricultural policy, by helping to:

(i)   scale down gradually production of surplus items and lighten the burden entailed by these for the taxpayer;

(ii) promote diversification and qualitative improvement in production, tailored to the requirements of the internal markets and consumer preferences;

(iii) support farming in areas where it is a vital aspect of regional development, the maintenance of social equilibria and the protection of the environment and the countryside;

(iv) promote increased awareness among farmers of environmental problems;

(v)   contribute to the development, within the Community, of firms processing agricultural products and thus involve farmers in the major technological changes of our time.

Under the rules of competition of the Treaty, the Commission will, of course, as in the past, bear in mind the need for the Member States to find solutions for economic problems arising from situations not yet covered by the particular regulations governing the common agricultural policy.

§ 7 — Aid for fisheries

General developments

290.   The table below summarizes progress on a number of aid cases with regard to fisheries, and the Commission's work in this area. The figures for the last two years show a sizeable reduction in the number of cases requiring examination. Almost all these cases related to general aid schemes which, once implemented, are modified only where this is required as a result of developments within the fisheries sector. The adoption in October 1983 of a series of measures in the context of the common policy on structures, [1] and the adoption by the Commission in July 1985 of guidelines for the examination of State aids in the fisheries sector created a clear framework for defining the activities of the Member States in this area and, consequently, have probably led to greater stability in the Member States' aid policies. The need to resort to new national aid measures has decreased of its own accord.

Year	Total	of which:		Decision to close the procedure under Article 93(2)[2]	Final decision under Article 93(2)[2]
		No objections	Procedure under Art. 93(2)		
1982	23	16	7	—	—
1983	15	10	5	3	· 5
1984	18	13	5	3	—
1985	12	8	4	2	2
1986	9[1]	6	—	2	2

[1]   Three cases were still being examined at the end of the year.
[2]   In the majority of cases, the decision to initiate proceedings was taken in previous years.

The Commission, acting with the two new Member States, carried out an initial analysis of the aid schemes existing in Spain and Portugal at the time of accession. It proposed that these schemes be modified or adjusted so as to adapt them to Community law and to guarantee compliance with the guidelines for the examination of State aids in the fisheries sector.

---

[1]   On 17 December 1986, the Council adopted a Regulation defining the structural policy for fisheries over the next 10 years.

Individual cases

Federal Republic of Germany

291. In June 1986, the Commission adopted a final decision under Article 93(2) of the EEC Treaty with regard to aid granted to organizations of producers in Germany engaged in inshore and cutter fishing. This aid consisted of converting into subsidies the market stabilization loans granted to these organizations under Article 6 of Regulation (EEC) No 3796/81 on the common organization of the markets in fishery products. The aid was granted on the condition that a single marketing organization be set up to market jointly the output of all the producer organizations concerned.

The Commission considered that the aim of the scheme is desirable in itself and is in accordance with the objectives of the common organization of markets, but that by forgoing reimbursement of these special loans granted under a provision relating to the common organization of markets and under the strict conditions laid down by that provision, the German Government is acting in contravention of the above-mentioned Regulation.

In July 1986, the Commission decided not to make any objection to two cases of aid granted by the German Government to the deep-sea fishing sector. The first case related to initial aid to two new deep-sea fishing companies for 1986, the second to transitional aid covering the years 1986 and 1987 for fishing off Greenland. These schemes are budgeted at DM 12 million in the case of the initial aid and DM 13 million in the case of the transitional aid. In both cases, the aid is being granted because of substantial losses of income due to bad weather conditions off the coast of Greenland where the fleet carries out a large proportion of its activities.

The Commission considered that these two aid schemes were covered by the derogation set out in Article 92(2)(b) of the EEC Treaty. The transitional aid scheme also includes a figure of DM 10 million for 1988. The Commission reserved the right to assess this final portion of the aid in the light of the economic situation of the deep-sea fleet and the amounts actually paid in respect of this aid in 1986 and 1987.

France

292. In July 1986, the Commission also adopted a final decision under Article 93(2) of the EEC Treaty with regard to aid granted in France in the form of a system of ceilings on the price of diesel fuel for fishermen, introduced for the first time in 1982. This scheme consists of a mechanism for adjusting diesel fuel prices for fishermen so as to offset large increases in fuel prices, whereby the increase paid by fishermen was limited to the variation in the general consumer-price index drawn up monthly by the Institut national de la statistique et des études économiques. Fishermen thus pay less for their fuel than other consumers during periods of adjustment.

Since other fishermen in the Community are not able to benefit from the same favourable conditions, the aid having been granted without any real reciprocal concession by the recipients, it has a direct influence on competition and trade between the Member States. Consequently, the Commission believes that it amounts to an operating aid incompatible with the common market.

Chapter II

Public undertakings

Greece: insurance

293.   After the Greek Government had failed to comply with the Commission's decision of 24 April 1985 [1] under Article 90(3) of the EEC Treaty on a piece of legislation which unduly favoured State-owned insurance companies, [2] the Commission decided to institute Article 169 proceedings and on 8 April 1986 gave the Greek Government notice to submit its observations.

The legislation (Article 13 of Act No 1256/82) provided that all public property in Greece must be insured with a Greek State-owned insurance company and also obliged State banks to recommend customers seeking a loan to take out the insurance they required in connection with it, with a State-owned company.

By failing to take steps to remove the discrimination against foreign insurance companies, the Greek Government had infringed Articles 5 and 189, of the EEC Treaty.

In its reply to the opening of proceedings, the Greek Government said it intended to amend the offending provisions in a new insurance act. When this did not materialize, however, the Commission went on to serve a reasoned opinion.

Federal Republic of Germany

294.   After intervention by the Commission under Article 90(1) in conjunction with Articles 37 and 86 of the EEC Treaty, [3] the German Government informed it on 30 July 1986 that the telecommunications regulations had been amended on 18 July to allow modems (both separate and integrated in more complex

---

[1]   OJ L 152, 11.6.1985.
[2]   Fourteenth Competition Report, point 286; Fifteenth Competition Report, point 258.
[3]   Fifteenth Competition Report, point 261.

equipment, such as personal computers) to be supplied by independent firms as well as by the Bundespost.

Hitherto, only the Bundespost had had the right to supply modems that were to be connected to the public telephone network. This not only prevented users from selecting the type of modem best suited to their needs, but also restricted the market open to suppliers of modems imported from other Member States to those used in private networks.

The Commission considered that the legislation giving the Bundespost a monopoly of supply of modems infringed Article 90(1) in conjunction with Article 37, because it both deprived users of a choice between modems available from several suppliers and denied suppliers direct access to a very large market. The tying of the sale or leasing of modems to the provision of telephone network services was also an abuse of a dominant position contrary to Article 86.

Belgium

295.   The Commission received a complaint about the exclusive rights given to the Belgian posts and telecommunications authority to import and supply low-speed modems and first telex terminals. After being informed that the monopoly was incompatible with the EEC Treaty because it denied suppliers of equipment from other Member States direct access to the Belgian market, the Belgian Government told the Commission that it intended to reform the provisions within three years.

Italy

296.   A similar complaint was made about a monopoly of importing and sale of modems and first telex terminals in Italy.

Here, modems and first telex terminals to be connected to the public network may be supplied and installed only by the DCST (Direzione Centrale Servizi Telegrafici) and the SIP (Società Italiana per l'Esercizio Telefonico). This arrangement affects imports of modems and telex terminals from other Member States as the manufacturers of such equipment in other countries cannot approach Italian users directly.

After intervention by the Commission, the Italian Government announced that it was going to reform the provisions.

297.   The Commission is continuing its investigations of PTT's monopolies to supply terminal equipment connected to the public telephone network also in other Member States.

Ireland

298.   The Commission also pressed ahead with its action on international courier services. In some Member States the postal authorities' mail-carrying monopoly was regarded as extending to courier services, even though private courier companies provided a standard of service, in terms of speed and reliability, which the postal authorities could not match. [1]

The company holding the postal monopoly in Ireland, An Post, still refused to allow international courier services to operate there, basing itself on section 73 of the Postal Act 1983. Its position was supported by the Government.

The Commission is examining the situation in the light of the solution agreed in Germany. [2]

---

[1]   Fifteenth Competition Report, point 259.
[2]   See point 294 of this Report.

Chapter III

Adjustment of State monopolies of a commercial character

France

299. In 1979, when the French Government reformed its State oil distribution regime to bring it into line with the monopoly provisions of the EEC Treaty, it had agreed with the Commission objective criteria for licensing oil distributors. [1]

In 1985, the Commission received a complaint from an oil company that was seeking a licence to sell jet fuel at Paris-Roissy airport. The company had been refused such a licence in 1982 and was afraid of being again refused in the 1986 licensing round, because of a restrictive interpretation of the licensing criteria.

During its investigation of the complaint the Commission found that the Paris airports authority had, with the Government's approval, changed the requirements for jet fuel distributors so that only those holding a licence for importing and refining crude oil could be licensed to distribute jet fuel at the airports. This meant that to obtain a licence, a company had to have refining facilities in France.

Judging that this requirement went beyond the criteria that had been agreed in 1979, the Commission pressed the French authorities in accordance with Articles 90 and 37 of the EEC Treaty to drop the new requirements.

As a result, the French Government informed the Commission via the Paris airports authority that the additional requirement had been abolished from 1 March 1986.

The French Government also removed the original cause of complaint, the alleged arbitrary and discriminatory application of the licensing criteria, when it granted the complainant a licence on 27 June 1986. [2]

---

[1]   Ninth Competition Report, point 205.
[2]   *Journal officiel de la République française*, 29 June 1986, p. 8096.

300. In connection with the French potash fertilizer monopoly, the Commission had in 1984 instituted Article 169 proceedings[1] against the French Government for still requiring import declarations for potash products from third countries that had already been admitted for free circulation in the Community by other Member States. This maintained monopoly importing rights, contrary to Article 37 EEC Treaty.

After being served with the reasoned opinion, the French Government announced that it was doing away with the import declarations system.

Greece

301. In October 1985, when the Greek Government introduced safeguard measures under Article 109 EEC Treaty as part of an economic recovery programme, it undertook to complete the reform of all its commercial monopolies, except for oil products, by 1 January 1986,[2] so as to meet its obligations under Article 40 of the Accession Treaty and Article 37 EEC Treaty.

The Commission has established that some monopoly importing and marketing rights for products from other Member States have now been abolished, as promised. The reforms cover especially former monopoly products, such as matches and cigarette paper, about which the Commission had received complaints.

The Commission is checking that the new legislation is in conformity with Community law.

302. The necessary reforms of the Greek oil monopoly are still under examination.

A programme for reform was laid down by Act 1571/85 and decrees containing detailed provisions were drafted. The decree dealing with imports of oil products however provided for only 15% of the market to be opened up to imports in 1986.

On 2 June 1986, the Commission therefore served notice of the institution of Article 169 proceedings against the Government for infringement of Articles 37 and 30 EEC Treaty.

---

[1]   Fourteenth Competition Report, point 288.
[2]   Fifteenth Competition Report, point 263.

In its reply, the Greek Government stated that the liberalization of 15% of the market that had taken place in 1986 would be followed by another 20% in 1987 and 20% more from 1 January 1988, so that 55% of the market would be open to imports by that date.

It also said the relevant ministerial decrees were being amended to meet the Commission's objections.

The Greek reply is still under examination.

303.   The Commission is also looking at the reforms that have to be made to the commercial monopolies in Spain and Portugal under Articles 48 and 208 of the Accession Treaty.

Spain

304.   Under Article 48(1) of the Accession Treaty, Spain is required to progressively adjust the monopolies so that by the end of 1991 products from other Member States can be imported and marketed freely. Exclusive exporting rights were to be abolished from 1 January 1986 (Article 48(2)). For imports from Member States, quotas are laid down which increase each year (Article 48(3) and Annex V).

305.   The Spanish Government has sent the Commission legislation (Decree-Laws 5/1985 and 2401/85) containing plans for the reform of its oil monopoly. The monopoly is administered by Campsa, which us 56% State-owned. The main outstanding problems are:

(i)   the fact that until new legislation for the retail trade is enacted, importers of oil products from other Member States cannot distribute them themselves on the Spanish market but have to sell them to the monopoly;

(ii)   the ban on importers supplying gas oil and fuel oil to large industrial consumers such as fertilizer manufacturers and gasworks.

306.   The tobacco products monopoly is administered by the 53% State-owned company Tabacelera.

A start was made on reforming the monopoly by Act 38 of 22 November 1985, which abolished the monopoly exporting rights for tobacco products and opened import quotas. However, a ministerial decree still has to be issued on the retail trade.

Portugal

307. In Portugal, the oil monopoly also covers refining. This is delegated to the State-owned company, Petrogal.

There is a monopoly of importation of petrol, kerosene, gas oil and fuel oil, for which annual import and distribution quotas for the Portuguese market are allocated to Petrogal (which is allowed to supply between 60 and 80% of the market, depending on the product), Mobil, Shell and BP.

There are no monopoly rights for retailing.

Under Article 208 of the Accession Treaty, Portugal is required to progressively adjust its monopolies so that by the end of 1992 products from other Member States can be imported and distributed freely on its market. For oil products it is required to open import and marketing quotas.

A framework for reform of the oil monopoly has been laid down by Decree-Law 525/85 and Decree 969/85.

The Commission is now scrutinizing the legislation in relation to Article 208 of the Accession Treaty.

308. The Portuguese alcohol monopoly, administered by the Administraçao Geral do Acucar et do Alcool (AGA), covers the production, importing, exporting and marketing of alcohol.

Under the joint declaration on the elimination of monopolies existing in the new Member States in the sphere of agriculture, Portugal is committed to reforming this monopoly in accordance with Article 208 of the Accession Treaty by opening annually rising import quotas. The Government has sent the Commission a decree (No 505/85) fixing a framework for the liberalization, which is now under scrutiny.

Chapter IV

Main decisions of the Court of Justice in aid cases

309. In 1986 the Court of Justice gave judgment in six aid cases and made orders in two cases.[1] Some of the decisions raised issues of general significance.

Right of appeal by third parties

310. The procedural judgment given on 28 January 1986 in Case 169/84 (*Compagnie française de l'azote (Cofaz) and Others v Commission*) is important for the clarification it has brought to the right of third parties to appeal against positive decisions in aid cases, here a decision to close the Article 93(2) procedure against an aid proposal. The Court's interpretation of the second paragraph of Article 173 of the EEC Treaty in this case, coupled with the Commission's own moves to provide more information about cases and schemes and about its monitoring methods,[2] will strengthen the safeguards for third parties affected by aid decisions.

The Commission had decided to close the Article 93(2) procedure against Dutch natural gas tariffs. Cofaz appealed under the second paragraph of Article 173 of the EEC Treaty against the Commission's decision.

The Commission submitted that its decision was not of sufficient individual concern to the applicants for their appeal to be admissible under the second

---

[1] (1) Case 52/84 *Commission v Belgium*, judgment of 15 January 1986 (not yet reported).
(2) Case 169/84 *Compagnie française de l'azote (Cofaz) SA and Others v Commission*, judgment of 28 January 1986 (not yet reported).
(3) Case 310/85 R *Deufil GmbH & Co. KG v Commission*, order of 6 February 1986 (not yet reported).
(4) Case 57/86 R *Greece v Commission*, order of 30 April 1986 (not yet reported).
(5) Case 234/84 *Belgium v Commission*, judgment of 10 July 1986 (not yet reported).
(6) Case 40/85 *Belgium v Commission*, judgment of 10 July 1986 (not yet reported).
(7) Case 282/85 *Comité de développement et de promotion du textile et de l'habillement (DEFI) v Commission*, judgment of 10 July 1986 (not yet reported).
(8) Case 253/84 *Groupement agricole d'exploitation en commun v Council and Commission*, judgment of 24 September 1986 (not yet reported).
[2] See point 204 of this Report.

paragraph of Article 173. Whilst it did not maintain that a decision to close the Article 93(2) procedure could not be appealed by third parties in other circumstances, in the present case the Commission considered that the appeal should be dismissed.

The Court held, referring to its earlier judgment in Case 25/62 *Plaumann v Commission,* that 'persons other than those to whom a decision is addressed may claim to be concerned within the meaning of the second paragraph of Article 173 only if the decision affects them by reason of certain attributes which are peculiar to them or of circumstances which place them in a different position from all other persons, and is thereby of similar specific importance to them as it is to the addressee'.

In general, an appeal was open only to firms able to show that their market position was substantially affected by the aid measure on which the decision was taken. In Cofaz's case, the Court thought the company had adduced pertinent reasons to show that the Commission's decision could adversely affect its legitimate interests by substantially altering its position on the relevant market.

The judgment is significant in that it was the first time the Court had agreed to consider an appeal by a third party against a Commission decision to close the Article 93(2) procedure after the third party had demonstrated that the decision was of direct concern to it.

Right of appeal by quasi-governmental organizations

311. In its judgment delivered on 10 July 1986 in Case 282/85 *Comité de développement et de promotion du textile et de l'habillement (DEFI) v Commission,* the Court dismissed as inadmissible an appeal by the quasi-governmental organization responsible for administering a French textile levy scheme against Commission Decision No 85/390 of 5 June 1985 prohibiting the scheme. The judgment is interesting for the light it throws on the right of appeal by bodies whose interest in a decision is indistinguishable from that of the Member State concerned. It also confirmed the Court's practice of dismissing appeals by organizations representing the collective interests of operators affected by a decision.

The Commission submitted that DEFI did not have a legitimate interest or, at any rate, that its interest was indistinguishable from that of the French State, so that it was not directly concerned by the decision for the purposes of the second paragraph of Article 173 of the EEC Treaty. The Court agreed, basing itself not on abstract principles but on the practical ground that in view of the organization's close links with the State its interest in the case was indistinguishable from that of the State, by which an appeal was already pending. The judgment leaves the question open whether a quasi-governmental organization would have a right of appeal under the second paragraph of Article 173 if the facts of the case showed it to have an interest distinct from or at least complementary to that of the State.

Stays of execution of Commission decisions

312. The order made by the President of the Court on 6 February 1986 in Case 310/85 R *Deufil GmbH & Co. KG v Commission* confirmed the Court's practice of assessing the urgency of applications for stays of execution under Article 83(2) of the Court's Rules of Procedure in the light of the likelihood of the applicant's suffering serious and irreparable damage if the application is not granted. After referring to the fact that under Article 185 of the Treaty actions brought before the Court do not have suspensory effect, the Court dismissed the application for a stay of execution on the ground that the applicant had not shown the requisite degree of urgency. On 30 April 1986 an application by Greece for an injunction restraining execution of another Commission aid decision was dismissed for the same reason (order by the President of the Court in Case 57/86 R *Greece v Commission*). The decisions clarify the conditions the Court imposes for injunctions against Commission decisions.

Subscriptions of capital in ailing businesses

313. In two judgments handed down on 10 July 1986 in appeals by Belgium against Commission decisions (Cases 234/84 and 40/85), the Court further [1] clarified the position regarding the applicability of Article 92 of the EEC Treaty to rescue aid in the form of injections of equity capital. The judgments also developed the case law on the procedural requirements for negative decisions under Article 93(2) (see below 'Substantiation of decisions and rights of the defence').

---

[1] See Case 323/82 *Intermills v Commission* [1984] ECR 3809 — Fourteenth Competition Report, points 200 and 201 — and Joined Cases 296 and 318/82 *Netherlands and Leeuwarder Papierwarenfabriek v Commission,* Fifteenth Competition Report, point 176.

The two Commission decisions of April 1984 [1] and October 1984 [2] had ordered Belgium to withdraw the aid it had provided to Meura, a firm manufacturing mainly brewery equipment, and Boch, a crockery and ceramic sanitaryware manufacturer, in the form of subscriptions of new equity by the Wallonian Regional Investment Corporation (SRIW).

The Commission had decided that the capital subscriptions amounted to rescue aid, which was ineligible for an exemption under Article 92(3)(c) EEC.

The Court agreed with the arguments of the Commission in the decisions and rejected the submission of the Belgian Government. It held: 'To ascertain whether such a measure is in the nature of State aid, it is right to apply the criterion set out in the Commission's decision (and not contested by the Belgian Government), based on the company's ability to raise finance on the private capital markets. In the case of a company almost all of whose shares are held by State bodies the major question is whether a private shareholder would in similar circumstances, in the light of the company's prospects of future profitability, have invested the capital without regard to social, regional or industrial policy considerations.' [3]

The Court also accepted the Commission's evidence that the difficulties of the companies were of more than a passing kind and a restructuring would not have made them profitable again. In Meura's case the company had been heavily lossmaking for several years and to keep it afloat the Belgian authorities had had to inject new funds to recapitalize it on several previous occasions also. Furthermore, the company was in an industry suffering from overcapacity.

Substantiation of decisions and rights of the defence

314.   The same two judgments also confirmed the requirements regarding the substantiation of decisions: 'The reasons given for an adverse decision must be such as to allow the Court to verify its legality and to provide those concerned with sufficient information to judge whether or not the decision is soundly-based.' [4] To enable the Commission to discharge this requirement, the Member States must give it their active cooperation during the scrutiny process under the Article 93(2) procedure. If they failed to do so, the Commission was entitled to take its decision on the facts known to it at the time.

---

1   Fourteenth Competition Report, point 252.
2   Fourteenth Competition Report, point 250, and Fifteenth Competition Report, point 211.
3   Case 234/84, point 13.
4   Cases 234/84 and 40/85, point 21 in both judgments.

The Court also held that 'the safeguarding of the rights of defence in any proceedings taken against a person that are capable of leading to an adverse decision against him is a fundamental principle of Community law and must be observed even in the absence of specific rules on the matter in the procedure in question.'[1] A proper observance of the principle requires the sending to Member States of the documentary evidence on which the Commission bases its view that aid is incompatible with the common market. If the Commission considers that the Member State concerned cannot be given access to documents or observations received during the Article 93(2) procedure because this would breach trade secrets protected by Article 214 of the EEC Treaty, this evidence cannot be used in its decision against that State.

Withdrawal/recovery of illegal aid

315. In 1983 the Commission informed the Member States by notice in the Official Journal[2] that it had decided to put into practice the principle established by the Court in its judgment in Case 70/72 that illegally paid aid was refundable.

Strong support has been given for the Commission's policy by the Court's judgment in Case 52/84 *Commission v Belgium,* an action for a declaration that Belgium had failed to fulfil its obligations under the EEC Treaty by not complying with the Commission's decision ordering it to withdraw aid from Boch.

The Court rejected the Belgian Government's argument that it was impossible to implement the decision properly: 'The fact that on account of the company's financial position the Belgian authorities could not recover the entire sum paid does not mean that implementation was impossible, because the Commission's objective was to withdraw the aid, and as the Belgian Government itself admits that objective could be attained by proceedings for winding up the company, which the Belgian authorities, in their capacity as shareholder or creditor, could institute.'[3]

---

[1] Case 234/84, point 27.
[2] OJ C 318, 24.11.1983; Thirteenth Competition Report, point 220.
[3] Case 52/84, point 14.

However, the Court did not rule out the possibility of unforeseen or unforesee-able difficulties arising in implementing a Commission decision ordering the withdrawal of aid. In such a case, the Commission and the Member State should, in keeping with Article 5 of the EEC Treaty, 'work together in good faith to overcome the difficulties in full compliance with the provisions of the Treaty, and in particular those on aid'. [1]

---

[1]   Case 52/84, point 16.

Part Four

The development of concentration, competition and competitiveness

Introduction

316. This part of the Report first gives some idea of the changing economic background to the Commission's competition policy with the latest statistics on mergers, acquisitions and joint ventures in the Community.

The analysis of the data on such activity, and particularly mergers, in industry, the distributive trades, banking and insurance gathered from the specialist press indicate that there might be a greater role for competition policy in some, though not all, areas. Spectacularly large mergers in particular have shown the limitations of traditional competition policy and prompted reviews of previous practice in some Member States.

A rethinking of old ideas and the development of new strategies in competition policy are also the purpose of the Commission's programme of studies, whose results are reported in Section 2.

For example, this year's studies included work on shared dominance, which extends the traditional concept of dominance, and on predatory pricing. These could point towards better ways of exploiting the scope afforded by Article 86.

The changes in the distributive trades brought about by increasing concentration and new forms of retailing also demand new responses from competition policy. Studies on concentration in retailing and the resulting accumulation of buying power and on franchising in selected retail trades provide empirical material on which to base these new responses.

Finally, to break down the widespread aid mentality in the Community by a consistent enforcement of the aid rules it is necessary to develop stricter, economically based criteria. Two of this year's studies contribute to the development of such criteria.

§ 1 — Mergers, acquisitions and joint ventures involving Community-scale firms in 1985/86

317. This section analyses the incidence of mergers, acquisitions and joint ventures in the industrial sector, the distributive trades, banking and insurance, in an effort to identify changes in the structure of the Community economy, to explain the reasons for them and to grasp their implications for competition. The analysis is based on data gathered from the specialist press on operations involving at least one of the 1 000 largest firms in the Community, according to their financial data. This year, the results of the analysis of operations involving the top 1 000 firms were also compared with a wider sample covering all the operations reported in the press.

The operations were placed in three categories:

(i)   mergers (including both takeovers and voluntary amalgamations) and acquisitions of majority holdings in companies;

(ii)   acquisitions of minority holdings; and

(iii)   industrial and commercial joint ventures.

The reference period is June 1985 to May 1986.

General picture (Table 1)

318. The total number of operations recorded in the three categories was considerably up on the previous year, at 561 compared with 480 in 1984/85, indicating the density of the links between firms in Europe.

Mergers and acquisitions of majority holdings accounted for about half (53%) of the cases, acquisitions of minority holdings for about 29% and joint ventures for about 18%. Compared to last year there was a sharp rise in the number of acquisitions of minority holdings. As the acquisition of a minority stake in a company can be a prelude to a takeover this finding could signal a future wave of merger activity.

The majority of mergers and acquisitions of minority holdings involved firms from the same country, whereas firms from different countries were involved in more than half of joint ventures. Among operations of all three types involving firms from different countries those involving other Community firms predominated only in the case of mergers. Firms from non-EEC countries were as often as not involved in minority acquisitions or the other partner in joint ventures.

In general, a trend towards an internationalization of the links forged by European firms emerges. This development has a positive side: it may reflect the increased integration of the European market and indicate more widespread technology transfer both between Community countries and from non-EEC countries.

By sector, mergers were relatively more frequent in distribution and insurance than in industry and especially banking, where minority acquisitions and joint ventures also showed up prominently.

TABLE 1

National, Community and international mergers (a), acquisitions of minority holdings (b) and joint ventures (c) in the Community in 1985/86

Sector	National			Community			International			Total			Grand total
	(a)	(b)	(c)	(a)	(b)	(c)	(a)	(b)	(c)	(a)	(b)	(c)	
Industry	144	88	34	52	20	20	30	22	27	226	130	81	437
Distribution	27	7	3	6	1	1	0	0	1	33	8	5	46
Banking	12	10	10	4	3	6	9	8	0	25	21	16	62
Insurance	5	4	0	3	0	0	4	0	0	12	4	0	16
Total	188	109	47	65	24	27	43	30	28	296	163	102	561

Mergers, acquisitions and joint ventures in industry

Mergers (including acquisitions of majority holdings)
(Table 2)

319. The total number of industrial mergers was again up, but the increase (9%) was much less than in previous years.

All the increase was accounted for by Community and international operations. This was different from the picture found between 1982 and 1984, when purely national mergers had increased much faster than those involving other Community or non-Community firms.

TABLE 2

National, Community and international mergers
(including acquisitions of majority holdings)
in the Community in 1982/83, 1983/84, 1984/85 and 1985/86

Industry

Sector[1]	National				Community				International				Total			
	1982/1983	1983/1984	1984/1985	1985/1986	1982/1983	1983/1984	1984/1985	1985/1986	1982/1983	1983/1984	1984/1985	1985/1986	1982/1983	1983/1984	1984/1985	1985/1986
1. Food	1	7	20	25	2	2	1	7	0	2	1	2	3	11	22	34
2. Chem.	10	21	25	23	13	13	23	28	3	11	5	6	26	45	53	57
3. Elec.	5	9	13	10	3	2	5	0	7	2	4	3	15	13	22	13
4. Mech.	12	16	24	19	5	3	4	3	2	4	3	7	19	23	31	29
5. Meta.	7	9	13	14	1	0	3	1	2	0	1	2	10	9	17	17
6. Trans.	2	5	8	6	0	3	2	0	1	2	0	4	3	10	10	10
7. Pap.	7	11	10	18	1	1	5	4	1	1	3	5	9	13	18	27
8. Extra.	4	4	7	7	3	2	0	3	2	2	0	0	9	8	7	10
9. Text.	4	5	7	7	3	0	0	1	2	0	0	1	9	5	7	9
10. Cons.	6	13	14	12	4	3	1	2	0	1	0	0	10	17	15	14
11. Other	1	1	3	2	3	0	0	3	0	0	0	0	4	1	3	5
12. Comp.[2]	0	0	2	1	0	0	0	0	0	0	1	0	0	0	3	1
Total	59	101	146	144	38	29	44	52	20	25	18	30	117	155	208	226

[1] Key:
Food: Food and drink.
Chem.: Chemicals, fibres, glass, ceramic ware, rubber.
Elec.: Electrical and electronic engineering, office machinery.
Mech.: Mechanical and instrument engineering, machine tools.
Meta.: Production and preliminary processing of metals, metal goods.
Trans.: Vehicles and transport equipment.
Pap.: Wood, furniture and paper.
Extra.: Extractive industries.
Text.: Textiles, clothing, leather and footwear.
Cons.: Construction.
Other: Other manufacturing industry.
Comp.: Computers and data-processing equipment.
[2] In 1982/83 and 1983/84 included under mechanical engineering (Mech.).

This internationalization of merger activity was repeated in a large number of individual industries. It was especially marked in the chemicals industry, which as in previous years had the highest number of mergers overall, and in the food and drink industries which also saw a sharp rise in the overall number of mergers.

A similarly sharp increase in the number of mergers in the wood, furniture and paper industries was mainly due to national operations, however. Finally, the reduced prominence of the engineering industries (both electrical/electronic and mechanical) in merger activity should be noted.

The incidence of merger activity in each industry was also studied by relating the number of mergers to the number of firms in the sample for that industry. The chemical industry was also found to have the highest proportion of mergers — the number was more than half the number of firms in the sample — followed by the wood, furniture and paper industries, where there were also more than half as many mergers as firms in the sample. The lowest incidence was observed in vehicles and transport equipment and in textiles and clothing.

However, absolute figures for mergers do not automatically permit conclusions as to the trend of concentration in an industry.

The impact of mergers on concentration mainly depends on the size of the firms involved. Mergers between the largest groups will have different effects from those between firms in the smallest size category of the sample. In Table 3, the 1985/86 merger figures are broken down by the combined turnover of the firms involved.

This shows that the sharpest increase was in the largest size category, i.e. among firms with a combined turnover of over 1 000 million ECU, unlike last year when smaller-scale mergers increased most. The increase in large-scale mergers was most noticeable in the chemicals and food and drink industries. Nationally, the largest number of mergers in the 1 000 million ECU plus category was centred in Germany, with 33 cases. The UK, France and Italy had 24, 23 and 16 cases respectively. This represented an increase in such mergers in Germany and Italy, and a fall in the UK, which may reflect the already high level of concentration of UK industry.

A clearer idea of the part played by the very biggest firms is given by the fact that the firms classified on a turnover basis among the biggest in their industry (3.5 % of the total sample) were involved in about 10 % of mergers. Moreover, three-quarters of these cases involving the very largest firms were horizontal mergers, which increases the danger of a reduction in the intensity of competition.

TABLE 3

Breakdown of mergers (including acquisitions of majority holdings) by combined turnover of firms involved

Industry

Sector[1]	< 500 m ECU				500 to 1 000 m ECU				> 1 000 m ECU				Turnover n.a.			Total			
	1982/1983	1983/1984	1984/1985	1985/1986	1982/1983	1983/1984	1984/1985	1985/1986	1982/1983	1983/1984	1984/1985	1985/1986	1983/1984	1984/1985	1985/1986	1982/1983	1983/1984	1984/1985	1985/1986
1. Food	—	—	7	8	—	1	2	7	3	10	13	17	—	0	2	3	11	22	34
2. Chem.	4	7	15	13	2	2	11	6	20	28	23	33	8	4	5	26	45	53	57
3. Elec.	1	3	6	3	—	1	5	0	14	8	8	9	1	3	1	15	13	22	13
4. Mech.	2	6	6	5	5	5	5	4	12	9	17	17	3	3	3	19	23	31	29
5. Meta.	1	1	7	9	—	1	1	2	9	5	7	4	2	2	2	10	9	17	17
6. Trans.	—	2	4	3	1	2	1	4	2	5	2	3	1	3	0	3	10	10	10
7. Pap.	1	4	8	12	1	2	2	4	7	3	4	5	4	4	6	9	13	18	27
8. Extra.	—	3	0	1	—	—	0	1	9	4	7	7	1	0	1	9	8	7	10
9. Text.	4	1	3	5	—	1	2	1	5	2	0	2	1	2	1	9	5	7	9
10. Cons.	2	2	3	2	2	3	2	3	6	10	8	8	2	2	1	10	17	15	14
11. Other	1	—	3	1	2	—	0	1	1	1	0	2	—	0	1	4	1	3	5
12. Comp.[2]	—	—	0	1	—	—	0	0	—	—	3	0	—	0	0	—	—	3	1
Total	16	29	62	63	13	18	31	33	88	85	92	107	23	23	23	117	155	208	226

[1] For key, see Table 2.
[2] In 1982/83 and 1983/84 included under mechanical engineering (Mech.).

These results show the threat to competition posed by an increase in concentration resulting from mergers, especially those involving very large firms. They also point to the need for Community control of mergers.

Acquisitions of minority holdings (Table 4)

320. The number of acquisitions of minority holdings, at 130, was 94 % up on last year and the same sharp increase was observable in all three categories of operation, national, Community and international.

The sectoral distribution of such acquisitions differed markedly from previous years, when they had shown little sectoral variation and traditional industries were fairly strongly represented. In 1985/86 the increases showed strong sectoral variation, being concentrated in the chemical, metal and construction materials industries.

TABLE 4

National, Community and international acquisitions of minority holdings in the Community in 1982/83, 1983/84, 1984/85 and 1985/86

Industry

Sector[1]	National				Community				International				Total			
	1982/ 1983	1983/ 1984	1984/ 1985	1985/ 1986	1982/ 1983	1983/ 1984	1984/ 1985	1985/ 1986	1982/ 1983	1983/ 1984	1984/ 1985	1985/ 1986	1982/ 1983	1983/ 1984	1984/ 1985	1985/ 1986
1. Food	3	3	9	7	0	1	1	3	0	0	2	1	3	4	12	11
2. Chem.	0	4	4	16	3	1	4	5	1	2	0	6	4	7	8	27
3. Elec.	0	6	3	10	0	0	3	1	1	1	2	2	1	7	8	13
4. Mech.	2	6	13	13	0	2	0	3	1	1	4	1	3	9	17	17
5. Meta.	4	2	2	18	1	3	0	1	0	2	0	4	5	7	2	23
6. Trans.	1	3	2	4	0	0	1	3	1	0	2	3	2	3	5	10
7. Pap.	4	5	5	5	0	0	0	1	0	1	1	1	4	6	6	7
8. Extra.	2	2	3	4	0	1	0	0	0	1	0	0	2	4	3	4
9. Text.	3	3	2	1	1	0	1	0	0	1	0	1	4	4	3	2
10. Const.	1	3	0	7	2	0	0	2	0	0	0	1	3	3	0	10
11. Other	0	0	1	2	2	0	0	0	0	0	1	2	2	0	2	4
12. Comp.[2]	—	—	1	1	—	—	0	1	—	—	0	0	—	—	1	2
Total	20	37	45	88	9	8	10	20	4	9	12	22	33	54	67	130

[1] For key, see Table 2.
[2] In 1982/83 and 1983/84 included under mechanical engineering (Mech.).

Minority acquisitions thus appear to be becoming more important. From the point of view of the acquiring firm, minority stakes can serve various purposes, ranging from gaining effective control over the target company (a majority stake or a complete merger is not always essential for this purpose) to putting cooperation between the companies on a more stable basis.

The extremely fast growth in acquisitions of minority holdings, coinciding as it does with a slower increase than previously in the numbers of mergers and acquisitions of majority holdings, suggests that the two types of transactions are to some extent interchangeable.

Another explanation is to see acquisitions of minority stakes as the first step to a takeover. From a position as minority shareholder the acquiring company can complete the takeover with the benefit of more detailed information, and possibly at less cost. If this explanation proves the more correct, a new wave of takeovers could be in prospect.

Joint ventures (Table 5)

321. The number of joint ventures recorded was stable, at 81, in marked contrast to the increase in mergers and acquisitions.

As in the case of acquisitions of minority holdings, there were substantial changes in the sectoral distribution of cases. The number of joint ventures in the chemical industry almost doubled, putting this industry into the lead for joint ventures as well as for mergers and minority acquisitions. A sharp increase in joint ventures was also seen in electrical and electronic engineering and office equipment. There were again, however, few cases in the food and drink industries, in contrast to the large number of mergers there. In general, the picture was confirmed that joint ventures tend to be found in high-technology sectors rather than in traditional industries.

TABLE 5

Joint ventures in the Community in 1982/83, 1983/84, 1984/85 and 1985/86

Industry

Sector[1]	Total															
	National				Community				International				Total			
	1982/ 1983	1983/ 1984	1984/ 1985	1985/ 1986	1982/ 1983	1983/ 1984	1984/ 1985	1985/ 1986	1982/ 1983	1983/ 1984	1984/ 1985	1985/ 1986	1982/ 1983	1983/ 1984	1984/ 1985	1985/ 1986
1. Food	1	2	1	2	—	1	0	1	—	—	1	1	1	3	2	4
2. Chem.	4	4	5	7	1	2	0	7	3	5	7	9	8	11	12	23
3. Elec.	4	8	3	10	1	1	3	4	5	10	7	5	10	19	13	19
4. Mech.	3	5	8	5	1	1	3	1	1	3	5	4	5	9	16	10
5. Meta.	2	6	8	5	3	3	1	1	2	1	1	4	7	10	10	10
6. Trans.	2	3	3	0	—	1	1	3	—	3	2	1	2	7	6	4
7. Pap.	2	—	4	0	2	1	4	0	—	3	2	0	4	4	10	0
8. Extra.	2	2	3	2	—	—	1	0	1	—	1	0	3	2	5	2
9. Text.	—	—	0	0	—	—	1	0	1	—	0	0	1	—	1	0
10. Const.	1	2	2	3	—	1	1	2	1	—	1	0	2	3	4	5
11. Other	2	—	0	0	—	—	0	0	1	1	0	2	3	1	0	2
12. Comp.[1]	0	0	3	0	0	0	0	1	0	0	0	1	0	0	3	2
Total	23	32	40	34	8	11	15	20	15	26	27	27	46	69	82	81

[1] For key, see Table 2.
[2] In 1982/83 and 1983/84 included under mechanical engineering (Mech.).

An increasing proportion of joint ventures involved partners from other Community countries. This increase was matched by a fall in purely national ventures.

Main motives for the mergers and joint ventures (Table 6)

322. A comparison of the main motives cited for the mergers and joint ventures showed that both could be used as a vehicle for rationalization in industry; however, mergers were much more commonly undertaken for this reason. On the other hand, R&D was a more frequent motive for joint ventures, reflecting presumably both a desire to spread risks and to pool the partners' complementary technology or know-how.

Looking at the overall distribution of motives compared with last year, rationalization had declined somewhat in frequency while the offensive types of operation, such as expansion, diversification and R&D, had increased. This could reflect an improvement in the financial position of firms in some industries, which often seems to lead to a policy of external growth.

TABLE 6

**Main motives for mergers
and joint ventures in 1985/86**

Mergers (including acquisitions of majority holdings)		Joint ventures	
Expansion	29	Production	12
Diversification	20	R&D	10
Specialization	3	R&D and production	6
Strengthening of market position	18	Strengthening of market position	7
Complementarity	23	Complementarity	5
Rationalization	56	Rationalization	10
R&D	4	Expansion	7
Other	7	Other	5
Not specified	66	Not specified	19

Extension of analysis to wider sample

323. The above analysis of operations involving the 1 000 largest Community firms was repeated for a wider sample comprising all the operations reported in the European specialist press including those involving smaller firms. These numbered nearly 2 300 cases in 1985/86.

The wider sample showed some illuminating differences from the smaller one with respect to the types of operation, the nationality of the parties and the sectoral distribution of cases.

From the point of view of type of operation, mergers were commoner in the wider sample, accounting for 64% of the total as against only 53% when only those involving the largest firms were taken. Conversely, acquisitions of minority holdings represented only 20% of the wider sample against 29% in the smaller one. Joint ventures were also significantly less numerous in the larger sample (16% as against 18%). These differences between the two samples could indicate that cooperation figures more prominently in the strategies pursued by the largest firms, whereas slightly smaller firms tend to follow the merger or takeover route to external growth.

If this is correct, mergers — which may be a response to technical or economic requirements such as the realization of economies of scale — may well help to make the structure of industry more balanced and to intensify competition in it.

As far as the nationality of the parties is concerned, the preference for links with firms from the same country is even more marked in the wide sample. The proportion of national operations ranges from 75% in the case of acquisitions of minority holdings (as against 68% of the smaller sample), through 67% for mergers (64%) to 50% for joint ventures (42%). It is thus the largest Community firms that appear to be leading the internationalization of supply through link-ups with foreign firms.

Differences in the sectoral distribution of the operations in the two samples probably partly reflect the structure of the industries as well as the strategies of firms in them. However, in highly concentrated industries such as chemicals, vehicles and transport equipment, and electrical and electronic engineering and office equipment [1] the differences appear to be largely strategic.

(i) In the chemical industry the largest firms were more active in all types of operation than those in the immediately following size category. This could indicate that the largest firms are here pursuing a multiple strategy of both external growth and specialization and rationalization. It points to a need for close monitoring of the situation from the point of view of competition policy.

(ii) In the vehicles and transport equipment industries, however, the largest firms were most prominent only in the case of acquisitions of minority

---

[1] Thirteenth Competition Report, point 295.

holdings. Mergers and joint ventures were more frequently among the 'second-division' firms surrounding the major players. External growth and expansion by this group could reduce the disparities with the dominant oligopoly and help intensify competition.

(iii) In the electrical and electronic engineering and office equipment industries, the very large firms were mainly involved in joint ventures while the smaller ones were most active in mergers and acquisitions. This could indicate different strategies on the part of the two groups, the larger firms being intent on specialization and the smaller ones on external growth. As in the previous case, this trend could help to improve the balance of power in the industries.

(iv) Relatively concentrated industries such as wood, furniture and paper were much more strongly represented in the wider sample. In fact, contrary to the received wisdom, they appeared to have quite high incidences of such operations, especially mergers, which did not show up in the sample only covering the largest firms. Some of the operations probably involved takeovers of ailing firms.

The extension of the analysis to a wider sample was thus useful in several respects:

(i) The comparison of the two samples shed light on possible correlations between the size and strategy of firms and on changes in the structure of an industry.

(ii) The wider sample was more informative about what was happening in industries insufficiently represented in the top 1 000.

(iii) The analysis also showed that some of the activity could be good for competition in so far as it strengthened the position of firms barking at the heels of the 1 000 majors. On the other hand, the large number of operations involving smaller firms point to a need for competition policy not to confine its surveillance to the industries that are already highly concentrated.

Mergers, acquisitions and joint ventures in services

324. Like last year, the three service sectors studied were distribution, banking and insurance.

Mergers (including acquisitions of majority holdings)
(Table 7)

325.   The number of bank mergers increased sharply, whereas in distribution and insurance the number fell. A striking feature of the bank mergers was the number involving non-EEC banks. Like in industry, the barriers to the internationalization of links between financial services firms appear to have receded. In the distributive trades, however, mergers continued to be predominantly national affairs.

The mergers were also analysed by the size of the firms involved, using the criteria adopted in the proposed merger control regulation, namely:

(i)   in the distributive trades, the parties' combined turnover;

(ii)   in banking, one tenth of the parties' assets; and

(iii)   in insurance, the parties' combined premium income (Table 8).

This year almost half of the cases involved firms at the top end of the size scale. However, the proportion was smaller than last year, owing to falls in the numbers of large mergers in distribution and insurance. Whether this indicates that a saturation point has been reached in mergers between large firms in these industries remains to be seen.

Acquisitions of minority holdings
(Table 9)

326.   The number of acquisitions of minority holdings reported was about 15% down on 1984/85. This contrasted with the sharp increase in such operations in industry. The largest number of cases was found in banking. In distribution and insurance, however, minority acquisitions played a secondary role.

In terms of the nationality of the parties, the same trend was observable for minority acquisitions as for mergers: in both cases links with firms from outside the EEC were the only category to show an increase.

TABLE 7

National, Community and international mergers (including acquisitions of majority holdings) in the Community in 1984/85 and 1985/86

Services

Sector	National		Community		International		Total	
	'84/85	'85/86	'84/85	'85/86	'84/85	'85/86	'84/85	'85/86
Distribution	30	27	3	6	1	0	34	33
Banking	10	12	6	4	2	9	18	25
Insurance	7	5	7	3	1	4	15	12
Total	47	44	16	13	4	13	67	70

TABLE 8

Breakdown of mergers (including acquisitions of majority holdings) by combined turnover[1] of firms involved

Services

Sector	< 500 m ECU		500 to 1 000 m ECU		> 1 000 m ECU		*	Total	
	'84/85	'85/86	'84/85	'85/86	'84/85	'85/86		'84/85	'85/86
Distribution	11	10	2	8	21	10	5	34	33
Banking	3	5	5	2	10	18		18	25
Insurance	5	4	1	2	9	6		15	12
Total	19	19	8	12	40	34	5	67	70

*   Turnover n. a.
[1]   One tenth of assets in the case of banks and premium income in the case of insurance companies.

TABLE 9

National, Community and international acquisitions of minority holdings in the Community in 1984/85 and 1985/86

Services

Sector	National		Community		International		Total	
	'84/85	'85/86	'84/85	'85/86	'84/85	'85/86	'84/85	'85/86
Distribution	7	7	2	1	0	0	9	8
Banking	10	10	6	3	5	8	21	21
Insurance	5	4	3	0	0	0	8	4
Total	22	21	11	4	5	8	38	33

Joint ventures (Table 10)

327.   Joint ventures showed an increase of around 17% over 1984/85. All the increase was due to ventures with partners from other EEC countries.

TABLE 10

Joint ventures in the Community in 1984/85 and 1985/86

Services

Sector	National		Community		International		Total	
	'84/85	'85/86	'84/85	'85/86	'84/85	'85/86	'84/85	'85/86
Distribution	3	3	1	1	0	1	4	5
Banking	9	10	2	6	2	0	13	16
Insurance	1	0	0	0	0	0	1	—
Total	13	13	3	7	2	1	18	21

Results

328. The main findings emerging from the analysis of mergers, acquisitions and joint ventures involving the 1 000 largest Community firms reported in the specialist press in 1985/86 were as follows:

(i) The number of mergers continued to increase, but by less than in previous years. However, this general trend masked variations between different groups of firms. Very large industrial firms were involved in a higher proportion of mergers than last year. This suggests that the increase in concentration in the Community is continuing.

(ii) Acquisitions of minority holdings in industry increased sharply, with a shift in their sectoral distribution towards the high-technology sectors. Hence, the potential impact on competition of such acquisitions is tending to increase.

(iii) A general trend towards the internationalization of mergers and other links was visible. This may be a positive sign, indicating that national markets are becoming more open. It may also be due to the saturation of possibilities on national markets resulting from the high levels of concentration in some Member States.

(iv) The relative importance of the motives for mergers and other links changed. Rationalization was less often cited as a motive, probably reflecting the more buoyant economic climate in some industries.

(v) The operations in the banking sector indicated a greater degree of internationalization of links in this sector than in insurance. In the latter sector, the barriers to trade between Member States appear to be as great as ever. In the distribution sector, the majority of cases were mergers with other firms in the same country.

§ 2 — The programme of studies and its results

Objectives of the 1986 programme of studies

329.   In 1986 the Commission maintained the approach of its programme of economic studies, seeking in the main to analyse general problems of competition policy without, however, ignoring certain aspects of the evolution of concentration in particular industries.

The studies were commissioned from universities and independent consultants, who are responsible for the data and views set out therein. They are published as working papers, of which copies are available.

The studies fell within three broad subject areas: the first covers the application of the competition rules to enterprises in general; the second relates more specifically to the distributive trades, and the third to government assistance to enterprises.

Studies concerning the application of the competition rules to enterprises

330.   Many of the Community's markets are characterized by a small number of large producers. The Commission considered it appropriate to undertake three studies having a bearing on related aspects of importance in this context:

(a) the concept of shared dominance and its relevance to competition policy;

(b) predatory pricing practices in the Community; and

(c) the definition of the relevant market in Community competition policy.

(a)   The concept of shared dominance and its relevance to competition policy

The concept of shared dominance

331.   The two essential features of shared dominance are:

(i)   the fact that a small number of enterprises account for most of the turnover in the market in question without any single enterprise having a dominant position;

(ii)   the high degree of interdependence among the decisions of the enterprises.

One of the aims of competition policy is to ensure that certain types of behaviour by the enterprises concerned do not preclude a sufficient level of competition in such markets. In the case of a tight oligopoly, the reduction in the intensity of competition does not necessarily lead to the appearance of tacit collusion. Tacit collusion may, however, arise from the fact that members of the oligopoly become aware of their interdependence and of the probably unfavourable consequences of adopting a competitive attitude.

Factors explaining the emergence of stable collusion

332.   The authors of the study found that there is an increased probability of collusion between oligopolists where:

(i)   Price elasticity of demand is weak, which increases the overall benefits to be derived from the collusion and lessens the incentive for each enterprise to adopt a competitive attitude.

(ii)   The environment is relatively stable. A surge in demand, or rapid technological progress encourages non-collusive behaviour.

(iii)   The enterprises are structured in such a way that their investments cannot be used for the production of other goods or services. Each oligopolist is thus more vulnerable to retaliatory action in response to attempts to break up any collusion over prices. More generally, barriers to entry to or exit from the market, whether they be of an economic nature (large economies of scale favouring established producers) or whether they be due to government policy (e.g. import restrictions), limit the effect of potential competition.

The existence of surplus production capacity may have more complex effects. On the one hand, this situation may render the advantages derived by all producers from the collusion more decisive. On the other hand, there is a stronger incentive for the individual producer to cease colluding and try to increase his share of the market.

Mergers may help bring about collusion: horizontal mergers because they reduce the number of competitors, and vertical or conglomerate mergers because they block the entry of new companies.

Implications for competition policy

333.   Abuse of shared dominant positions may have many unfavourable consequences for the economy as a whole, including the final consumer (e.g. higher prices, a slowdown of technological progress, imposition of unfair terms of trade).

Although Article 86 may be applied in order to punish such conduct, it should be the aim of competition policy to prevent situations arising which form a hotbed for tacit collusive behaviour. This is one of the objectives of the proposal for the prior control of mergers at Community level.

(b) Predatory pricing practices

Predatory pricing and the reasons underlying it

334.   Predatory pricing involves, for a producer, fixing artificially low prices so that a competitor is either eliminated or disciplined. According to some economists, the strategy of predatory pricing is irrational from the point of view of the one who employs it, the cost being inevitably higher for the predator than for the prey. It would appear, therefore, that predatory pricing is rare.

One of the aims of the study was to determine under what circumstances a predatory pricing strategy may be rational from the aggressor's point of view:

(i)   it must be a multiproduct firm which can make up, in one or more markets, for the losses incurred in the market in which the aggression took place. The aggressor reduces his prices when a competitor tries to enter one of these markets;

(ii)   where a predatory price is applied, the present value of the entrant's future profits is smaller than its fixed sunk entry costs so that it cannot survive in the long run;

(iii) the victim is not sure that the price cut is predatory; it may come to the conclusion that there is no room for it in the market under competitive conditions.

Empirical evidence

335.   There is little available information on the extent to which predatory pricing is practised. Statistics on private anti-trust litigation in the United States between 1973 and 1983 indicate that 10% of cases include a complaint alleging predatory pricing practices. In 1983, this figure fell to 5%. Alleged predation is not, however, proved predation.

Implications for competition policy

336.   From the point of view of competition policy, the lowering of price levels as a result of predatory behaviour is not in itself cause for concern. The ensuing consequences, namely the elimination of, albeit competitive, competitors or the restriction of potential competition, may, however, have serious side-effects, in particular a renewed rise in prices.

One policy attitude advocated by some economists is to do nothing, since punishing predatory pricing may accidentally condemn and discourage competition.

A second attitude is to apply a *per se* rule, according to which the limit of predatory pricing is set, for example, at the marginal cost level, any prices above this being presumed legitimate. Irrespective of the difficulty of determining with certainty the level of costs, this rule is not above criticism on theoretical grounds. Thus, for example, at certain times of crisis, firms may set their prices below marginal costs, without necessarily pursuing a short-run predatory policy.

Predatory pricing practices must be regarded as part of an abusive global strategy aimed at eliminating other producers in an anti-competitive manner, or at restricting their freedom of action. A firm's strategy has many dimensions (products, marketing, investments) and price is but one element among others.

Consequently, a policy of deterring predatory pricing which does not take account of the context might cause certain firms to have recourse to different methods in order to achieve the same goals. In the ECS/AKZO decision,[1] the Commission applied this global approach to a strategy which sought to force the exit of a competitor.

(c) Definition of the relevant market in Community competition policy

Applications of the relevant market concept

337.   Although the concept of relevant market may also be used to assess the effects of agreements between enterprises or of State aids, the importance of the concept is mainly apparent in the case of the application of Article 86.

---

[1]   See Fifteenth Competition Report, point 82.

Need to resort to the relevant market concept

338. The application of Article 86 to cases of abuse of a dominant position presupposes that such a position can first be identified. In some cases, different approaches may be followed, for example by directly proving unrestrained conduct on the part of the dominant business. The case-law of the Court of Justice has, however, confirmed the fundamental importance of the relevant market concept. The discussion about the need to resort to this concept is linked, moreover, to the more general question of the importance that should be atached to analysis of the structure of markets when dealing with competition matters.

Analytical framework for definition
of the relevant market

339. One of the aims of the study was to define an analytical framework which makes it possible to take into account systematically all the variables and factors which might affect the relevant market, as regards both the product aspect (notably the different variables affecting the substitutability of other goods and services, potential competition) and the geographical dimension (for example, change in prices and market shares in different geographical areas, barriers to the transfer of supply and demand between areas, barriers to entry). This framework was then applied to various cases, including certain decisions of the Commission and the Court of Justice.

Limits of the relevant market concept

340. When a relevant market is referred to, it is primarily the dominance linked to horizontal expansion that is highlighted. A company which relies mainly on vertical integration or diversification strategies will not necessarily experience an increase in its horizontally defined market shares.

When considering dominant positions of a vertical or conglomerate nature, a somewhat artificial definition of relevant market is sometimes required. Recourse to the concept of obligatory trading partner, which concerns the relationship of dependence which may exist between two economic operators owing to their commercial dealings, may prove to be useful.

The Commission is studying the possibility of employing this concept as a supplementary tool of cases of abuse of dominant positions.

Studies on distribution

341. The Commission has for a long time been concerned about the distribution aspect of competition policy owing, in particular, to the development of certain methods of distribution and the evolution of concentration in this sector. The Commission has carried out two studies, one on franchising in certain branches of trade in the Community and the other on concentration in the distribution of consumer goods in the Community and its impact on buying power.

(a) Franchising in certain branches of Community trade

Objectives of franchising

342. The franchisor's aim is primarily better penetration of the market with the help of an organization which makes it possible to spread and export a brand image and increase the public's awareness of the goods or service offered for sale. From the point of view of the franchisee, the principal advantage of franchising is that it offers more chance of success and of making a profit than does a venture undertaken in isolation or within the framework of other forms of cooperation. These results can be achieved thanks to marketing and management techniques which are not normally available to small and medium-sized businesses.

Development of franchising in the Community

343. In 1983, there were approximately 1 600 franchise systems and 83 500 franchisees in the Community. This gives some idea of the importance of this method of distribution. Franchising is most widespread in France (around 500 franchisors and 25 000 franchisees). French franchise networks are also the most extensive in the Community. Franchising has developed more slowly in Germany (260 franchisors and 28 000 franchisees) and in the United Kingdom (283 franchisors and 12 000 franchisees).

Franchise systems originating in non-member countries and operating in the Community are primarily American, although some Swedish and Swiss franchisors have also established themselves in several Member States.

Implications for competition policy

344. The study's findings highlight the nature of franchising from the economic point of view and in particular its international repercussions. The special features of this method of distribution have induced the Commission to adopt a specific approach to this phenomenon, involving in particular the drawing up of a block exemption regulation (see point 31 of this Report).

(b) Evolution of concentration in the distribution of consumer goods in the EEC and its impact on buying power

Structural evolution of trade in consumer goods

345. As a result of the development of their networks and their advanced marketing techniques, the large distribution firms have increased their market share at the expense of small family businesses and cooperatives, Cooperation between small distribution firms has not as a rule played a decisive role in the structural evolution of trade in consumer goods.

This evolution cannot be analysed in isolation from the evolution of concentration in the production of consumer goods. The structure of this industry has changed in that the market shares of the industry leaders have increased. This development has led to numerous takeovers (see Section I of Part Four of this Report), in the foodstuffs sector, for example, particularly in the United Kingdom and France.

Purchasing policy in consumer goods trade

346. The authors noted a change in purchasing policies, more and more weight being given to the favourable terms that can be obtained through bulk buying. The result has been an increase in the number of purchasing associations. According to the authors, this increased buying power of distributors has, in general, not been abused.

Outward signs of buying power

347. Trading conditions between the food industry and distribution firms have become more complex and less transparent, which makes it more difficult to assess the impact of distributors' buying power. The authors noted the increased size of quantity discounts and of turnover-related rebates and the defraying by producers of advertising costs for the promotion of their products.

Implications for competition policy

348.   From the point of view of competition policy, the main aim is to ensure that the savings due to the distributors' buying power are passed on to the consumer through the maintenance of a sufficient level of effective competition at the level of distribution.

As assessment of the buying power of distribution firms having a large turnover cannot be based on their market share alone but must take account of the competitive situation and the structure of supply.

Since it is not possible to establish exhaustive criteria for an appraisal of abusive practices linked to buying power, a case-by-case evaluation is essential. The vertical dimension of instances of buying power means that the obligatory trading partner concept (see point 1(c) above) is a useful element with which to supplement an analysis based on the relevant market.

Studies relating to government support for enterprises

349.   With a view to improving the economic bases of its methods of monitoring certain State aids, the Commission has considered it appropriate to study more closely the calculation of the aid element both of State acquisitions of company capital and of soft loans.

(a) The amount of aid involved in State acquisitions of company capital

350.   The study starts from the premise that, although the Commission has clearly established [1] — with the support of the Court of Justice [2] — that State acquisitions of capital may under certain conditions constitute aid, major methodological obstacles arise when it comes to measuring the intensity of the aid. However, these obstacles must be overcome if one is to be able to compare the aid element of a State acquisition with other measurable State aids such as grants or soft loans.

The authors of the study consider that the aid element of a State acquisition is the difference between the value of the shares acquired and the amount paid by the State. The problem then arises of how best to assess the value of the

---

[1]   Cf. Bull. EC 9-1984, point 2.1.30.
[2]   Cf. OJ L 223, 9.8.1986.

shares. Referring to the principal methods proposed by financial theory, the authors of the report opt for use of the market value of the shares, where they are quoted on a stock exchange, or, failing that, their intrinsic value. It is proposed that the latter be calculated — over a period of between four and seven years — as the sum of the present value of future dividends and the present value of projected net assets per share. The authors consider that such a method — which is tested on some 10 concrete examples of State acquisitions in the United Kingdom and France — is internally consistent, theoretically acceptable and capable of application in practice.

The main objection to this procedure is that, like any method involving a share valuation technique, it means having to forecast company performance, which is particularly difficult in the case of troubled companies which the State hopes to see placed on a sound financial footing at the end of its aid programme.

The possibility of using the proposed approach in practice is therefore being examined by the Commission's departments, which have already entered upon a similar study of its application in other Member States of the Community (Federal Republic of Germany and Italy).

(b) Calculation of the aid element corresponding to the grant of soft loans

351.   The Commission's established method of calculating the aid element of soft loans is to measure the difference between the rate of interest applied and a reference rate, which is an estimate of the market rate. [1]

A large part of the study is devoted to analysing the characteristics of these national rates from the point of view of their economic significance, their evolution during the period 1979-85 and the extent to which they represent the true cost of access to credit for firms. The study's authors point out that, except in the case of the Netherlands, Denmark and Luxembourg, the reference rates correspond to the rates defined by national institutions of a public character and are therefore not necessarily representative of market rates. An alternative possibility envisaged by the study's authors would be to define each national

---

[1]   Since 1979, these reference rates have been defined within the framework of the principles of coordination of regional aid systems (OJ C 31, 3.2.1979).

reference rate using econometric methods; these estimated reference rates would be theoretical rates representing the economic conditions determining or reflecting the actual cost of credit in the various Member States of the Community.

This research may be put to good use when the Commission, in conjunction with the Member States, reviews the principles of coordination of regional aid systems.

Annex

Resolution on the Fifteenth Report of the Commission of the European Communities on Competition Policy

Opinion on the Fifteenth Report on Competition Policy of the Commission of the European Communities

  I — Competition policy towards enterprises — List of Decisions, other measures and Rulings
    1. Pursuant to Articles 85 and 86 of the EEC Treaty
    2. Administrative letters sent following publication of a notice pursuant to Article 19(3) of Regulation No 17
    3. Decisions concerning Articles 65 and 66 of the ECSC Treaty
    4. Rulings of the Court of Justice

 II — Competition policy and government assistance to enterprises
    1. Final negative Decisions adopted by the Commission following the Article 93(2) EEC procedure
    2. Judgments and orders delivered by the Court of Justice
    3. Aid cases in which the Commission raised no objection
    4. Aid cases in which the Commission decided to open the Article 93(2) EEC procedure
    5. Aid cases in which the Commission decided to close the Article 93(2) EEC procedure

III — Competition policy and government assistance in the agricultural sector
    1. Aid cases in which the Commission raised no objection
    2. Aid cases in which the Commission adopted negative opinions under Article 93(2), first sentence
    3. Aid cases in which the procedure provided for in Article 93(2) of the EEC Treaty was initiated
    4. Aid cases in which the procedure provided for in Article 93(2) of the EEC Treaty was closed
    5. Final Commission Decisions taken following procedures under Article 93(2) of the EEC Treaty
    6. Rulings of the Court of Justice
    7. Council Decisions under Article 93(2) of the EEC Treaty

IV — List of studies published in 1986 and to be published

RESOLUTION
on the Fifteenth Report of the Commission of the European Communities on Competition Policy

The European Parliament,

A. having regard to the Fifteenth Report of the Commission of the European Communities on Competition Policy (Doc. C2-44/86),

B. having regard to the motion for a resolution by Mr Kuijpers and others on a Community policy regarding competition rules for mass media (Doc. B2-1245/85),

C. having regard to its previous resolutions on competition policy,

D. having regard to the report of the Committee on Economic and Monetary Affairs and Industrial Policy and the Opinion of the Committee on Legal Affairs and Citizens' Rights (Doc. A2-136/86);

General conclusions

1. Emphasizes the continuing vital role of Community competition policy in establishing fair competition between individual undertakings, between the public and private sectors, and between the different countries of the Community. Also believes that this constitutes the best way of protecting the consumer, of creating long-term employment, and of ensuring a stronger European economy;

2. Considers that vigorous application of the Community rules of competition, as described in the Commission's Annual Report, is essential in achieving these objectives;

3. Considers that the rigorous application of Community rules on competition enjoys credibility with the peoples of the Community and is effective in achieving its goals only when there is sufficient information and control with respect to the monopoly situations on the markets, otherwise it is likely to have the opposite effect;

4. Stresses that the most significant distortions of competition are caused by the fact that:

(i)   the Community's internal market is not complete,

(ii) internal competition is distorted by national subsidies,

(iii) world trade is distorted by protectionism, and

(iv) there are government monopolies in public procurement;

5. Considers that the following are further problems for Community competition policy that emerge from the Fifteenth Report:

(i)   the continuing deadlock as regards the application of the Community rules of competition in the field of air transport,

(ii) the need to draw up new Community guidelines in the fields of know-how, franchising and joint venture agreements,

(iii) the disgraceful lack of progress at Council level on the Commission's amalgamation and merger control proposals,

(iv) the regrettable procrastination by the Commission as regards submission of a proposal for a ninth directive on company law,

(v) the special problems for competition policy posed by research and development agreements and by State aids to research and development,

(vi) the expanding role of State monopolies and public authorities and the need for cooperation with industry in the field of telecommunications in an era of rapid development of telecommunications technology, and of associated products and services,

(vii) the need to encourage more expansive application of Community competition law by national courts, possibly by means of a Directive harmonizing practices in the Member States as regards injunctions, damages and other matters,

(viii) the need to draw up the criteria for rapid implementation of a two-tier system of judicial review, with the establishment of a specialized Community competition law tribunal,

(ix) the need greatly to improve the Commission's handling of confidential documents, as evidenced in the Stanley Adams and AKZO cases,

(x) the fact that it is impossible for the Commission to exercise effective supervision of the repayment of State aid incompatible with the common market,

(xi) rivalry among the Member States as regards tax relief for multinational undertakings, and the formulation of a Community fiscal policy to combat fraud;

6. Considers that if fair competition is to be ensured within the Community it will be necessary not only to apply the rules of competition, but also to achieve progress at Community level in many other areas, such as:

(i) gradual and balanced liberalization of the capital market,

(ii) reinforcement of the EMS and associated financial measures,

(iii) coherent Community strategies for specific industrial sectors, especially for reconversion of traditional industries, and the promotion of greater European competitiveness in the new technologies,

(iv) achievement of a common transport policy,

(v) reduction of regional and social disequilibria within the Community through strengthened Community regional and social policies and other measures,

(vi) application of strict standards in the field of environment and consumer protection,

(vii) a strengthened common commercial policy,

(viii) Community initiatives to reduce international protectionist practices and other international distortions of competition;

7. Emphasizes, therefore, that progress on completing the internal market and a vigorous Community competition policy must go hand in hand;

8. Observes in particular that fiscal approximation is not only vital in order to eliminate fiscal frontiers, but also in order to remove substantial distortions of competition and calls upon the Commission to give greater weight to this consideration in the future;

9. Considers that the application of Community competition policy and of these other Community policy objectives must be as carefully coordinated as possible;

10. Further considers that the actions of the Community and of the individual Member States must also be coordinated in order to render more effective the application of competition policy at Community level;

11. Emphasizes, as regards the adequacy of application of Community competition policy, the following points:

(i)   the need to ensure adequate levels of staffing for the Commission's Directorate-General for Competition,

(ii)   the need for the Commission to receive adequate information about possible competition policy abuses, whether from the Member States about their often not very transparent national aids, or from other sources,

(iii) the need to ensure rapid Commission procedures,

(iv)   the need to ensure fair Commission procedures,

(v)   the need to ensure the maximum degree of legal certainty,

(vi)   the need to reduce the workload of the European Court of Justice on competition policy matters of detail;

12.   Insists, as regards the methods of Parliamentary 'oversight' of Community competition policy:

(i)   that the Parliament has a formal role in the elaboration of block exemption regulations, as called for in paragraph 39 of its resolution on the Fourteenth Report and paragraph 63 of its resolution on the Thirteenth Report, and that, at the least, any forthcoming draft block exemption should be automatically submitted to the Parliament for its comments subject to a previously determined and reasonable time limit in order not to hold up the Commission,

(ii)   that future Annual Reports be always submitted before the end of April of each year, in order to give adequate time for in-depth parliamentary scrutiny,

(iii) that a special report be drawn up on Commission competition policy procedures, and also a hearing be held as called for in paragraph 50 of its aforementioned resolution on the Fourteenth Report.

(iv)   that procedures be established to monitor developments in competition policy on a periodic basis, backed by adequate research,

(v)   that its annual rapporteur on competition policy matters be entrusted with ensuring the necessary follow-up to its resolution for the rest of the year, aided, where appropriate, by a task force of interested members of the committee and reporting periodically on this matter to the Committee on Economic and Monetary Affairs and Industrial Policy;

Scope of competition policy

13.   Has noted the European Court of Justice's recent decision in the 'Nouvelles Frontières' case that Articles 85 and 86 of the Treaty are applicable to air transport in the absence of a Community air transport policy, but regrets that the Council has not yet proved able to formulate a sound policy; repeats its call for the Commission to draw up more realistic proposals in this connection;

14.   Reiterates that there must be gradual and balanced liberalization without the possible detrimental effects of ill-conceived deregulation;

15.   Calls, therefore, for agreement on the necessary measures of liberalization as regards inter-airline capacity, tariff fixing and revenue sharing that would permit agreements conforming to these minimum conditions to be exempted from application of the competition laws; supports the Commission's proposals in this regard (COM(86) 338/fin.) that would also protect public service obligations;

16.   Regards improvement of interregional air transport as highly important;

17.   Considers, however, that should the Council fail to reach an agreement before the end of the year, the Commission should then take direct action against Member States for violation of the competition laws, on the lines of the initiative recently announced by the Commission;

18.   Believes, moreover, that the Commission should be given the full powers necessary to conduct investigations in the air transport sector, which is currently excluded by Council Regulation 141/62; calls upon the Council to take a decision at long last on the amendments to the regulation which have been submitted by the Commission to this effect;

19. Notes that five years have gone by since the Commission first put forward its proposals for applying the rules of competition to maritime transport, and considers it essential that progress be rapidly made;

20. Calls for a fuller summary than that provided by the Commission as to the state of competition in the banking and insurance sectors, which pose particular problems for the application of competition policy because of their special regulatory regimes;

21. Welcomes the Commission's decisions providing for the first formal applications of the competition rules to commodity future markets;

Competition policy and private firms

22. Notes that a considerable number of block exemptions have been adopted by the Commission in recent years. Considers that examination of whether they are proving to be successful and whether they need to be revised, should constitute an important element of future competition resolutions from the Parliament;

23. Recalls that paragraph 19 of its resolution of 10 June 1983 on the block exemptions for exclusive distribution and purchasing agreements called for the Commission to produce a document itemizing the distortions caused to competition in the brewery sector, but that the Commission has not yet met this request; calls for the Commission, in order to ensure successful implementation of Title II of the block exemption on exclusive purchasing agreements, to draw up a full study of the state of competition in the beer sector, including consideration of the internal market aspects;

24. Notes that the Commission's economic research on R&D agreements within the Community has shown that the average turnover of the participants is extremely high, and that there is a very real danger of such agreements being used for anti-competitive purposes; calls, therefore, for vigilance by the Commission in applying the block exemption to such research and development agreements, and for it to ensure that smaller firms are taking fuller advantage of the exemption;

25. Further notes that the Court of Justice in its decision in the maize seeds case (258/78) appears to have taken a more sympathetic view towards licence restrictions than did the Commission in its block exemption on patent licences, and requests more information as to how this block exemption is working in practice;

26. Calls for the forthcoming Commission criteria for judging the competition implications of know-how agreements to be clearly spelled out in next year's Annual Report;

27. Notes that the Court has recently taken an important decision in the Pronuptia case (161/84) as regards distribution franchises; calls for the Commission to report back to the Parliament as soon as possible on how it is planning to deal with this fast-growing phenomenon of franchising agreements, and their as yet uncertain implications for competition policy;

28. Calls for the Commission's working document on a suggested policy framework for joint ventures to be transmitted to the Parliament, for it to give its views on the proposed criteria for judging whether the effects of such joint ventures influence competition;

29. Considers that the Commission should end the 13 year-old deadlock in Council on its proposals on amalgamation and merger controls by withdrawing them forthwith, in order that a fresh start can be made on filling this important gap in the Community's competition policy;

30. Welcomes the Commission's continued inclusion in its Annual Reports of a special chapter on the effects of EEC competition policy on small and medium-sized enterprises, and calls for further vigorous action to ensure that they are made fully aware of their rights and obligations under Community competition law;

31. Calls for the Commission to inform the Parliament of the latest situation as regards the status of the suspended IBM case, as requested in paragraph 44 of last year's resolution;

32. Considers that there are considerable potential dangers to competition in the fast-growing and increasingly complex area of the media, which is increasingly supranational in scope, and where interlocking ownership of newspapers, magazines, television stations and cable and satellite interests is becoming increasingly frequent;

calls, therefore, for a special section in next year's Annual Report to be dedicated to the problems of competition and the media, focusing not just on the situation within individual sub-sectors but also on the increasing interrelationships between them;

welcomes the Commission's decision to conduct a study of this area as requested by Parliament (paragraph 15 of its resolution of 10 October 1985 on the economic aspects of the common market for broadcasting);

calls finally on the Commission to formulate a policy framework regarding competition rules for the mass media;

33. Requests the Commission to examine carefully the potential problems for competition posed by the increasing concentration in the retailing sector as well as in other service sectors not traditionally analysed, such as tourism, industrial consulting on advertising, on taxation, on legal and social affairs and on investment, and the liberal professions;

34. Notes the important implications for competition policy of copyright issues, and expresses its surprise that controversial copyright provisions have been included in the Commission's recent proposal for a Directive on broadcasting (COM(86) 146/fin.) before the Commission has presented its long-awaited Green Paper on copyright questions;

35. Notes that the Commission's proposals for uniform rules governing commercial agents have been consistently deferred and calls therefore upon the Commission to make exceptional efforts to submit these proposals;

Competition policy and the State

36. Welcomes the Commission's decision to attempt a comprehensive survey of State aids in the Community, including concealed subsidies to loss-making nationalized industries sometimes disguised as increases in capital, and considers that the resulting White Paper will give a great opportunity to examine the strengths and weaknesses of current Community State aids policy;

37. Believes that the most intractable problem that the Commission will encounter is that of hidden State aids, and trusts that the survey will help to improve Community information-gathering systems concerning such aids; calls for this to focus on shipbuilding and on ports;

38. Notes that the number of aids notified to the Commission has fallen off sharply in 1985 and considers that this trend should be carefully monitored to see to what extent it is due to real decreases in State aids and to what extent to less transparent aids;

39. Welcomes the Commission's new procedures as regards State aids, and, in particular, its special notification procedure for significant cases of multiple aid awards under different schemes, and also the increased information that it intends to provide about the details of Article 93(2) procedures;

40. Suggests, in this latter context, that the Commission should consider publishing a series of special guides to Commission practice on State aids to particular sectors, including not just the latest version of any Commission framework for State aids to that sector, but also all of its decisions affecting the sector;

41.   Notes that the Commission has recently published a new Community framework on State aids for research and development, and that such aids now constitute one of the largest forms of intervention by government in support of industry. Believes that the criteria contained in the Commission's new guidelines will need to be applied most rigorously and carefully reviewed in a few years' time to see how they are working out in practice, and considers, moreover, that follow-up studies should be made to examine the extent to which the results of authorized R&D aid programmes meet their alleged objectives;

42.   Considers, as regards regional aids, that they need to be better concentrated than at present on peripheral and other priority areas of the Community and to be better coordinated at Community level to prevent, for example, major discrepancies of treatment between adjacent border areas in neighbouring countries, genuine improvements in communications with peripheral regions being necessary if fair competition is ever to become reality;

43.   Supports the inclusion of State aids to agriculture and to fisheries in the Annual Report, and believes, in spite of these sectors' distinctive features, that there are strong arguments for not treating them as completely separate areas of Community activity;

44.   Regrets the continuing breach of competition policy principles in the case of the preferential tariff charged to glasshouse growers for natural gas in the Netherlands, awaits the decision of the European Court of Justice in this matter, but considers that extremely tough measures need to be taken in the event of repeated abuses of the Community laws of competition;

45.   Takes the view that the Commission does not enjoy sufficient supervisory powers to take a tough line and insist on the repayment of unlawful aid; points out that this situation benefits Member States which engage in all sort of machinations to conceal State aid from the Commission and is therefore causing the incidence of such hidden State aid to rise;

46.   Welcomes the Commission's important decision to extend the application of its Directive (80/723/EEC) on the transparency of financial relations between Member States and their public undertakings to include the previously excluded sectors of public water authorities, energy, posts and telecommunications, transport and credit. Calls for the Commission to take vigorous action to maintain its rights to examine the justification of financial transfers from Member States to these enterprises as well;

47.   Recalls its previous request (in paragraphs 21 and 22 of its resolution of 29 March 1984 on telecommunications) concerning the liberalization of State monopolies in the field of telecommunications, and emphasizes the need for substantial progress in this field;

welcomes, therefore the actions taken by the Commission over the last year to prevent unjustified extensions of the PTT's monopolies in such products as cordless telephones and modems, and by the Court of Justice, in the British Telecommunications (BT) Case, that the latter held no monopoly over the provision of ancillary services such as the retransmission of messages on behalf of third parties;

calls for further vigorous action by the Commission in this sector;

48.   Welcomes the fact that in both the BT case and in the Telemarketing case the Court of Justice has made a clear distinction between a public undertaking's carrying out of its official duties and its business activities, in which latter case the competition rules should fully apply and there should be equal treatment of the public and private sectors;

49.   Requests the Commission to examine to what extent its principles of competition policy and its specific recommendations on public procurement could be applied to defence procurement;

Links between Community and Member States' competition policies

50.   Welcomes the fact that the Commission has devoted a special section of this year's report to encouraging more extensive application of Community competition law by national courts, though this must not replace policy-making through political decision-making procedures;

51. Points out the central need for uniform application of Community law in the Member States, but that there are currently substantial differences between the Member States on such matters as availability of injunctions and awards of damages, and that some Member States have no tradition of competition policy enforcement at all, e.g. the recently adopted provisions on driving and rest times in the transport sector, in which widely divergent application of common rules is distorting competition;

52. Calls upon the Commission to carry out a thorough study of these differences, and to report back next year on the advisability of a Community Directive harmonizing national practices in this sphere;

53. Considers that the Commission should pay special attention to the adjustment process for Spain and Portugal with regard to the application of competition rules in accordance with the provisions of the respective treaties of accession, maintaining an open and responsible attitude to the adjustment problems of the new Member States;

Competition policy procedures

54. Welcomes the progress outlined in the Fifteenth Report towards ensuring speedier resolution of cases, and the Commission's statement that a record number of files were closed in 1985, though believing that the procedures must be speeded up further, suggests, however, that all future Annual Reports include a precise breakdown of the cases that are still open, in terms of the categories in which they fall, so that the main problem areas can then be examined by the Parliament;

55. Calls on the Commission to improve demonstrably the transparency of procedures and results of its aids monitoring;

56. Notes that a new 'opposition procedure' has been introduced in recent block exemptions, providing for accelerated individual exemptions for certain agreements which do not meet all the terms of the block exemption. Calls upon the Commission to report on whether this 'opposition procedure' is being frequently used, and whether it is proving to be effective;

57. Recalls its past requests for the establishment of a new two-tier system of judicial review with a special competition law tribunal of first instance and with appeals on matters of fundamental principle to the Court of Justice itself. Notes that this request has been given additional force by the decisions of the Member States at the intergovernmental conference on 16-17 December 1985, that a new article be added to the Treaty providing for this possibility;

calls upon the Commission to report back in next years' Annual Report on what steps have been taken at Community level to implement this idea, and on the criteria to be established for permitting final appeals to the European Court of Justice;

58. Expresses its concern about the serious shortcomings that have emerged over the last year as regards the treatment of confidential information by the Commission, as a result of the decisions by the Court of Justice in the Adams and AKZO procedural cases;

considers that the Commission will have to take firmer action to improve its procedures in this regard, if its reputation is not to suffer;

The Commission's economic research

59. Welcomes the Commission's change in emphasis in its economic research towards making the research more applicable in practice, as called for in several of Parliament's previous resolutions;

60. Considers, however, that for the change to be a really meaningful one, the Commission's economic research section on competition policy matters should be reinforced, the subjects chosen for research should,

where possible, be mutually agreed between researchers and DG IV 'practitioners', and DG IV's decisions should more readily acknowledge economic research conclusions;

61. Calls, as it has in the past, for the Commission to provide a short summary of the conclusions of its external studies which are listed at the back of each Annual Report;

*

*   *

62. Instructs its President to forward this resolution and the report of its committee to the Council, the Commission, the parliaments of the Member States, the national anti-trust authorities and the Cartel and Monopolies Commission.

OPINION

on the Fifteenth Report on Competition Policy of the Commission of the European Communities

(86/C 333/01)

On 20 June 1986 the Commission of the European Communities decided to consult the Economic and Social Committee on the above-mentioned report.

The Section for Industry, Commerce, Crafts and Services, which was responsible for preparing the Committee's work on the subject, adopted its opinion on 3 September 1986.

At its 240th plenary session (held on 23 October 1986), the Economic and Social Committee unanimously adopted the following opinion with four abstentions.

Foreword

It is now generally recognized that competition policy is vital for the smooth running and promotion of the free market, and for the protection of consumer rights and freedom.

The present assessment of the Fifteenth Report on Competition Policy is conducted in the light of the changes underway in the Community and world economies.

An active realistic competition policy will have to take account of two factors currently of particular importance: the advent of world-wide markets and innovation.

1. The world economic context: world-wide markets and innovation

1.1. Against a world economic backdrop of rapid change in all sectors, the Committee endorses the Commission's conviction that 'the promotion of dynamic, innovative competition will continue to be a key yardstick in applying Articles 85 and 86 to restrictions of competition'. (Introduction to the Fifteenth Report).

This conviction must be acted upon consistently in all political or administrative action taken towards companies, States or international organizations.

1.2. Two factors have broken the existing balances: the growth of world-level markets, and the acceleration of innovative technological change.

Faced with this new and rapidly evolving situation, companies are obliged to adapt their strategies in the short term by restructuring and rationalization, and above all by innovation.

1.3. During this period of swift and radical change, the guardians of free competition must take account — particularly by adopting the necessary social measures — of the pressing need to adapt companies and economic, financial and legal structures; they should act to encourage and smooth these processes while ensuring the necessary control and coordination.

The changed scale of the markets and the phenomenon of innovation mean that rigid analyses of behaviour are no longer possible. In applying and interpreting the rules, the Commission must find new criteria which are better geared to the changed situation.

1.4.   Against this backdrop of major change, the creation of a single market, as gradually as may be necessary, is a vital and urgently needed tool for the new Community strategy in which competition has a key part to play, working in close and consistent collaboration with the other Community policies (see also point 7).

2.   The scale of the market — Cooperation between companies

2.1.   Integration is essential both for the necessary rationalization of Europe's production system and for new initiatives. Removal of internal barriers is the prerequisite for development of the Community's domestic market.

2.2.   The continued existence of national economic areas is an anachronism when it comes to achieving a sufficient degree of real competitiveness, or assessing or defining relevant markets. The smallest possible geographical yardstick is now the Community, and even then the world dimension cannot be disregarded.

Although the Treaty of Rome cites a 'substantial part' of the common market (but only as an alternative to the common market; and today this alternative applies only to very few minor cases), the common market is the smallest possible geographical unit for consideration. However, in a number of sectors it too is no longer large enough, for example when assessing the market position of a company or group of companies which compete with non-Community firms.

2.3.   The real unit today is the world even though economic and commercial integration at Community level are the main forces for ensuring the competitiveness of European industry.

2.4.   In such a situation, cooperation between companies must be encouraged.

2.4.1.   The Committee thus fully endorses point 26 of the Fifteenth Report, which states that: 'The Commission hopes to be able to speed up the rate of structural change by facilitating cooperation between firms, while maintaining a competitive environment'.

The Committee and economic circles await the promised guidelines on joint ventures. From the point of view of legal certainty, their effectiveness will depend on their success in the following areas: firstly, solution of the problems of 'relevant markets' and of yardsticks and reference thresholds; secondly, definitive abandonment of the imprecise criterion of potential competition; thirdly, a proper definition of 'structural effects'.

2.5.   The Commission proposal on merger control, though amended, has not yet met sufficient consensus for adoption by the Council. The Committee refers back to its detailed opinion issued at the time of this proposal, and urges the Council to adopt the proposal as soon as possible.

National and international situations have meanwhile changed, and alongside field of application, thresholds and yardsticks, and procedures, a clearer definition is needed of the Commission's powers under Article 86, whilst remembering the differing situations of the Member States.

Here too the necessary clarity and legal certainty can only help create conditions which will favour company initiatives during the changes underway.

3. Innovation

3.1.   The shift towards a world-scale market is flanked by the rapid growth of innovation, primarily in the most advanced sectors but also in the 'creative' ones. Its effects are widely felt, not least in the services sector and in employment.

3.2.   In its opinion on the Thirteenth Report (page 12, indent d), the Committee stated clearly that the term 'innovation' should be used in the broad sense to include both the technological development of the product (improved quality and performance) and of the process (lower costs), and the development of new finished products or components, or of new materials.

3.3.   A strategy to develop Community industry and the services sector must hinge on the promotion of innovation: the ability to create and incorporate innovation is today the key factor determining a company's competitive success on the world market.

Competition policy has a part to play in this Community strategy, stimulating innovation by creating conditions favourable to investment in research and development.

3.4.   Innovation is a complex phenomenon which affects all sectors to some degree, and which involves all stages of the production process. Encouragement of investment in research and development (R&D), including a favourable attitude to cooperation, which is vital in cases where enormous expenditure is needed, must therefore not be limited to pre-competitive research, but must include applied research and industrialization itself. Innovation can thus be present throughout the production process.

Regulation 418/85 provides Commission R&D policy with a suitable instrument for monitoring and promotion; this policy must at all events guarantee continued effective competition and technical progress.

4. State aids

4.1.   Growth — both industrial and non-industrial — is a major concern of national economic-industrial policy in all developed countries.

The problems of international competitiveness are so serious that they are unlikely to be resolved by firms acting alone. This is amply demonstrated by the Community shipbuilding sector which, despite the major drive to restore productivity and competitiveness, still requires aid: the prospect of a sector which can stand on its own two feet is still some way off.

4.2.   It is impossible to remain competitive without innovation, and there can be no innovation without R&D. State support for R&D, and thus for innovation, is indispensable. We have to be realistic about this.

4.3.   The Commission has adopted a code for State support, setting out principles, criteria and possible contingencies. The Community's approach is thus known. Because of the multifarious practical instances, and the diversity of national circumstances, the practical application of this approach is less well known, less identifiable and fraught with difficulty.

4.4.   Some points should be made about the (in some cases) 'relative' character of the general principles and criteria. The total amount of concessionary financing and grants provided by the State for R&D is important, regardless of whether it goes to industry, public laboratories or universities. A company has an advantage over its rivals in other countries if it operates in a 'richer' scientific environment.

The scale of support for industrial R&D consequently has to be evaluated in the light of national circumstances, and of the situation in other countries.

4.5. The Committee would point to another aspect of discrimination, resulting from the competition policy approach to aids.

As a result of the continuing tax differences between Member States, even carefully planned aids can generate competition distortions.

It would be wrong to look at State aids in isolation when assessing whether they are compatible with the Treaty. They have to be considered in their overall context, i.e. in terms of the difference between the tax burden of the firm or sector concerned and that of rival firms based in countries with a smaller or differently patterned tax burden.

The Committee certainly does not think that it is the task of aids to offset tax or structural differences between Member States.

The inadequate, indeed insignificant progress towards harmonization of tax systems makes it difficult to implement a correct, balanced policy not only on State aids but also in many other areas. No competition policy, however bold and far-sighted, can obviate the resultant imbalances and distortions.

4.6. Small firms await the launch of a series of specific measures to ensure that true free competition is respected. These measures should not just consist of exemptions in favour of small firms, but should provide an overall action programme.

The recent appointment of a Commissioner with special responsibility for small firms is undoubtedly a step in the right direction, but small firms await specific rules to implement an overall policy.

4.7. The Committee realizes how difficult it is for the Commission to implement an aids strategy as part of a coherent competition policy.

Resisting the temptation to recommend a rigid automatic system, the Committee endorses the pragmatic approach adopted by the Commission but urges that account be taken of the factors mentioned above.

4.8. It is especially necessary to be circumspect when making comparisons between countries, as it is not always easy to obtain full, adequate information on the effective national situation.

It suffices to point out that alongside State aids, i.e. aids provided by the central government, there are also aids provided by local authorities; these are harder to identify and their background is more complex. The fact that circumspection is needed does not mean that the problem should be neglected or, worse, underestimated. The Commission is right to attempt to compile an aids inventory. But apart from issuing the official results of any inquiries — which then prove outdated because of the slowness of bureaucratic procedures — the Commission should keep the current, coherent policy regarding national and regional aids under close review, with a view to reconsidering and changing its intervention policies (inclusing the use of the Community's funds).

4.9. More up-to-date, accurate information and increased vigilance are needed to ascertain the circumstances surrounding each aid measure, whatever its form.

It is not easy to establish a theoretical definition of 'State aid'. But neither is it easy to establish an adequate inventory or vetting criteria. Two examples: firstly, existence of public contracts, which is a potential cause of distortions in itself, since one firm may be a party to more such contracts than another.

A second weakness, in some cases, is the automatic exclusion from checks of firms which receive aids but whose business does not affect trade between Member States. After all, such firms may supply major exporters.

A pragmatic approach, combined with up-to-date accurate information, can improve and render effective a theoretical reference system which serves to remind everybody — State and firms — of the Commission's criteria and thinking with respect to measures adopted under Treaty Articles 92 and 93. In its opinion on the Thirteenth Report, the Committee urged the Commission to 'carefully consider the need for one or more Council Regulations to help reach the vitally necessary consensus between the Member States on correct implementation of the basic concepts contained in Articles 92 and 93'.

5. Public undertakings — State monopolies

5.1.   Blanket extension to all public-enterprise sectors of the 'transparency' directive should at least provide the Commission with the information and factors it needs to make considered evaluations.

The Committee is alive to the difficulties caused for the Commission by the reticence of the Member States, but hopes that it will nevertheless be possible to achieve satisfactory results, especially if the Commission ensures that the responsibility of the member governments in this matter becomes public knowledge.

5.2.   The difficulties posed by the national monopolies, especially the fiscal monopolies, are still more serious, as the close link with the structure of revenue, and thus with the central-government budget, makes it difficult to dismantle them.

Support should nevertheless be given to the Commission's endeavours to at least reduce the impact of these State monopolies on trade. But the Committee reiterates that the real problem is the inadequate harmonization of tax systems in the Community, and trusts that an overall approach to the issue will yield new, realistic proposals. At all events, where State monopolies exist, they must respect the rules of the market.

6. Specific sectors — air and sea transport

6.1.   The competition rules apply to all production and service sectors, both public and private.

The steps taken by the Commission to ensure compliance with the rules of open competition have already had positive results and should be encouraged.

6.2.   In the air transport sector, the Commission is hampered by the complexity of the problem and the structured-association system at world level.

Government behaviour is a further obstacle to a solution for this sector, which has been described as a 'microcosm of anti-competitive practices'.

The Committee looked at the air transport issue in its opinion of September last concerning the Commission's memorandum 2 on the whole problem of civil aviation.

The Committee would however reiterate its concern about the way the issue of air transport remains in a state of deadlock at the Council.

The recent ruling by the Court of Justice should have cleared the obstacles impeding the Commission. Indeed, this ruling should prompt the long-awaited legislative initiative. Progress must be made gradually, taking account of the many aspects of the problem. There will also be tangible effects for the consumer, at least as regards tariffs.

6.3.   Turning to sea transport, the Committee refers back to the relevant Committee opinion and trusts that the Council will make rapid progress in this sector too, particularly in view of the beneficial effects which this will have on the internal market.

7. Co-relation with other common policies

7.1. Competition policy must develop in accordance with the Treaty, like the other policies — social, trade, tax, transport, and the overall policy on consumer protection.

Competition policy, which should be dynamic and innovative, is seriously constrained by the lack of harmonization and coordination.

7.2. The Single Act provides for social harmonization, and the Committee hopes that this will occur at the highest level. But as part of this overall strategy for the social sector an effective competition policy must also take account of any distortion resulting from differing social situations, and avoid creating new imbalances. This applies not only within the Community — where the Commission can operate most effectively — but also in dealing with non-member countries.

7.3. A Community policy geared to the harmonization of fiscal systems, which is still at the initial stage, is likewise an essential component of an effective competition policy.

The competition distortions caused by differing tax situations and structures in the Member States, and by certain national measures which overfavour firms or producers in free zones, cannot be eliminated unless the Commission makes more vigorous use of its powers and of its right to put forward proposals.

7.3.1. The Member States are still separated by fully-fledged frontiers. The competition distortions caused in frontier regions by differing national value-added tax (VAT) and excise rates are a striking, concrete example. These distortions affect small firms in particular.

7.3.2. The White Paper admittedly provides for a gradual alignment of excise rates, while allowing modest differentials. The standstill proposal adopts the same line for VAT. But an effective harmonization policy designed to reduce or eliminate competition distortions will affect the structure of national budgets and the relations between the various types of taxes. Only if this is achieved will competition policy play its full role as a control and stimulus.

7.4. A competition policy which guarantees free trade, and free choice by consumers, will have tangible and increasing beneficial impact if consumer protection policy is closely coordinated with other common policies.

7.5. The Committee trusts that the Commission will react vigorously whenever the delays, uncertainties or setbacks of other policies threaten to hamper the achievement of genuine open competition, which is the prerequisite for effective economic integration and thus the competitive edge of the Community's economy internationally.

8. Legal procedure; certainty in legal relations

8.1. The Committee notes the substantial procedural improvements (speed, guarantees for adversary parties).

8.2. The plan to introduce a double legal control, in order to provide better guarantees for the rights of defendants, is to be welcomed.

8.3. Decentralization to national courts of the implementation of Articles 85 and 86 is likewise to be endorsed. More frequent and widely disseminated information is clearly valuable here.

Particular attention must nevertheless be paid to the varying circumstances obtaining in the Member States, to ensure that competition rules are not in practice applied non-uniformly and 'with varying degrees of effectiveness', as the Commission fears could be the case (point 41 of the Fifteenth Report).

The disadvantages of further discrimination and distortions should not be set against the advantage of speed and possibilities of damages at national level.

8.4.   The Committee welcomes the increased use by the Commission — perhaps encouraged by the endorsement in the Committee's opinion — of communications and guidelines to notify companies and Member States of its approach, thus providing them with a benchmark which will help to clarify the law and make for certainty in legal relations.

9.   Competition policy — role and means

9.1.   Competition policy has a key role to play in the unification of Europe, and a direct impact on the behaviour and decisions of companies and governments. The Commission should draw up a comparative study of the various national competition policies, providing a vital source of information for the completion of the internal market.

The application of the policy mapped out in Articles 85 and 86, and 92 and 93, often requires more on-going evaluation and action — even on individual, highly complex cases — than that of other Community policies.

9.2.   In the past, the Committee has stressed the need to strengthen the various units of the General Directorate for Competition. Experience confirms the urgent need to provide this General Directorate with more skilled staff and physical resources, so as to equip it to cope properly with its highly responsible and important tasks.

The economic and social interest groups represented within the Committee are familiar with the complexity and trickiness of the cases which have to be investigated, vetted and straightened out. They realize what human and physical resources are needed.

The Committee therefore trusts that this repeated reference to the vital need for greater resources — coupled with the similar recommendations by the European Parliament — will lead to prompt action by the authorities.

10.   Relations with international organizations

10.1.   Mention must be made of the increasing importance of active participation by the Community in the work of the international organizations, particularly on matters covered by Community policies.

10.2.   Greater integration and cohesion would give the Community a more powerful voice at international meetings.

10.3.   The prospective negotiations in GATT will give the Community an opportunity to exploit its importance as the world's leading trading unit. Reciprocity and/or safeguard clauses should confirm the principles of the Rome Treaty and the legitimate interests of Community consumers, and lay down the appropriate implementing measures.

Conclusion

The Committee states its appreciation of the Commission's Annual Report on Competition Policy.

The Annual Report is not just of interest to those who work directly on competition policy. The report makes it possible to ascertain the current state of progress within the Community towards free trade, which is essential for economic and social integration and increased competitiveness.

Our opinion concentrates this year on the accelerated pace of change throughout the socio-economic system, and in particular on two stimuli, namely larger markets and innovation.

The Community competition policy will be a success if it accommodates these two forces for change, which are the true challenges of our time.

Done at Brussels, 23 October 1986.

The Chairman
of the Economic and Social Committee
Alfons MARGOT

I — Competition policy towards enterprises

List of Decisions, other measures and Rulings

1. Pursuant to Articles 85 and 86 of the EEC Treaty

Decision of 23.4.1986 on a proceeding under Article 85 of the EEC Treaty 'Polypropylene'

OJ L 230, 18.8.1986, p. 1
IP (86) 191, of 24.4.1986
Bull. EC 4-1986, point 2.1.50

Decision of 10.7.1986 on a proceeding under Article 85 of the EEC Treaty 'Roofing felt'

OJ L 232, 19.8.1986, p. 15
IP (86) 377, of 28.7.1986
Bull. EC 7/8-1986, point 2.1.62

Decision of 14.7.1986 on a proceeding under Article 85 of the EEC Treaty 'Optical fibres'

OJ L 236, 22.8.1986, p. 30
IP (86) 369, of 17.7.1986
Bull. EC 7/8-1986, point 2.1.65

Decision of 25.9.1986 on a proceeding under Article 85 of the EEC Treaty 'Peugeot'

OJ L 295, 18.10.1986, p. 19
IP (86) 453, of 25.9.1986
Bull. EC 9-1986, point 2.1.52

Decision of 30.9.1986 on a proceeding under Article 85 of the EEC Treaty 'Vifka'

OJ L 291, 15.10.1986, p. 46
IP (86) 462, of 1.10.1986
Bull. EC 10-1986, point 2.1.65

Decision of 30.9.1986 on a proceeding under Article 85 of the EEC Treaty 'Irish banks' Standing Committee'

OJ L 295, 18.10.1986, p.28
IP (86) 461, of 1.10.1986
Bull. EC 10-1986, point 2.1.64

Decision of 26.11.1986 on a proceeding under Article 85 of the EEC Treaty 'Meldoc'

OJ L 348, 10.12.1986, p. 50
IP (86) 580 of 27.11.1986
Bull. EC 11-1986, point 2.1.76

Decision of 2.12.1986 on a proceeding under Article 85 of the EEC Treaty 'Fatty acids'

OJ L 3, 6.1.1987, p. 17
IP (86) 585 of 4.12.1986

Decision of 4.12.1986 on a proceeding under Article 85 of the EEC Treaty 'International Petroleum Exchange of London Limited'

OJ L 3, 6.1.1987, p. 27
IP (87) 1 of 6.1.1987

Decision of 4.12.1986 on a proceeding under Article 85 of the EEC Treaty 'ENI/Montedision'

OJ L 5, 7.1.1987, p. 13
IP (86) 600 of 5.12.1986

Decisions of 10.12.1986 on a proceeding under Article 85 of the EEC Treaty 'The Gafta Soya Bean Meal Futures Association' 'The London Grain Futures Market' 'The London Potato Futures Association Limited' 'The London Meat Futures Exchange Limited'

OJ L 19, 21.1.1987, pp. 18-30
IP (87) 2 of 6.1.1987

Decision of 10.12.1986 on a proceeding under Article 85 of the EEC Treaty 'VEB/Shell'

IP (86) 631 of 19.12.1986

Decision of 11.12.1986 on a proceeding under Article 85 of the EEC Treaty 'Association belge des banques'	OJ L 7, 9.1.1987, p. 27 IP (86) 619 of 17.12.1986
Decision of 12.12.1986 on a proceeding under Article 85 of the EEC Treaty 'ABI'	OJ L 43, 13.2.1987, p. 51 IP (86) 620 of 17.12.1986
Decision of 15.12.1986 on a proceeding under Article 85 of the EEC Treaty 'X/Open Group'	OJ L 35, 6.2.1987, p. 36 IP (86) 625 of 18.12.1986
Decision of 15.12.1986 on a proceeding under Article 85 of the EEC Treaty 'Boussois/Interpane'	OJ L 50, 19.2.1987, p. 30 IP (86) 636 of 23.12.1986
Decision of 17.12.1986 on a proceeding under Article 85 of the EEC Treaty 'Pronuptia'	OJ L 13, 15.1.1987, p. 39 IP (86) 634 of 22.12.1986
Decision of 17.12.1986 on a proceeding under Article 85 of the EEC Treaty 'Yves Rocher'	OJ L 8, 10.1.1987, p. 49 IP (86) 634 of 22.12.1986
Decision of 17.12.1986 on a proceeding under Article 85 of the EEC Treaty 'Mitchell Cotts/Sofiltra'	OJ L 41, 11.2.1987, p. 31 IP (86) 635 of 23.12.1986

2. Administrative letters sent following publication of a notice pursuant to Article 19(3) of Regulation No 17

Notice pursuant to Article 19(3) of Regulation No 17 concerning a request for negative clearance or the application of Article 85(3) of the EEC Treaty 'ICL/Fujitsu'	OJ C 210, 21.8.1986, p. 3

3. Decisions concerning Articles 65 and 66 of the ECSC Treaty

Decision of 5 February 1986 on a proceeding under Articles 65 and 66 of the ECSC Treaty authorizing Röchling Eisenhandel G, Ludwigshafen ('Rochling') and Possehl Eisen- und Stahl GmbH, Mannheim ('Possehl') to set up the 'Stahlcenter Röchling-Possehl GmbH & Co. KG' as a 100% subsidiary of Saarlux	Bull. EC 2-1986, point 2.1.60
Decision of 18 March 1986 on a proceeding under Article 66 of the ECSC Treaty authorizing the British Steel Corporation, London (BSC) and Guest Keen & Nettlefolds, Redditch (GKN) to group their activities in the engineering steel sector in a joint subsidiary to be called United Engineering Steels Ltd (UES)	Bull. EC 3-1986, point 2.1.65
Decision of 21 March 1986 on a proceeding under Article 65 of the ECSC Treaty authorizing some 30 wholesalers from Northern Ireland—the Northern Ireland Coal Importers Association (Nicia)—to manage an agreement strictly analogous to joint-buying covering their purchases of solid fuel for domestic purposes from the National Coal Board, London (NCB)	Bull. EC 3-1986, point 2.1.64

Decision of 2 April 1986 on a proceeding under Article 66 of the ECSC Treaty authorizing Klöckner & Co. KG., Duisburg (Klöckner) to acquire the majority of the share capital of 's Gravendeel Holding BV, 's Gravendeel (Heuvelman)

Decision of 26 May 1986 on a proceeding under Article 66 of the ECSC Treaty authorizing Usinor, Paris to acquire the Creusot-Marrel and Mécanique spécialisée divisions of Creusot-Loire

Bull. EC 5-1986, point 2.1.53

Decision of 4 June 1986 on a proceeding under Article 66 of the ECSC Treaty authorizing Ryan International plc, Cardiff and Consolidated Gold Fields plc, London, to set up a joint 50/50 owned subsidiary 'Ryan Consolidated Ltd'

Bull. EC 6-1986, point 2.1.88

Decision of 7 July 1986 on a proceeding under Article 66 of the ECSC Treaty authorizing Ulan Coal Mines Ltd to acquire 50% of the share capital of Hargreaves (Antwerp) NV, a 100% subsidiary of Hargreaves Group plc

Bull. EC 7/8-1986, point 2.1.66

Decision of 25 July 1986 on a proceeding under Article 66 of the ECSC Treaty authorizing Saarstahl Völklingen GmbH to appoint certain officials from Arbed SA and Forges et Aciéries de Dillingen (Dillinger Hüttenwerke) to the Board of Directors of Saarstahl for the period of one year

Decision of 29 July 1986 on a proceeding under Article 66 of the ECSC Treaty authorizing Ruhrkohle Handel GmbH to acquire the wholesaling coal business of Haniel Handel GmbH in the cities of Duisberg, Mannheim, Frankfurt and Nürnberg

Bull. EC 7/8-1986, point 2.1.67

Decision of 12 November 1986 on a proceeding under Article 66 of the ECSC Treaty authorizing the Coalite group to acquire the Hargreaves group

Bull. EC 11-1986, point 2.1.79

Decision of 25 November 1986 on a proceeding under Article 66 of the ECSC Treaty authorizing Acenor SA, Bilbao and United Engineering Steels Ltd, Rotherham, to set up a joint subsidiary, Gekanor SA (Madrid)

Bull. EC 11-1986, point 2.1.78

Decision of 4 December 1986 on a proceeding under Article 66 of the ECSC Treaty authorizing Klöckner Stahl GmbH, Duisburg, to acquire 26.4% of the share capital of Hellenic Steel Co., Athens

Bull. EC 12-1986, point 2.1.108

Decision of 12 December 1986 on a proceeding under Article 66 of the ECSC Treaty authorizing Saarlor to act as a joint-selling agency of solid fuel from Houillères du Bassin de Lorraine and Saarbergwerke

Bull. EC 12-1986, point 2.1.110

Decision of 17 December 1986 on a proceeding under Article 66 of the ECSC Treaty authorizing C. Walker & Sons Ltd, Blackburn, to acquire the share capital of GKN Steelstock Ltd, Wolverhampton

Bull. EC 12-1986, point 2.1.109

Decision of 17 December 1986 on a proceeding under Article 66 of the ECSC Treaty authorizing Lauerweg GmbH to acquire 50% of the share capital of Gesellschaft zur Rückgewinnung von Rohstoffen mbH

Bull. EC 12-1986, point 2.1.107

Decision of 19 December 1986 on a proceeding under Article 66 of the ECSC Treaty authorizing Nuova Italsider to transfer its shares held in the company 'Consorzio Genovese Acciaio SpA' (Cogea) to the groups Leali, Lucchini, Riva, Bellicini, Regis and Sassone

Bull. EC 12-1986, point 2.1.106

4. Rulings of the Court of Justice

Ruling (28.1.1986) in Case 161/84
'Pronuptia/Schillgalis'

OJ C 44, 26.2.1986, p. 6

Ruling (25.2.1986) in Case 193/83
'Windsurfing International/Commission of the European Communities'

OJ C 79, 8.4.1986, p. 8

Ruling (30.4.1986) in joined Cases 209-213/84
'Ministère Public/Asjes and Others (Air tariffs)'

OJ C 131, 29.5.1986, p. 4

Ruling (24.6.1986) in Case 53/85
'AKZO Chemie BV and AKZO Chemie UK Ltd/Commission of the European Communities and Engineering & Chemical Supplies Ltd'

OJ C 196, 5.8.1986, p. 6

Ruling (23.9.1986) in Case 5/85
'AKZO Chemie BV and AKZO Chemie UK Ltd/Commission of the European Communities'

OJ C 265, 21.10.1986, p. 4

Ruling (22.10.1986) in Case 75/84
'Metro SB Großmärkte GmbH/Commission of the European Communities, Saba and Federal Republic of Germany'

OJ C 296, 22.11.1986, p. 8

Ruling (11.11.1986) in Case 226/84
'British Leyland/Commission of the European Communities and Merson'

OJ C 318, 11.12.1986, p. 4

Ruling (18.12.1986) in Case 10/86
'VAG France SA/Magne SA'

OJ C 23, 30.1.1987, p. 4

II — Competition policy and government assistance to enterprises

1. Final negative Decisions adopted by the Commission following the Article 93(2) EEC procedure

Federal Republic of Germany

Decision (87/15/EEC) of 19 February 1986 on the compatibility with the common market of aid under the German Federal/*Land* Government joint regional aid programme (Joint programme for the improvement of regional economic structures) in six labour market regions

OJ L 12, 14.1.1987, p. 17
Bull. EC 2-1986, point 2.1.61

Decision (86/509/EEC) of 21 May 1986 on aid granted by the Federal Republic of Germany and the *Land* of Bavaria to a producer of polyamide and polyester yarn situated in Deggendorf (Textilwerke Deggendorf GmbH)

OJ L 300, 24.10.1986, p. 34
Bull. EC 5-1986, point 2.1.54

Decision (87/98/EEC) of 28 July 1986 on aid proposed by the Rheinland-Pfalz state government for a metalworking firm in Betzdorf (Schäfer Werke AG und Fritz Schäfer KG)

OJ L 40, 10.2.1987, p. 17
Bull. EC 7/8-1986, point 2.1.68

Decision (87/99/EEC) of 29 July 1986 on aid proposed by the Rheinland-Pfalz state government for a fibre-processing firm in Scheuerfeld (Lignotock Fasertechnik GmbH & Co. Produktions KG)

OJ L 40, 10.2.1987, p. 22
Bull. EC 7/8-1986, point 2.1.68

Belgium

Decision (86/366/EEC) of 10 June 1986 concerning aid which the Belgian Government has granted to a ceramic sanitary ware and crockery manufacturer (Boch)

OJ L 223, 9.8.1986, p. 30
Bull. EC 6-1986, point 2.1.97

Decision (86/593/EEC) of 29 July 1986 on a proposal by the Belgian Government to grant aid for investments by a flat-glass producer at Auvelais (Glaceries de St Roch)

OJ L 342, 5.12.1986, p. 32
Bull. EC 7/8-1986, point 2.1.74

Decision (87/48/EEC) of 22 October 1986 concerning aid in Belgium in favour of the brewery equipment industry (Technibra-Meura)

OJ L 20, 22.1.1987, p. 30
Bull. EC 10-1986, point 2.1.73

Decision (87/195/EEC) of 3 December 1986 on a proposal by the Belgian Government to grant aid for investments by a flat-glass producer at Moustier (Glaverbel)

OJ L 77, 19.3.1987, p. 47
Bull. EC 12-1986, point 2.1.118

France

Decision (87/194/EEC) of 12 November 1986 on a FIM loan to mineral water and glass bottle manufacturer (Société générale des grandes sources d'eaux minérales françaises)

OJ L 77, 19.3.1987, p. 43
Bull. EC 11-1986, point 2.1.84

Italy

Decision (87/16/EEC) of 23 April 1986 on a proposal by the Italian Government to grant aid to a firm in the chemical industry (producing industrial auxiliaries, intermediates and pesticides) (ENI-Chimica)	OJ L 12, 14.1.1987, p. 27 Bull. EC 4-1986, point 2.1.52

2. Judgments and orders delivered by the Court of Justice

Judgment (15.1.1986) in Case 52/84 'Commission v Kingdom of Belgium' OJ C 37, 18.2.1986, p. 7

Judgment (28.1.1986) in Case 169/84 (Compagnie française de l'Azote (Cofaz) SA v Commission' OJ C 44, 26.2.1986, p. 6

Order (6.2.1986) in Case 310/85 R 'Deufil GmbH & Co. KG v Commission' OJ C 52, 6.3.1986, p. 6

Judgment (10.7.1986) in Case 40/85 'Kingdom of Belgium v Commission' OJ C 196, 5.8.1986, p. 8

Judgment (10.7.1986) in Case 282/85 'Comité de développement et de promotion du textile et de l'habillement v Commission' OJ C 209, 20.8.1986, p. 6

Judgment (10.7.1986) in Case 234/84 'Kingdom of Belgium v Commission' OJ C 209, 20.8.1986, p. 3

3. Aid cases in which the Commission raised no objection

Federal Republic of Germany

3.1.1986	Aid scheme to promote innovation by small firms in Frankfurt
20.1.1986	Tax relief for takeover of business in difficulty (machine tools — Leitz)
21.1.1986	Aid scheme for investment by small firms in Bremen
5.2.1986	Tax relief for takeover of business in difficulty (animal feed — Hakva)
20.2.1986	Tax relief for takeover of business in difficulty (clocks and watches — Kienzle)
27.2.1986	Aid scheme to promote exports by small firms in Bremen
7.3.1986	Aid scheme for apprenticeship training in Saarland
19.3.1986	14th General Plan of joint Federal/state regional aid programme (part)
19.3.1986	Aid by Hamburg to shipyard (Blohm & Voss)
9.4.1986	Bavarian state regional aid programme (part)
14.4.1986	Aid by Rheinland-Pfalz to caravan manufacturer (Haselwarter)
23.4.1986	Business start-up scheme in Hamburg
5.5.1986	Aid scheme to promote innovation by small firms in Hamburg
5.5.1986	Tax relief for takeover of business in difficulty (automotive parts — Erpe-Ernst Pelz Vertriebs GmbH)
21.5.1986	Aid for R&D by Siemens and Philips
23.5.1986	Extension of joint programme regional aid in Heide-Meldorf
23.5.1986	Aid under joint programme special Bremen scheme to Lufthansa
10.6.1986	Aid to shipyard (Harmstorf)
18.6.1986	Amendments to Effluent Discharges Levy Act
2.7.1986	Extension of aid scheme for start-ups of high-technology businesses
16.7.1986	Extension of assisted status of Essen-Mühlheim and Special Steel Scheme under North Rhine-Westphalia regional development programme
23.7.1986	Environmental technology innovation scheme in Hessen
29.7.1986	Regional aid to households textiles manufacturer (ADO-Gardinenwerke)
29.8.1986	Aid scheme for small firms in Marburg and Marburg-Biedenkopf rural district
29.8.1986	Tax relief for takeover of business in difficulty (liquid gas — Willersinn & Walter)
18.9.1986	LKB Kredit employment creation scheme in North Rhine-Westphalia
8.10.1986	Addition of Emsdetten to North Rhine-Westphalia regional development programme
8.10.1986	Tax relief for takeover of business in difficulty (corrugated board — Wellpappenwerke Bruchsal)

9.10.1986	Aid scheme to support introduction of new technology in Rheinland-Pfalz
22.10.1986	Aid scheme for marine science and technology research
5.11.1986	Aid for meeting stricter air pollution standards in power stations and combustion plants
14.11.1986	Aid scheme for investment by small firms in Hamburg
19.11.1986	Extension of joint Federal/state aid programme for construction of coal-fired power stations and district heating networks
16.12.1986	Aid under joint programme special Bremen scheme to aerospace firm (Erno)
17.12.1986	Amendment to Investment Grants Act (part)

Belgium

16.7.1986	Aid scheme for re-employment of long-term unemployed in Wallonian region
10.9.1986	Aid for information technology project (Swift)
5.11.1986	Economic Recovery Act 1984 (part)

France

19.2.1986	Special Employment premium scheme in Nord-pas-de-Calais region (part)
20.2.1986	FIM loans to aircraft engine manufacturer (Snecma)
20.2.1986	FIM loans to aerospace firm (Aérospatiale)
11.4.1986	Long-term loan scheme for small firms
7.5.1986	Regional planning grant to Creusot-Loire
19.11.1986	Electronics Industry Scheme

Ireland

2.7.1986	Technology Acquisition Grants Scheme
31.7.1986	Employment grants for small industry projects
8.9.1986	Inner-city aid scheme

Italy

20.2.1986	Extension of aid scheme under Act 696/83 for purchase of high-technology equipment by small firms
10.3.1986	Assistance under Act 46/82 to moped manufacturer (Piaggio)
19.3.1986	Industry aid scheme under Act 1007 (part)
14.5.1986	Aid to aerospace industry
16.5.1986	Assistance under Acts 1089/68 and 46/82 to electronics and telecommunications enterprise (Telettra)

18.6.1986	Sicilian small industry aid scheme
24.6.1986	Extension of Special Innovation Fund under Act 46/82
24.6.1986	Extension of Applied Research Fund under Acts 1089/68 and 46/82
1.7.1986	Assistance under Act 46/82 to tyre manufacturer (Pirelli)
22.7.1986	Industry aid scheme under Act 710/1985
22.7.1986	Assistance under Act 46/82 to motor manufactures (Iveco-Fiat)
20.8.1986	Aid for closures in steel foundries industry
20.8.1986	Aid for closures in welded pipe industry
12.9.1986	Aid scheme to promote tourism in Calabria
8.10.1986	Aid scheme for local commerce in Sicily
22.10.1986	Assistance under Acts 1089/68 and 46/82 to telecommunications enterprises (Cselt, Italtel)
7.11.1986	Assistance under Act 46/82 to telecommunications enterprise (Sip)
14.11.1986	Aid scheme for rural tourism in Umbria
27.11.1986	Assistance under Acts 46/82 to electronics and telecommunications firm (Marconi)
3.12.1986	Industry aid scheme under Act 57
3.12.1986	Aid scheme for cooperatives (Act 49/1985)

Netherlands

10.2.1986	Changes to scheme to support costs of consultancy services
2.4.1986	Extension of scheme for pollution-control investment in galvanizing industry
21.4.1986	Aid for R&D in microelectronics (ASM)
21.5.1986	Aid for R&D in electronics (Philips)
18.6.1986	Aid for R&D in software production
18.6.1986	Changes to IPR regional aid scheme
2.7.1986	Aid for R&D in biotechnology (Unilever)
2.7.1986	Changes in tax incentives for cars meeting stricter exhaust emission standards
29.7.1986	Aid for R&D in electronics (Philips)
29.7.1986	Aid for R&D in chemical industry (Dow, AKZO, DSM)
8.10.1986	Shipbuilding aid scheme 1985-86
15.10.1986	Aid for R&D in medical engineering (Medtronic)
22.10.1986	Aid scheme for research into wind energy
3.10.1986	Aid scheme for re-employment of long-term unemployed
19.10.1986	Changes to scheme to support cost of consultancy services

Portugal

8.10.1986   Regional aid scheme

United Kingdom

14.4.1986   Extension of regional aid scheme (Blackpool)

10.6.1986   Extension of regional aid scheme (Penzance and St Ives)

18.6.1986   Shipbuilding aid 1984/85

16.7.1986   Small firms merit award for research and technology (Smart) scheme

29.7.1986   Extension of regional aid scheme (Forres and Upper Moray)

12.9.1986   New Workers' Scheme

24.9.1986   Changes in regional aid scheme (cumulation of BIS investment aid with regional develop-
                   ment grant)

8.10.1986   Electronics manufacture scheme

19.11.1986   Assistance for Cornish tin mines

Belgium/France/Luxembourg

5.11.1986   European development zone

4. Aid cases in which the Commission decided to open the Article 93(2) EEC procedure

Federal Republic of Germany

29.1.1986	Aid by Baden-Württemberg to aluminium producer (BUG)
19.3.1986	14th General Plan of joint Federal/state regional aid programme (part)
9.4.1986	Bavarian state regional aid programme (part)
29.10.1986	Aid by Baden-Württemberg state government and Rastatt local authority to car manufacturer (Daimler-Benz)
5.11.1986	Aid to firms in difficulties under Baden-Württemberg economic development programme
17.12.1986	Amendment to Investment Grants Act (part)

Belgium

13.1.1986	Aid under Economic Expansion Act 1959 to flat-glass producer (Glaverbel)
29.1.1986	Aid scheme for brewery equipment industry (Technibra)
21.5.1986	Aid for R&D by pharmaceutical companies
29.7.1986	Pharmaceutical industry aid scheme
29.7.1986	Aid to a steel pipe and tube producer (Tubemeuse)
24.9.1986	Tax concessions for textile and clothing and glass firms
5.11.1986	Economic Expansion Act 1984 (part)

Denmark

9.12.1986	Changes to regional aid scheme

France

15.1.1986	Tax incentives for investment in French-language film productions
29.1.1986	FIM loans to electrical car equipment manufacturer (Valeo)
12.2.1986	FIM loans to telecommunications manufacturer (Thomson)
12.2.1986	Assistance for restructuring of farm machinery business (Tenneco)
12.2.1986	Aid to glass container manufacturer (Verrerie Ouvrière d'Albi)
19.2.1986	Special Employment Premium Scheme in Nord-pas-de-Calais region (part)
25.3.1986	Assistance for restructuring of tractor tyre business (Kleber)
23.4.1986	Aid scheme for energy conservation and award under this scheme to paper manufacturer (Maurice Franck)
23.4.1986	Textile and clothing industry levy scheme
7.5.1986	Aid to chemicals company (CDF-Chimie)

10.6.1986	Retention of certain areas in Regional Planning Grants (PAT) scheme
8.7.1986	Aid to plasterboard manufacturer (Escogypse)
8.7.1986	Leather and footwear industry levy scheme
8.7.1986	Furniture industry levy scheme
8.7.1986	Aid to copper foil manufacturer (Eurocel)
22.7.1986	Aid to trailer manufacturer (Trailor)
29.7.1986	Aid to domestic appliance manufacturer (Electrolux-Arthur Martin)
29.7.1986	Aid to car manufacturer (Renault)
5.11.1986	Construction materials industry levy scheme
5.11.1986	Aid cumulation notification arrangements
19.11.1986	Aid to wood processor (Isoroy)

Greece

29.10.1986	Business Reconstruction Organization
5.11.1986	Aid cumulation notification arrangements

Italy

29.1.1986	Assistance under Act 675/77 to textile and clothing group (ENI-Lanerossi)
29.1.1986	Tax incentives for investment in Italian-language film productions
19.3.1986	Industry aid scheme under Act 1007 (part)
9.4.1986	Assistance under Act 675/77 to automotive components manufacturer (Pai-Demm)
2.7.1986	Stock relief scheme for shipbuilders
20.8.1986	Aid for investment in seamless tubes sector

Netherlands

9.12.1986	Aid scheme for solid board manufacturers

United Kingdom

22.10.1986	Aid to a synthetic yarn texturizing firm (Crimpfil Ltd)
17.12.1986	Aid for commercial vehicle operations (Rover Group)

5. Aid cases in which the Commission decided to close the Article 93(2) EEC procedure

Federal Republic of Germany

19.3.1986	Lower Saxony loan guarantees scheme
29.10.1986	Aid to car manufacturer in Bremen (Daimler-Benz)
17.12.1986	Film industry aid scheme

Belgium

26.2.1986	Aid to aluminium and aluminium alloy semis producer (Sidal)
26.2.1986	Aid to brewery equipment manufacturer (Meura)

France

26.2.1986	Aid to paper manufacturer (Chapelle Darblay)
23.4.1986	Aid to pulp mill (Cellulose de Strasbourg)
10.6.1986	Shipbuilding aid scheme 1985-86
8.7.1986	Aid scheme for spirits producers
16.7.1986	Machine tool plan
5.11.1986	Aid to a zinc foundry (Asturienne)
5.11.1986	Aid to glass container manufacturer (Verrerie Ouvrière d'Albi)
19.11.1986	Microelectronics industry support programme
19.11.1986	FIM loans to consumer electronics manufacturer (Radiotechnique)
3.12.1986	FIM loans to rubber goods manufacturer (Hutchinson)
3.12.1986	FIM loans to computer manufacturer (Bull)
3.12.1986	FIM soft loans to electronic components manufacturer (Matra-Harris)

Italy

12.2.1986	Assistance of State-owned man-made fibres producer (Anicfibre)
25.3.1986	Aid to domestic appliances manufacturer (Zanussi)
23.4.1986	Assistance under Act 46/82 for R&D in chemicals industry (engineering plastics — ENI)
8.7.1986	Aid scheme for young entrepreneurs in Mezzogiorno

24.9.1986	Aid scheme for port development works
5.11.1986	Industry aid scheme under Act 1007 (part)
17.12.1986	Aid for restructuring of State-owned aluminium industry

Luxembourg

| 29.1.1986 | Aid to polyester film producer (Dupont de Nemours) |

III — Competition policy and government assistance in the agricultural sector [1]

1. Aid cases in which the Commission raised no objection

Federal Republic of Germany

7.2.1986	*Bavaria:* Reconstitution of vineyards destroyed by frost
7.2.1986	Action to improve agricultural structures, in particular as regards conservation of the countryside
7.2.1986	*Baden-Württemberg:* aids to promote consumer information on products and their improvement
24.2.1986	*Schleswig-Holstein:* aids for the purchase of private woodlands and land for afforestation
24.3.1986	*Schleswig-Holstein:* aid to the development and plantation of woodlands
26.3.1986	*Baden-Württemberg:* grant of premiums for the maintenance of 'Hinterwälder' cattle. This scheme comes under the 1985 programme of *Länder* measures outside FRG 'common projects'
2.4.1986	*Lower Saxony:* aid for the maintenance and protection of permanent grasslands in nature areas and natural parks
22.4.1986	*Baden-Württemberg:* improvement of the marketing of slaughter cattle (construction of a slaughterhouse at Bretten)
2.5.1986	*Palatinate:* aid to the growing and use of pulses
15.5.1986	*Hesse:* financial aids to farms for survival
16.6.1986	*Schleswig-Holstein:* Amendment of the Directive on 'encouragement of green areas, with a view to protecting the environment'
16.6.1986	Aid to offset calf birth losses following treatment ordered by the authorities
7.7.1986	*Rhineland-Palatinate:* Compensation for losses suffered by wine-growers joining producers' associations
7.7.1986	Improvement in dairy structures in Westphalia. Measures to cut down dairy product processing capacity
10.7.1986	*Lower Saxony:* aids for loss of cattle following disease, and payment of costs to control certain diseases
15.7.1986	*Rhineland-Palatinate:* Draft law exempting farmers from social security contributions in agriculture
15.7.1986	Draft decree on a subsidy in respect of contributions to retirement allowances for farmers
23.7.1986	Improvement in agricultural structures. These are various measures including assistance to the training of young farmers and forestry holdings
30.7.1986	*Bavaria:* directive on support for measures to pursue the agricultural landscape
1.8.1986	*Lower Saxony:* abandonment aid for cultivated land left fallow

---

[1] This list does not include positions adopted by the Commission in connection with socio-structural provisions.

21.8.1986	*Rhineland-Palatinate:* Measures assisting adaptation of production and conversion from 'main occupation' holding to ancillary holding for wine-growers in Mosel-Saar-Ruwer, Mittelrhein and Ahr areas
28.8.1986	Measures underpinning resources of low-income farms
2.9.1986	*Bavaria:* construction of a cold store and dispatching facility. This is an aid for a dairy for the reorganization and diversification of cheese production
4.9.1986	*North Rhine-Westphalia:* measures for farmers living in less-favoured areas; aid to deer-farming
4.9.1986	*Bavaria:* measures to assist the construction of a slaughterhouse
9.9.1986	*Federation:* measures to assist the sale of wine
9.9.1986	*Lower Saxony:* aids for the organization of home help (aid to the rational utilization of staff needed by farmers at time of sickness)
25.9.1986	*Rhineland-Palatinate:* measures to promote the leasing or buying of land with reference quantities for milk deliveries
2.10.1986	*Lower Saxony:* aid measures for cattle losses following disease and payment of costs for control of certain diseases
20.10.1986	*Rhineland-Palatinate:* promotion of marketing programmes consisting of market research, market strategy development, product development of regional or quality character
20.10.1986	*Bavaria:* extension and improvement of soft cheese storage facilities corresponding to a reduction in facilities intended for the marketing of milk
27.10.1986	*Federation:* Compensation for damage resulting from the Chernobyl accident (general subsidies to agriculture and subsidies to vegetable growers and dealers)
8.11.1986	*Rhineland-Palatinate:* Interest subsidy for short-term operating credit to wine growers' groups
23.12.1986	*Schleswig-Holstein:* measures for green areas for the protection of the environment
23.12.1986	*Rhineland-Palatinate:* interest subsidies for loans for the construction of a public market in Rhineland-Palatinate
11.12.1986	*Schleswig-Holstein:* aids for the payment of interest for up to 10 years for short- and medium-term loans mainly relating to investments
12.12.1986	*Hesse:* aids for the development and maintenance of rare plants in meadows and fields, for the improvement of the environment

Belgium

25.3.1986	Aid to investment in rice products

Denmark

21.1.1986	Aid to reduce ochre content (iron oxide) in water courses
25.1.1986	1986 budget and amendment of 1985 budget for funds for the selection or promotion of sales for the following product groups: seeds, plants, potatoes, horses
25.1.1986	1986 budget and amended 1985 budget for funds for fruit and horticultural products and for the 'pro mille' fund
25.2.1986	Aid to rabbit farming
6.3.1986	1986 budget of the poultry-farmers' trade fund and amendment of the 1985/86 budget of the beef/veal trade fund
23.4.1986	1986 budget for the trade funds for cattle, milk and sheep

17.6.1986	1986 budget of the 'pro mille' fund
26.8.1986	Further State aid to the control of the herpes virus in cattle
8.9.1986	Budgets of the 'pro mille' fund and of the funds for cattle, milk, horses, sheep, seeds and crop improvement
5.12.1986	Amended 1985/86 budget of the pig fund and recording of expenditure concerning the potatoes fund

France

15.1.1986	Aids to horticulture (Oniflhor). These are measures for research, experimentation, development, and strengthening of economic organization
17.1.1986	Financing of the re-placing on the French market of 70 000 tonnes of intervention barley on special terms for stockfarmers who have been victims of the 1985 summer drought
27.2.1986	Ofival aids to increasing the production of horse- and rabbit-meat
19.3.1986	Exceptional aid to new potato producers' groups and advertising aid
2.4.1986	Loans made by the agricultural mutual credit funds to special crop products
22.4.1986	Special stockfarming loans (investments and purchases of purebred male breeding stock entered in herd books)
16.6.1986	Aids to the promotion of cherries and for pears of the Provence-Alpes-Côte d'Azur region
24.7.1986	Exceptional aid to beef/veal farmers to cover some of the cost of borrowing for investment
29.10.1986	Ofival aids to an increase in the production of horse-meat and rabbit-meat (aids to investments and miscellaneous aids to producers' groups)
4.9.1986	Financing of the guarantee fund against agricultural disasters (FF 400 million)
25.9.1986	Taxation relief of up to 50% of VAT on domestic oil used by farmers (thus yielding a total deduction of 100% of the VAT charged on this fuel)
8.10.1986	Seven draft decrees concerning the readjustment of the rates of subsidized loans to farmers, in particular for the purchase of farm land, and for the joint use of equipment in cooperatives
19.10.1986	Measures to assist farmers affected by the exceptional drought in certain departments of the south of France
23.12.1986	Aid to producers of young bulls on farms in financial difficulties
23.12.1986	Aid to the transport of grazing stock in areas suffering from the 1986 drought
28.11.1986	Aids to the modernization of wine-growing (research, technical support to wine-growing, improvement of land structures, improvement of processing, storage and bottling conditions)
28.11.1986	Individual sheep production development programmes (Ofival)
28.11.1986	Aid for poultry-farmers wishing to discontinue this enterprise, enabling them to stop producing eggs and dismantle their facilities
28.11.1986	Aids to the restructuring of the dairy enterprises

Greece

23.12.1986	— Aids because of fire, — Aids for natural disasters, — Measures for crop production

Spain

22.9.1986 Aids to wine-growers affected by April 1986 frosts

Ireland

5.3.1986 1985 Feed Voucher Scheme to offset effects of heavy rain in the summer of 1985

22.9.1986 Working Capital Scheme (short-term interest-rate subsidy for operating credit)

Italy

14.5.1986 *Sicily:* draft law concerning intervention as regards agricultural credit (Law of 27 June 1985, No 1000)

15.5.1986 Specific case of application of Law No 700 of 19 December 1983 concerning sugarbeet; this concerns the facilities of a sugar group located in the centre-north of Italy

23.6.1986 Measures contained in the Italian law No 887 of 22 December 1984 making arrangements for the formation of the annual budget of the State (guarantee in the form of insurance and exchange guarantee, creation of marketing centres abroad, implementation of commercial 'penetration' programmes and participation in fairs and exhibitions)

14.11.1986 Measures for the milling industry, subsidies for the demolition of mills

14.11.1986 *Mezzogiorno:* Law of 1 March 1986 No 64 laying down extraordinary measures for the Mezzogiorno having the objective of the creation of an agency for the promotion of development in the Mezzogiorno and links between the State and the regions. The Commission may, as appropriate, comment on the national and regional texts as regards the application of the Law

23.12.1986 *Sicily:* Forward budget for 1986 and 'multiannual' budget 1986-88. These are investment aids to agricultural production and aids for research and dissemination of information as regards genetics, teaching of artificial insemination techniques, and control of livestock mortality

23.12.1986 *Marches:* Draft Law No 78 on the financing of regional provisions for agriculture (reduced-rate loans to promote access to ownership, operating loans contracted by cooperatives and their groupings, subsidies to promote the mechanization of production and for the construction, enlargement and modernization of housing for cattle, sheep and goats, guarantees against marketing loans, funds supplementing electrification programmes in country areas)

19.12.1986 Decree of the President of the Council of Ministers of 29.2.1985 amending the Decree of the President of the Council of Ministers of 2.4.1982 concerning interest-rate subsidy rates to be granted in Italy for loan operation

Luxembourg

24.11.1986 Draft aid to wine-growers to offset some of the income losses because of the poor weather

Netherlands

30.1.1986 Measures to assist fruit-growers following the frost in 1984/85. These measures provide only for assistance in the cost of investment concerning the replanting of fruit trees and other tree species destroyed by the frost

19.8.1986 Alteration of the aid to slurry banks. This is a measure for the disposal of slurry with proper regard for the needs of nature protection

Portugal

2.9.1986   Supplementary aid to the construction or relocation of farm buildings or for land improvement provided for under the draft decree-law concerning national aids provided for in the Portuguese regulations relating to the application in Portugal of Council Regulation (EEC) No 797/85 of 12 March 1985 on improving the efficiency of agricultural structures

United Kingdom

2.6.1986   Home-grown Sugarbeet Fund (research and education); this is a modification of an existing aid scheme, through a reduction of the charge made to finance research work and the training of growers

13.6.1986   Potatoes, 1986 crop support arrangements; this is an aid in support of potato growing

19.6.1986   *Northern Ireland:* forestry measures; these are aids granted to encourage and improve private woodlands, for the broadleaved trees

13.8.1986   *Isle of Man:* — aid to mountain sheep farming,

26.8.1986   — 1986 farm improving scheme

17.9.1986   Agricultural and horticultural training scheme

17.9.1986   *Isle of Man:* aid to supply of lime for 1986; it is none the less proposed to pay the aid only if it is certain that the liming operation aided will serve lasting land improvement

10.10.1986   Measures for improvement in cereals marketing (Home-grown Cereals Authority)

31.10.1986   Aid to the Council for Horticultural Development, for research

31.10.1986   Aid to hill cattle-farming

2. Aid cases in which the Commission adopted negative opinions under Article 93(2), first sentence

United Kingdom

7.7.1986   *Isle of Man:* aid proposed under the Basic Slag Scheme 1986

France

29.10.1986   Aid to grouping of foals, by animal or by farm, and to purchase of stallions for production of horsemeat

3. Aid cases in which the procedure provided for in Article 93(2) of the EEC Treaty was initiated

FR of Germany

10.7.1986   The measure concerns compensation for livestock losses following disease or treatment

Belgium

27.1.1986   Measures to assist nurserymen and fruit-growers following frost damage in 1984/85

France

7.5.1986   Practical case of application relating to an investment for the modernization of a wheat-starch plant (loan from the Industrial Modernization Fund)

25.7.1986   Measures to assist a reduction in social security costs for the employment of occasional labour for certain farming operations and an aid to diversification in the horticultural sector

23.12.1986   Aid to dairy farmers in the form of the part-payment of social security contributions

Ireland

27.8.1986   Exchange guarantee granted, reflected in an interest subsidy for new agricultural products

Italy

7.2.1986   *Sicily:* regional law amending the Regional Law No 16 of 2 March 1981, concerning:
- (i) subsidies for the sterilization of land under cover, 50% of the costs; this subsidy is 60% for owner-occupiers and 80% for cooperatives and their associations;
- (ii) 7.5% interest subsidies to cooperatives not having received management loans for one or more of the preceding agricultural marketing years

19.2.1986   *Abruzzi:* amendment of Regional Law No 31 of 3 June 1982 by Regional Law No 25 of 11 April 1985, concerning, in particular:
- (i) extension by two years of the aid (Article 66) for purchasing cattle-feed;
- (ii) granting of an aid (Article 20) for the purchasing of male reproducing poultry.

14.4.1986   *Trento:* Draft Law No 101 amending a law of the province on agriculture
                 Measures objected to:
- (i) aid for the purchasing, construction, extension of facilities for the transport and preservation of milk;
- (ii) allowance for Alpine grazing of sheep;
- (iii) reduced-rate loans over 12 months for the purchase of store cattle;
- (iv) subsidies for the transport of milk to dairies;
- (v) interest subsidies for the purchase of machinery for the processing and marketing of agricultural products

7.5.1986	Aid to dealers for sugar in stock at the end of October 1984
16.6.1986	Circular from the Ministry of Agriculture No 21, 23 November 1985, applying Article 2 of the Law No 430/85: aid to the export of cattle and beef/veal to non-member countries
23.6.1986	Law No 887 of 22 December 1984 including provisions concerning the composition of the State annual and 'multiannual' budget (1985 Finance Act) and providing for the extension to the food-processing sector of provisions laid down in Italian Law Nos 265/82 and 227/82 and 227/72 (reduced rate discounting of medium- and long-term loans contracted in connection with exports to non-member countries)
17.10.1986	Measures to support the distillation of table wine and quality wine storage aids

Luxembourg

1.8.1986	Aid to the development of agriculture. The measures criticized concern aids to investment in the processing and marketing of agricultural products, the rates of which exceed the maximum normally authorized by the Commission

Netherlands

23.12.1986	The Commission decided to initiate the procedure laid down in Article 93(2) of the EEC Treaty against (98) aids financed by 'parafiscal' charges in the Netherlands, either in respect of the levying of charges and allocation of their yield for imported products or in respect of the aspect aids to Dutch agriculture

4. Aid cases in which the procedure provided for in Article 93(2) of the EEC Treaty was closed

FR of Germany

18.4.1986   *Hesse:* aid concerning measures to support the use of grasslands and to underpin employment in small and medium-sized farms

Denmark

8.4.1986   Law No 247 of 6 June 1985 reforming land credit

France

13.2.1986   Compensation for the abolition of transport aids

21.10.1986   Aid to advertising for Pineau de Charentes

Italy

11.2.1986   Draft law amending Regional Law (Molise) No 27 of 4 September 1979 for the improvement and development of animal husbandry

12.3.1986   *Calabria:* draft law refinancing, for 1985, Regional Law No 21 of 2 June 1980 on measures supporting to agriculture (partial closure)

22.5.1986   *Sicily:* aid concerning measures to assist farms damaged by bad weather in 1984 and 1985

24.7.1986   Draft Law No 1000 providing for new standards relating to farm credit and other measures supporting agriculture

25.6.1986   Regional Laws Nos 86 of 5 August 1982, 105 of 5 August 1982, 87 of 5 August 1982 and 97/81

                Closure of the procedure provided for in Article 92(2) of the EEC Treaty in respect of investment aids contained in these laws

17.10.1986   Refinancing for 1985 of Regional Law No 21 of 2.6.1980 supporting agriculture

17.10.1986   Regional Law No 583-547 on intervention as regards credit to industry, commerce, small firms, fisheries and cooperatives

5. Final Commission Decisions taken following procedures under Article 93(2) of the EEC Treaty

Conditional positive final decision

7.5.1986   Aids concerning measures for sugar producers

6. Rulings of the Court of Justice

Order of the President of the Court, 30 April 1986, in Case 57/86 R: 'Hellenic Republic v Commission of the European Communities', interest subsidy on export credit for all products except petroleum products — OJ No C 151, 17.6.1986, p. 2.

7. Council Decisions under Article 93(2) of the EEC Treaty

Decision	of 19.12.1985 on the grant of aids for table olives in Greece.
Decision	of 15.5.1986 on the grant by certain Member States of a short-term private storage aid for table wines and musts.
Decision	of 8.12.1986 on the grant of certain national aids as regards wine in Italy following a serious crisis because of the methanol scandal.
Decision	of 16.12.1986 on the granting of a national aid in the form of an advance payment against the ewe premium in France.

IV — List of studies published in 1986 and to be published

Documents

No	Title	Research institute	Expert(s)
ISBN-72-825-5896-7	Comparaison de la situation concurrentielle des entreprises privées et publiques dans trois secteurs industriels de la CEE	Université de Nice, Nice	J. Bernard Cl. Berthomieu L. Cartelier Cl. Charbit P. Mottard P. Romani
ISBN-92-825-6030-9	Kriterien zur wettbewerbspolitischen Beurteilung der Gründung von Gemeinschaftsunternehmen; eine Analyse aus der Sicht der Wettbewerbsregeln der Europäischen gemeinschaft	Institut für Angewandte Wirtschaftsforschung, Tübingen	Lothar Rall Rudi Kurz
ISBN-92-825-6424-x	Minority share acquisition: the impact upon competition	The Institute for Fiscal Studies, London	Shirley Meadowcroft David Thompson
ISBN-92-825-6700-1	Definition of the relevant market in Community competition policy	Fishwick Consultants, Bedford	Francis Fishwick
ISBN-92-825-6715-x	Predatory pricing	CORE, Louvain-la-Neuve Centre for Operations Research and Econometrics	Louis Phlips
ISBN-92-825-7125-4	The measurement of the aid element of State acquisitions of company capital	Huddersfield Polytechnic West Yorkshire	E.C. Lea
ISBN-92-825-7180-3	Franchising in ausgewählten Bereichen des Handels in der Gemeinschaft — Wettbewerbspolitische Analyse	Handelsinstitut Universität des Saarlandes, Saarbrücken	B. Tietz C. Arend U. Brauer F. Denger
ISBN-92-825-7145-9	Die Konzentration der Konsumgüterdistribution in der Gemeinschaft und ihre Auswirkungen auf die Nachfragemacht	IFO-Institut für Wirtschaftsforschung — München	U. Täger, J. Lachner H. Ullrich
ISBN-92-825-7146-7	Analyse des politiques de contrôle des prix dans certains secteurs sous l'angle de la concurrence et des échanges intra-communautaires	Institut des Sciences Economiques de Brest	M. Glais M. Hardouin E. Jolivet
ISBN-92-825-7144-0	Kollektive Marktbeherrschung. Das Konzept und seine Anwendbarkeit für die Wettbewerbspolitik	Institut für Industrie- und Gewerbepolitik der Universität Hamburg	E. Kantzenbach J. Kruse

No	Title	Research institute	Expert(s)
n.a.	La prise en compte de l'élément aide des prêts à taux réduits aux entreprises de la Communauté	Université d'Aix-Marseille III	G. Bramoullé
n.a.	The EEC telecommunications industry. Competition, concentration and competitiveness. The accession of Portugal and Spain	Istituto superior tecnico Lisboa	L.T. Almeida

European Communities — Commission

Sixteenth Report on Competition Policy

Luxembourg: Office for Official Publications of the European Communities

1987 — 286 pp. — 16.2 x 22.9 cm

ES, DA, DE, GR, EN, FR, IT, NL, PT

ISBN 92-825-6957-8

Catalogue number: CB-48-86-060-EN-C

Price (excluding VAT) in Luxembourg

ECU 11.60   BFR 500   IRL 8.90   UKL 8.30   USD 12

The Report on Competition Policy is published annually by the Commission of the European Communities in response to the request of the European Parliament made by a Resolution of 7 June 1971. This Report, which is published in conjunction with the General Report on the Activities of the Communities, is designed to give a general view of the competition policy followed during the past year. Part One covers general competition policy. Part Two deals with competition policy towards enterprises. Part Three is concerned with competition policy and government assistance to enterprises and Part Four with the development of concentration, competition and competitiveness.